SUN SIGN RISING

Maria Elise Crummere

BALLANTINE BOOKS • NEW YORK

To
Dolors Bonseigneur

Copyright © 1969, 1977 by Maria Crummere

All rights reserved, which includes the right to reproduce this book or portions thereof in any form whatsoever. Published in the United States by Ballantine Books, a division of Random House, Inc., New York, and simultaneously in Canada by Ballantine Books of Canada, Ltd., Toronto, Canada.

A different version of this book was first published by Avon Books, a division of The Hearst Corporation, 1969, as *Your Sun-Personality*.

ISBN 0-345-25322-1-195

Manufactured in the United States of America

First Ballantine Books Edition: January 1977

You Look Like Your Horoscope

You are your own astrological pattern, like a woven rug or an intricate design. Your horoscope is your blueprint, your map of destiny.

Your Sun-sign shows the heart's wish. But the position of your Moon shows the yearning of your soul. And your Rising Sign may show such force that it enriches your birth sign.

With this book, world-famous astrologer

MARIA ELISE CRUMMERE

shows how, through astrology, you can actually

CHANGE YOUR LIFE

Also by Maria Elise Crummere

*SUN-SIGN REVELATIONS
THE AGE OF AQUARIUS

Published by Ballantine Books

Contents

Preface ... vii

Introduction: Is This What You Think of Astrology? ... ix

Part One

1. How to Get a Good Reading ... 2
2. Here's How ... 25
3. You Are More Than One Sign ... 39
4. The Importance of Each Sign ... 54

Part Two

5. The Career Potential of Each Sign ... 58
6. Characteristics of Each Sign ... 68
7. The Big Wheel ... 79

Part Three

8. Aries: The First Sign ... 83
9. Taurus: The Second Sign ... 98
10. Gemini: The Third Sign ... 113
11. Cancer: The Fourth Sign ... 130
12. Leo: The Fifth Sign ... 145
13. Virgo: The Sixth Sign ... 161
14. Libra: The Seventh Sign ... 177
15. Scorpio: The Eighth Sign ... 195
16. Sagittarius: The Ninth Sign ... 212
17. Capricorn: The Tenth Sign ... 226
18. Aquarius: The Eleventh Sign ... 240
19. Pisces: The Twelfth Sign ... 255
20. Discovering Your Sun and Personality Sign ... 269

Preface

Because I am an astrologer, people have come to me over the years expecting to be told how exciting they are and about the great destiny in store for them. They expect astrology to trigger their great dreams pushbutton-style; to create a picture-book life by the mere turn of a phrase; to bring them an endless flow of wealth and the name of that magic street which can lead only to fame. They think, perhaps there is a blueprint here to a gold mine that is awaiting exclusive exploration, and only the stars can guarantee results.

Young men and women who resemble motion-picture stars, or heiresses who are both beautiful and gifted, all tell me they have supreme talents that need but the barest identification for real genius to burst forth from them. Alas, astrology is not black magic!

When I apply astrology to the power of their charts, I introduce them to themselves for the first time. I give them clues to know the *self* better and the means to expect more from life because of the wealth of talents still untouched within that self. I show them what may be holding them back; what has delayed their harmonious flow through life; why they have not had happier lives. I help them start a new life. I organize them.

Astrology can create marriages; bring about reconciliations that seemed hopeless; mend failing businesses that were thought to be lost; fulfill actual dreams by making them realities; put an end to chronic ailments; resolve indecisions; even surmount obstacles within hours. When I show my clients this, invariably they are surprised. Yet I have done nothing but show them how to solve their own probelms.

They simply did not know that astrology has the practical mechanics to show them the way out of trouble. Astrology has no peer in analysis. That it can show them a way to independence—so that they never again need help from anyone—seems incredible to them.

Yet it is true! There is no other form of problem-solver that can bring immediate help to the problem at hand so quickly or so adequately. To any question —how to deal with the present struggle; what to do in the relationships with a loved one; whether a chosen profession is suitable—astrology has the answer.

Astrology can and will show how to "time" every event in your life so that what you *will*, will endure. My purpose here is to make this clear in a language that you will understand, using only the astrological terms that must be used for identification. This will open up to you a simple path, the magic of which can free you forever from indecision, stagnation, and frustration, giving you a happier life and more time to do the pleasurable things you want to do.

Most people are under the impression that all this is a hit-or-miss proposition, the effects of which are not lasting. When they discover that it can be depended on through the years in the most severe tests and that it can reliably free them so that they never need a crutch again, they are overjoyed. Then astrology becomes the only logical way to deal with any problem, person, or situation.

Introduction

Is This What You Think of Astrology?

The image that the word *astrology* conjures up in the minds of most people is that of an old woman wearing a turban with a priceless jewel (synthetic of course) set in the center, with a black cat mewing at her heels and a parrot perched on her shoulder screeching out prophecies and formulated panaceas. The astrologer is the old girl straddling a broomstick on her way to one of the planets of which she is supposed to know so much. Low lights, burning incense, and various other atmospheric props are visualized. Magic symbols decorate the walls and hint at voodoo possibilities.

The mention of a birth date is supposed to pull a rabbit out of a magic hat—and the answer to any problem posthaste. If the astrologer does not give the answer in a wink, she is either a fake or does not know anything about star-science. The answer must be infallible too. All this, of course, is pure foolishness!

Most people know that, astrologically speaking, there are ten planets. But most people never think of consulting all their positions at the time of birth to guarantee a satisfactory picture of their destinies. When this is shown to them, it is thought to be magic. It is magic, but the kind of magic that requires intelligent handling. The wise answer can build; the wrong answer can destroy.

Astrology can open the mysterious doors of wealth, health, and happiness. It can give you the keys to open these doors. The greatest of all the occult sciences works its magic when Saturn is used to *time* the event you want and Jupiter is used to *ripen* it. Then nothing can cancel it.

A charming woman called me from the Plaza Hotel

one day for an appointment. When she arrived, she brushed past me and asked, "Where's the woman who consults here?" I said that I was the woman. She replied, "What could a little thing like you tell me?" When I said, "Mainly that you are this moment suffering from a blood condition," she stared at me. I continued, "That may account for your irritability and brusque manners!"

That was enough. She admitted that she had expected a great horse of a woman to fit her private impressions of what astrology was like. Her health was her purpose for coming. We had satisfactory results and became fast friends.

Another wand-waving client came to me through a friend. Her husband had become involved with another woman. She was on the verge of collapse, for he had demanded a divorce. She wanted a capsule type of advice, a quick, ready-made formula. This I could not give her, but I did tell her that her marriage was not over.

Next, in order to know how to maneuver in any battle, we had to learn the power of her enemy. Charts had to be drawn up and studied, both for the husband and the other woman. I learned that my client's marriage was a first-sweetheart thing, which meant that her husband had not sown his wild oats.

The other woman was a seasoned type who knew that the sands of youth were running out for her. She was using time. So would we.

My client was advised to put off going to Reno, but never—*never*—say that she was not going. This fooled the other woman. It gave the husband time to run the gamut of his infatuation. The other woman began nagging him. The husband became disillusioned under her harassment, especially when she abused him unsparingly for not hurrying his wife off to Reno. My job was to placate and keep the wife confident, for I knew that time was our friend and the other woman's enemy. We won of course. The husband returned.

As soon as the first wrong impressions are wiped out and the real power that astrology has is made clear, there is no end to the feats that can be accomplished through the medium. *The wonder of this science is all in application and interpretation.*

There are those who have said to me, "But I do not want to know what the future holds for me!" I tell these people this story:

Late one night, a friend telephoned me. He was quite excited. "There is a girl around the corner from you," he said, "who is contemplating suicide! Please go around and see what you can do. Take your ephemeris."

I did not look forward to this with relish. It was late and very cold, but I hurried to her home and found the girl in bed. She was very close to a nervous breakdown as a result of an unhappy love affair. Sitting beside her bed, I set up a chart and noted at once that a new opportunity was on its way to her through a friend, someone from another city.

I asked her if she had friends in another city. She said only that she came from Chicago. I asked her if a friend might be coming to town. "No," she answered as if that was the end of the matter. But being resourceful, I asked her to send notes to everyone she knew living in other cities. It was clear that she was not impressed. I persisted until she agreed to write the notes. I said, "Write pleasant letters. I will mail them for you."

She began to brighten as she wrote. I left but telephoned her every day to keep the idea and the enthusiasm alive. In about two weeks one of the recipients came to town and called her in response to her letter. He had just inherited some money from his mother. He and his wife invited her to take a trip to Mexico. While there, they introduced her to a friend who became the girl's lasting friend and sweetheart. The "opportunity . . . through a friend" was fulfilled.

To those who say, "I do not want to know the future," I say, "You do not know what wonderful things are in store for you!" My young friend had been completely demoralized by a man who had failed her. Just one effort, put into operation because of an astrological indication, gave the young girl a new outlook on life. Astrology did not bring back the man; it simply showed that something new could be had. Merely make yourself aware of the possibilities, and that alone may produce the results you want!

Suppose this had not been brought to the young lady's attention. Her days might have been less depressing because of the powerful uplift in her good-aspect period then, but we pressed it to the full for an answer and got over the finish line with effort and ideas. The application plus interpretation brought us one result—*magic*.

Another time a very beautiful Spanish girl came to me to select the best time to divorce her wealthy Viennese husband. While examining her chart, I asked if she had a child. She had a boy. I cautioned her that she must never let the child travel with his father because he had a very bad accident-chart. She said, "That's odd, for my husband flies everywhere. He owns his own plane." Then we agreed on a divorce time, for this is what she had come for primarily.

Months later, she returned to me with her sister. She told me that her husband had been killed on a flight to South America. He had wanted to take the child; but remembering my warning, she had obtained a court order to keep the boy from accompanying his father. Consequently, the child's life was saved. The father's chart had shown death on a journey. This is an example of preventative astrology.

The law of life gives one free will. There are many decisions to make and many paths to choose. Astrology can steer one into the right path or the ripe choice. Nothing *has* to be. There is no such thing as an all-bad chart or an all-good chart. There is not a single life or chart that does not carry a glimmer of hope or the possibility of improvement. Nothing is lost, only postponed. Men and women have come to me in great grief over the loss of a lover, and my standard answer is, "If he—or she—was once yours and is alive, he can be yours again!"

Remember the cases I've related to you thus far:

A girl despairing to the point of suicide was guided into a rewarding future by letting astrology solve her problem and work for her benefit.

The heart-broken wife had her husband and faith

restored to her by timing the end of a frivolous affair that could have ruined the lives of three people.

A child's life was saved, thanks to an alert mother and astrology.

Today, religionists are working overtime to restore faith in man so that he may live a happier life through spiritual communication with the Divine Spirit. Psychologists and psychiatrists are tirelessly using every instrument at their disposal to measure man's discontent and rid him of his many and varied psychological disturbances. Yet the struggle mounts rather than diminishes.

Why not give the oldest science in the world, starscience, a chance to redeem man? The stars are older than man. They are older than medicine and religion. They are still here as they were at the beginning of time and the universe. They *must* have some part in the divine plan too.

To quote from *The Theory of Celestial Influence*, by Rodney Collins, "Certainly the angle of the Sun's ray, the distribution of moisture and warm sea-currents are also factors of great importance. At the same time it is difficult to believe that these differences in speed of surface-movement are not primary cause in the enormous variations of life forms at different latitudes. And if we apply this principle to other planets and parts of planets, in search of a clue to possible life there, the results are—to say the least—*illuminating*."

The spiritual adviser advocates that you invoke the divine law of God when your life hits a snag to which you cannot adjust. This advice is foolproof of course, as Faith without works is dead. This points to some active measure that should be sought and used.

The psychologist tries to unravel the underlying reason for your problem through some "complex" that you have which you do not fully understand. But the spiritual side that the religionists advocate is left out to a large extent, just as the religionists do not pry open the inner door of your mind for you to show that subconsciously you cannot, or do not want, to solve the problem. Why can't they be united? Astrology provides the mechanics as well as the spiritual answer. Together with the forecast, astrological analysis can reveal to you the reason why you are in a state of confusion.

Astrology may tell you only one thing about yourself that could be the key to all you need to know. It might tell you that your last business venture had to fail because it was against your time. You would stop accusing yourself then of being a poor businessman. There is no such thing as a completely bad or afflicted life, just as there is nothing in life to guarantee security.

Two years ago in a restaurant, I met a man whom I had befriended years before. With the help of astrology, he had gained his position. He greeted me very coolly, entirely out of keeping with the kind of attitude my work with him during the previous years deserved.

Out of curiosity I later brought his chart up to date to see what was going on in his life and what his prospects were. I was not surprised to see that he would take a fall from his present position, that the fall would be complete, and that the affliction would last for many years. Through a mutual friend I sent him a message asking that he contact me.

There was no response. This man lacked vision, for he now ignored the very thing that led him to success. Had he sought the aid of astrology again, he might have staved off the public disgrace that followed. I do not believe that our meeting was mere chance. It was a warning. A warning that he threw away because he thought the bridge that had once carried him safely to his goal was not needed now.

Once these wheels were set in motion, nothing could have stopped the consequences; but two whole years could have been amended, and the unmistakable misfortune prevented.

So I say this to you about astrology: Try it! If it does not work for you, you can always return to your old habits. To quote Francis Bacon, "Men are rather beholden generally to chance."

Part One

1
How to Get a Good Reading

Astrology can enjoy greater popularity and importance once it is presented to the public more simply. The tendency of certain astrologers to make a mystery of the science has hindered the willingness of the average person to give it a hearing.

Astrology is a symbolic sign-language, simpler than a spoken language. You have the twelve zodiacal *signs* and the meanings of the twelve *houses* to remember. At this writing, there are only ten *planets* delegated to the twelve signs. (There may be two more planets out there that have not yet been discovered.) Once their basic meanings are memorized, you can begin to speak the most exciting, fascinating language in the world.

Astrology is everywhere. For example, the symbols of the language are in the churches: the holy cross is called the *square*, and the holy triune is called the *trine*, or good-luck symbol.

The *aspects* (the spatial relationship of one planet to another) make up the network of destiny. They translate your being into certain traits that indicate the way you will react to outside circumstances: the way the planets are moving from day to day will affect you greatly. The position of each planet in your horoscope at the time you were born will show how you will express love or the kind of love you will attract.

For example, a chart with many trines (two planets 120° apart—the best luck) shows that the person will have little trouble getting what he wishes in life, especially if the trines are backed up by strong planets. The square (two planets 90° apart—the more difficult aspect) shows the trials encountered in pursuit of a desired goal. The *conjunction* (two or more planets joined together in the same sign, even the same degree) is the beginning or initial point. If good planets are joined in this conjunction, so much the better. If one so-called good planet and one so-called difficult planet are in conjunction, a contradictory force results. This can be reconciled with knowledge.

The *crown* is the circle of the zodiac. It consists of 360° with each sign containing 30°. The *square,* which takes in the East-West, South-North points of the circle, represents foundation, as the circle represents the completion or results. The "jewels," or planets, set in the circle and square represent the desired identification drawn into play from the Universal Spirit to mark the event of the blessing of birth from the Deity.

You are your own astrological pattern, like a woven rug or an intricate design. *You look like your horoscope.* It is your blueprint, your map of *destiny*.

Think of what great fun it would be to know the color and plan of your pattern, whether you represent the warm shades or the cool ones, whether you—as a house—are built to give comfort or excite, remain in the suburbs or be a part of the teeming cities.

The signs will select the colors or impetus indicated for you. For example, a cardinal sign such as Aries will select strong, pure colors. Red is a daring color and suits the male sign Aries—Libra will select muted, soft, or light colors. Libra takes the casual way in life, hence the refined color. Timid Cancer picks shades so light that they appear faded; yet they suit the sensitive approach, for Cancer moves quietly through life, fearing to be noticed and hurt. Capricorn selects dark colors. Its ruler is Saturn, the planet that rules the church. Black, the habit of the clergy, represents the secrecy that the parables of the prophets were clothed in. The careful shades which Capricorn chooses (blues and blacks) show caution to be inherent and correct. Such are the laws of the church.

If astrologers would present astrological facts as simply as possible—as the doctor who, after examination, tells you what the x-ray means or what your blood count indicates—you would gladly allot the astrologer an hour of your time to learn these facts about yourself.

The average astrologer can detect at a glance the interplay of the different signs in the appearance and movement of the person. The variation of the planets appearing in different signs, and the signs themselves in the birth horoscope, is what makes the interesting personalities. The different qualities found in the destiny blueprint make this the most exciting of all the mystic arts. For instance, a slow-moving planet like Saturn, forcing its will on an active cardinal-type, say Aries, can turn the enthusiasm of this sign into a brutal, might-makes-right person. Or a fast-moving planet like Mars, transiting over a passive sign like Taurus, can stir this plodding and well-regulated sign into unusual activity that is entirely alien to its nature.

For example, if you have the good fortune to have the benefic planet Jupiter transiting either your Sun-sign (your birth sign) or your personality ascendant (the sign that was rising on the eastern horizon at the time of your birth), many opportunities would be on their way to you. If you knew this, you could immediately put the forces to work, for it would be another twelve years before Jupiter would be good to you again like this.

If Mars, the impulsive and quarrelsome planet, is making the same transit, it would be to your advantage to curb your temper or impulse lest you end relations with someone in bitterness. Also, energetic Mars can get you to work accomplishing those tiresome tasks you have been putting off, for now you would *want* to do them.

If astrology were brought to your attention and, after experimenting with it, it did not work for you, you could abandon it and return to your old ways. You would accept it if it made your life easier, simpler. You have only to remember a language of a few symbols. A child can remember the circle of twelve. You will not have to remember as many as twelve signs in your birth horoscope. You may have planets in only six or seven signs. No one has twelve. You could then begin the life of self-discovery and the pleasure of enjoying yourself.

There are three wheels moving from the moment you draw your first breath. The first wheel is your true and spiritual first self, the kind of character you may ultimately be expected to express. The second wheel is that which draws you away from the first, forming the outgrowth of the first wheel and directing you down the road to make your history or destiny. The third wheel, over which you have no control, is the wheel of every circumstance. This outside wheel of circumstance with which you must deal is life. Psychologists might call it the pressures of life.

There are three basic types, or frames of reference, that aid the astrologer in his analysis: the twelve signs are broken down into the cardinal, mutable, and fixed signs. If your Sun-sign in the big wheel is a fixed sign, the outside wheel or pressures of life will not deter you from the path you have chosen. It may bar your way, but only temporarily. You may have to detour, to retrograde, as the planets themselves do, or stand still; but you will get back on your path according to schedule, for you belong to the fixed signs.

The heavy artillery, the destiny individuals, are the fixed signs: Taurus, Leo, Scorpio, and Aquarius. The rub-with-life wheel, or outside circumstances, cannot possibly have the same effect on the destiny of a man once he comes to know *why* or at *what time* he can fail or succeed. Astrology, and only astrology, can *time* the events in your life as no other of the occult or mystic sciences can.

The cardinal signs—Aries, Cancer, Libra, and Capricorn—have a harder time controlling the third wheel of circumstance. They like to get into the fray. They are more inclined to join circumstances, like the prodigal son who could not resist the wheel. He took to the road with it.

The cardinal signs become somewhat dog-eared; they get buffeted about, wanting to see what is going on in the world. They pay the price. They want action; they get it. The kind of action? Well, that is something else. Rather than stand the test of time or wait for luck to change, they square their shoulders to this wheel; like Old Man River, they just keep rolling along with life. If there is an abundance of cardinal signs, their action is greater, and it is more difficult for these people to keep their course.

Money, according to the Freudians, is love or energy. The cardinals are inclined to spend their money, or love and energy, in action, fencing with life on that outside wheel of circumstance. Their chance of beating it is second to the fixed, the more determined signs.

Cardinals are doers. They learn by the greatest school of experience. If the life wheel is too severe, they take the mighty blow. If the wheel is traveling easily, they get things done. Army men are usually cardinal signs, as are organizers, leaders, and workers.

The wheel of circumstance finds easy pickings with the mutable signs. They are the dual people wishing to go both ways at once. When pressures or circumstances move against them, they swing with them, moving back and forth, trying to recover their original pattern, but still definitely agreeing with the distractions. As a consequence, they have more difficulty reaching their goals.

If the abstractions fascinate them for too long a period, they may never return to the chosen path; or having recovered the original pattern, they may find their return is too late to achieve the desired goal.

The mutable signs—Gemini, Virgo, Sagittarius, and Pisces—are the thinkers, teachers, lecturers, speakers, news reporters, and philosophers. Being dual, they may cover two or three of these endeavors. A mutable who starts out to be a teacher would write, then lecture; and he might find that lecturing is more satisfying to him and never return to teaching. Circumstances would have changed the path. This would be agreeable to the mutable, or common, signs.

The cardinals, for instance, would also enjoy the new idea for a while; yet as soon as the new idea grew old, they would be bored. Change finds cardinals easy converts, but converts who will be converted again very easily. The fixed signs will resist and return to the original program.

The zodiac is a dial; it is a timepiece. Man consults the time of day to arise and to retire. Why not consult the time of life to marry or enter into a new venture, rather as one might look at one's wrist watch to keep an appointment. You can keep your appointments with destiny with the same intelligence you use to select a house to live in or a mate to love and cherish.

Too often, astrology is eschewed because it promises so much. But it can keep these promises if the *way to use it* is made clear. The average person is suspicious of an art or science that seems all-knowing. That is why astrology is dubbed fortune-telling. This is a great mistake. Astrology is a science of potential. The possibilities are there or they are not there. One may wait for the right time and reap the rewards—or jump the gun and fail. This is not the fault of the stars, but the mistake of the person who has not timed the event for good or evil. Life is not canceled, just postponed. *Time* is the greatest factor in astrology.

Years ago, a client came to me with a wonderful idea to create an exciting earring. I gave her the exact time when the idea would be acceptable and even gave her the names of prominent department-store buyers who were my clients too. The buyers were all interested. The client, being an Aries birth sign, could not wait for the time that was indicated. She went ahead and had the earring manufactured at once. She was ahead of *time*. The buyers only ordered a few, for it was against their buying time. She could not understand why they had shown so much enthusiasm yet had ordered so few. The public did not react, so there was no reordering.

Later, the idea was tested again and it became a fad. Someone did improve on her original concept, but the time of introducing it was closer to the time we had decided on, the time for which she could not wait. This is an example of an impulsive, quick-acting, cardinal sign—Aries.

I remember going into court with a client. She wished to defend herself against an unfair divorce in which the husband did not wish to pay back money he had borrowed. The early part of the day was against her, so his lawyers gave her a really hard time.

She was ready to give up by the time court recessed for lunch. It took a lot of reassuring from me to get her to return to court to defend her rights. I told her that if she waited she would witness a complete change in the attitude of the court. The Moon would change signs at about four. It looked so hopeless that it was all the lawyer and I could do to keep her on the stand.

The lawyer was afraid that the judge would end the case before the time I had predicted. Knowing my client, I allowed for the breakdowns that her hysterical condition would consume. This would take time. The hands of the clock went past four. The lawyers for the husband showed impatience and began to abuse her. Unmerciful and totally indifferent to her rights, they aroused the judge. He gave her his direct attention, instructing her lawyer to her advantage.

The other side could not believe their ears, for they were sure they had everything their way. The later it became, the further the Moon went into Cancer where it has a very strong influence for a woman. The Moon had been in Gemini, the indecisive sign. The Moon represented people, or the court. The judge renewed his interest in the case from her side. Even her lawyer began to pick up steam and find more ideas to present in her behalf. The consciousness—the Moon at home and strong in Cancer manifested itself in a complete and unequivocal victory for her. Time got for us, I know, what justice could easily have lost, even though her cause was just!

Another extremely interesting case concerning a more severe planet and involving the time element is this one: A famous art director was summoned to report for army duty. His secretary telephoned me in great panic. He was in the midst of an advertising campaign which he did not want to leave. I asked her to call back, giving me a chance to set up a chart. Uranus—the planet that I call the Declaration of Independence—was about to make a very important aspect for the man's birth Sun in about twelve hours, but it would not be operative until the next morning. I suggested that she call the draft board and put the appointment off until the next morning. It worked! Congress passed a new amendment for the age limit! It was announced on the newscast that very night; he had escaped by minutes! Had he reported that afternoon, he would have been drafted. Here again time was the leading character. Destiny was not canceled, but it was planned. He was so delighted he drew a picture of me, making me a four-star general in drawing.

The weather man forecasts, for he has made observations of wind direction, the humidity, and cloud changes, giving him the right to say what *can* be.

A man born when the Sun's rays were in the cardinal sign Aries (March 21-April 19) has a different character that one born in the fixed sign of Taurus, (April 20-May 20), when the Sun's force is more fixed, determined, and powerful. This shows that the Sun's rays differ in potential, depending on the time of day and the place on earth upon which it pours forth its force.

Throughout world history, symbols of the fixed signs are seen. People worshipped the golden calf in the Taurian age. We see the statues of lions in the squares and plazas of Europe's capital cities, for kingdoms are indicated by the lion. The serpent—Scorpio—in the headgear of rulers symbolizes wisdom and invincible power. The last and fourth fixed sign seen in the ancient statues is that of man pouring water upon the land, the sign of Aquarius that is so often found in fountains. The sign most prominent in the Hall of Fame is Aquarius.

The other signs are just as important in the destiny of man; but the symbols of the fixed signs certainly behave differently from the cardinals and mutables and show that the Sun has a far different vibration or different role to play in each sign. The individual has his job or service to perform this time around. The sooner man comes to know this, and more, about himself and reconciles his attitude toward it, the sooner he will accomplish his mission happily.

The fixed sign always wants to be a big shot; he can and does go far in winning time, but often spills the effectiveness of his power and brings down on his head the greater tragedies. It is in keeping with this power that, should the tide turn, his fall is the greater. Seeking more, the fixed sign person has more to defend, must stand greater consequences, and bear greater responsibility. Thus, the perfect law is equalized.

The cardinal signs change power, for they seek change. Theirs is a greater variety of circumstances to enjoy. They are compensated, reversely, in that they do not enjoy the same things for as long a time as the fixed signs.

So perfect is the law that, even in the signs, the rewards and trials are exactly in accordance with the pleasure and pain which the sign has enjoyed. The mutable signs do not want things as determinedly as the fixed. Neither are their hardships or pleasures as deep-seated, lasting, and varied as the cardinals. Their casual touch in life being easier, they receive a lighter sentence in the court of human relationships. Mutables have less to show, and have suffered less, by keeping the ease with which they accept defeat or triumph.

There is no such thing as a pure-type chart, that is, all ten planets in the sign under which you were born. Ten planets cannot be in one sign. There is no such thing as an all-Aquarian or an all-Leo.

You may not look like your Sun-sign at all nor even give a hint of what your Sun-sign is in appearance. A Capricornian, a short sign, can be very tall if the rising sign, or personality, which controls one's appearance is a tall sign like Aquarius. Or reversely, put the short sign Capricorn as the rising sign on the tall Aquarian and you will have a short Aquarian.

This is another reason why the superficial interpreter of astrology, who does not know these things, gives astrology up as hopeless. Many times the sign in which the Moon is found will emphasize one's appearance—if, for example, the Moon happens to be closer to the personality, or rising sign, and the Sun is setting on the western half of the horoscope. This brings us to the most important phase of astrology.

The time of birth will tell whether the Sun was rising or setting. If you look like the position of your Moon rather than your Sun-sign, then the Moon should be emphasized in your reading; and the best of life's work can be expressed through the mentality or consciousness rather than through the Sun-sign.

There is no end to the possibilities inherent in using your horoscope to better the situations in your life and in interpreting what your life can be against what you let it be; it can apprise you of your potentials, program them into a practical plan, and make them work for you.

This brings me to the point that I have maintained for years, that the *exact time* of birth should be placed on the birth certificate, for someday astrology will be taught in the schools as an essential asset to one's education. This time will come!

Astrology stands unheeded because it is regarded as a mystery—an enigma. It is a language composed of symbols to be seen and translated. (It was proven during World War II that men understood and remembered symbols and visual instruction better than the spoken word. The eye will register a scene and reset it in the mind's eye.) A symbol may and can represent many ideas that will describe the objective for the interpreter much more than words.

Your own sign will begin to spell out things for you, increase your awareness, heighten your ability to express yourself with greater assurance, pay off the dividend of a single symbol of the self's potential. Think of the importance of this alone.

Add this advantage to nine others, accounting for ten planets, and you have ten times more knowledge for ten more advantages. Suppose you were born under the sign of Capricorn, a sign that has the reputation of arriving at goals late in life. This may discourage you. If you found that you had many planets in the sign behind Capricorn—Sagittarius—this awareness would change your destiny at once; this venturesome sign gets around and gambles with life. You need no longer take a back seat. On the contrary, you would then need to know that what you have uncovered should be organized with an eye to making it pay off. Capricorn rules government; Sagittarius travels: hence, you would be a splendid type to travel either for the government of your country or as trouble-shooter for an organization or company.

You might think, if you learned you were a Taurian, that your only business is in the counting house, the bank where money is stored. But on seeing that you have two or three planets in the sign of Gemini, the most versatile sign of the mutables, you might sing through Taurus, but play the piano and compose your own songs through Gemini. Taurus has a lovely voice; Gemini can do anything with the hands. To the plodding Taurus, known for its singleness of purpose, Gemini would give even more. There would be no end to your accomplishments. That is why seeing the symbols, their many variations and potentials, would open up a whole new world for you.

Astrology can rediscover for you ideas that you have forgotten, that lay deep in some little cubbyhole of your subconscious mind, and that you meant to take up one day like a forgotten dream. I call these naggings the "divine discontent."

One good look at the horoscope can uncover many things at once. Psychiatrists all over the world are kept busy digging these things out of the debris of man's mind. Why can't you do it for yourself? You don't have to bare your soul to a stranger to find out why you fail yourself.

If you were planning a garden, you would buy the implements and read all you could about the kind of flower you preferred, especially the ways to plant and grow it. You would head for the hardware and seed stores!

Astrology cannot be more taskful. It is just as fruitful, particularly if it is treated as an idea that you mean to use and apply to your everyday problems; it tells you something more about yourself which would improve your life and lead you progressively into smoother waters. On the other hand, if you planted a seed, and the flower which grew from it did not appeal to you, you need never plant it again.

Astrology should be treated as an idea that may help you, give you higher hopes. If it is found wanting, like the seed you planted, you could abandon it, put it aside as a thing that had no value for you. You might find numerology more to your liking, or graphology, or palmistry. But only astrology can, up to the last day of your life, tell you something about the great plan of your destiny.

For his own protection, everyone should have a map of his destiny set up by a competent astrologer. The reading should be demonstrated to you. As far as I know, I am the only astrologer who places your chart on a blackboard before you, like an easel holding a picture. It is indeed your heavenly picture instead of your physical portrait. It shows you the exact position of every one of your planets—and why and how they influence your life.

A client may be entirely ignorant of the science, but he still benefits much from this method, having seen what frequently cannot be remembered.

For example, the native with many planets above the horizon will certainly lead a more public life than one whose planets lie below in the earth. The planets above the earth are high and naturally lift that person out, up, and into a public life. Also, he will receive more credit for his efforts and talents. The least fortunate native, with planets below the horizon, may be sacrificed.

Thomas Edison had four of his important planets below the earth, keeping him in the laboratory of investigation. He, the man, seldom appeared before the people, but what he discovered did appear. He was an Aquarian, the sign of investigation or invention, with Scorpio, the sign of research or detection, for personality. He fulfilled to the height the two powerful signs and reconciled them. Aquarius, to invent, and Scorpio, to do research, brought power to the world through light, even though his Sun-sign was below the earth (but in the house of fame after death).

To be a public figure, one must have a planet high in the chart. Franklin D. Roosevelt's Moon (the people) and Mars (his action) had the brightest position in his chart.

These are the rewards of seeing your birthday placed before your eyes with a view of what you *can* be, how you can be *more* of what you are, and how you can get full credit on this planet for what you truly are. Then you will speculate no more. You will know for sure.

Another very satisfactory phase, after seeing on

which side of the circle of life you are, is to see how your planets are placed. If they were setting at your birth hour, or on the western side of the wheel of destiny, instantly it would be clear to you why your life seems all tied up in others, why so many are dependent upon you, and why you are seemingly dependent upon others. Once this is seen, if it is not to your liking, you can adjust it.

If your planets are rising, or all on the eastern side of the wheel of destiny, you will be happy to know that your life is in your own hands to do with it as you wish. Many more opportunities will come your way than to those whose western side is heavily tenanted. Your eastern planets will give you the choice to win or lose; you have a better choice of paths before you. But, of course, you have no one to blame if your life does not come off to your satisfaction. You cannot, like the western-side native, charge failure to anyone else.

Awareness of any situation, good or bad, instantly enhances or reduces its potential. Knowledge sets man free. Awareness is the clue to success.

I have read for those with bright and fortunate charts that they were letting their good days die, unaware of the important and wonderful destiny that lay ahead for them if they should exert only a little effort to bring it into full realization.

Being aware of his potentials, the individual can set out on the path to success, timing it with opportunity.

Most important in the satisfactory reading—after the values have been summed up——is the organization of a plan to conduct affairs in such a way as to get the very best out of every favorable aspect, avoid afflictions, and bring about maximum results toward whatever the client's goal may be.

The Sun-sign shows the *heart's* wishes. The position of the Moon, the mentality or the conscious and unconscious state, shows the yearning of the *soul's* desire—the mind of the matter. The two positions must be combined and reconciled.

Suppose one born under the sign of Leo, a lordly or kingly sign, has the Moon in the sign of Gemini. This person will have a maganimous heart, yet he may express himself so indecisively (Gemini) that the big part never gets a chance to express itself. It is a lost cause unless the second wheel, or destiny, projects into the person some mental attitude that coincides with the more determined Sun-sign.

I recall a man who came to me one Sunday. I told him it was my rest day, but he pleaded that his case was desperate. He had just lost a girl with whom he was deeply in love. He was a Geminian, the indecisive sign, with his Moon in Cancer. The girl had an Aquarian Sun, with her Moon, representing mentality, in Scorpio—one of the most determined combinations. She knew how to get rid of someone she no longer wanted. She was difficult to persuade, and his weak sign contributed to form a rather hopeless picture.

First, the man's demoralization had to be erased. The Aquarian influence and the placement of the girl's Moon in Scorpio (cruelty) had almost finished him off. The one thing he wanted most was to see her. I had to forbid this. His physical condition alone would have dismissed him from her life. Her Scorpio Moon would not have sympathized with this ruin. Scorpians, as soon as they have degraded you, find the ugly picture you make repulsive to them. They hate failure. Success is all they are interested in. The man was in torment over this verdict. He felt I could never help him.

When he saw I would not consider the case unless he followed orders, he promised to make no effort to see her. I knew I would have to watch him every step of the way, for our most important weapon was *time*.

I convinced him that his present mental state, corresponding to his Moon's position, put him in a very poor light in regard to his outward attitude. We had to bide time to get into a better bargaining position. His Moon also represented the girl.

I allowed one occasional brief telephone call, very tentative, in accordance with the traveling of the Moon in his chart but never overtaxing its potential. He began to see that her anger and hostility were waning which gave him renewed confidence to go on with his own affairs. The unhappiness of the loss of her love had diminished.

At the time of the first good aspect to his Moon, he went to see her. He was happily surprised by her relaxed attitude toward him and found her bitterness gone. I made him cut his visit short so as not to arouse the dormant hostility. He was quite pleased by the outcome. Time had indeed been our friend. Her fears died, and the doubt she had borne against him subsided.

Since I was going to Europe, I had to forbid frequent calls and visits. He was distraught that I was leaving. I pointed out that time had served us well; our plan was working. If he failed to carry it out, I would give it up. He acquiesced. When I returned, we again took up the cudgels of time. The result of this consultation ended happily.

His Moon had gained so in strength that he married her in May, as I had predicted.

Astrology does not get the hearing that it deserves because most astrologers are pressed into giving the kind of reading the client demands. Many of them cannot afford to practice the kind of astrology they would wish—that is, to give exact readings. If the reading is not optimistic, the client cannot understand it, as if the astrologer were responsible for the message read in the stars' positions! We are not magicians; we are interpreters. But often, the client comes to hear absurdities.

For example, if the client is living a useless, foolish life, the astrologer may still see many good aspects that could bring wonderful results. But what good are these aspects if the client does not make a move to bring them to fruition? A chart may for the moment show unhappiness. It is the duty of the astrologer to point this out to the client so that trouble can be prepared for and disaster warded off: the client can thus detour around trouble until good aspects reappear.

Years ago, a house guest of mine, newly separated from her husband in California, asked me to do a reading for her. First, I tried the reconciliatory aspects for a return to the husband. The woman, a difficult Aquarian, immediately wanted to telephone him. I advised against this because most of the trouble had centered around her extravagance, and long-distance calls are expensive. She insisted (you can never tell an Aquarian anything!); the husband, a Capricornian, responded in the negative, as I knew he would, and eventually they broke up.

I foresaw that this Aquarian woman would marry the first man who came along and offered to care for her—and that it would last exactly four years. At the end of four years, after she had married as I had predicted, I telephoned her to warn her that her marriage was in a state of test. At first, she pretended to have forgotten me. (I represented a part of the past that psychologically she preferred to forget.) When I showed an inclination to agree with her and was about to hang up, she was suddenly very glad to hear from me, no doubt curious why I had telephoned. I explained that her marriage needed closer attention, but she laughed it off. Having done my duty, I ended the conversation after she vainly told me (she had Libra rising, a vain personality) that her husband was still crazy about her and that she also had another rich admirer waiting to marry her the very moment her present alliance was over. She was an Aquarian, who welcomes a new mate.

However, something must have occurred during the night, for she called me the next morning, making an appointment for an interview. She was leaving for Florida, so I agreed to see her at once. She then admitted that she was planning to divorce her present husband. This verified the four-year bet that I had made silently to myself.

Quite naturally, if a certain aspect takes away a man, it is clear that the same aspect can create an odd situation for a new associate, particularly if there is no good aspect for the new friend. I informed her of this fact, explaining that she had better be very sure that the new man's chart showed a marriage because her chart did not show marriage. She went to Florida, but her first letter to me was very disturbing.

Her husband told her in a letter that he did not wish her to return to him under the same circumstances as they had been living. Again her aspects were proving that this prediction was being fulfilled. In the meantime, another woman telephoned me and asked for an appointment. When I asked her who had recommended me, she mentioned the name of the first woman's husband. I immediately called him to verify the reference and he surprised me by saying that it was very important that I see him too!

When the second woman arrived, she was hysterical. The reason was obvious. She was engaged to none other than the same man whom my Aquarian friend was planning to marry. In her hysteria, she had asked the latter's husband to help her solve the disappearance of the much-sought-after man. In his effort to console her and from the information that she offered, the husband realized that his wife was involved with this man, too. After all the facts were known, the husband sought my aid by sending his wife's rival to me.

In unraveling the situation, it turned out that the bad aspects which my Aquarian lady was undergoing had attracted an equally unattractive association with this new man. He was the type who preyed on married women, but who was ready to leave the scene hurriedly when a victimized married woman began to force the ring. So the same aspect which I had predicted would end the marriage also brought out the new man's perfidious intentions.

Had my client been less vain and not so divorce-prone (this was her fourth marriage), and had she not possessed Libra vanity plus Aquarian love of change, I could have saved her good marriage, mended the situation, and saved at least three people from unhappiness. Instead, many lives were needlessly torn by the refusal of one person to accept the influences of her chart. Her own fixed sign (Aquarius) made her determined to have her way. She ignored the wonderful potential of this great science which could have planned her course and led her into safety had she given it a hearing and abided by it.

It is a satisfying life in that it is the duty of the astrologer to warn. This is the most sincere and, ultimately, the most satisfactory form of offering astrology. On the other hand, it is a great pleasure to tell good news and impart joy (or to be able to train the client to accept the wonders of astrology), knowing that if his first impression does not suit him—the oldest and most helpful of the mystic sciences will be lost.

However, a client can contribute to the wrong type of practice by demanding to be told only the flattering things rather than the truth. The chart shows the kind of person for whom you are interpreting. It is up to the astrologer to establish a rapport between the aid that is meant to be given and the truth concerning how the client stands with the intelligence of destiny's clock.

I remember a Swiss banker whose marriage I had brought about, even though the difference of both religion and social position had raised a problem. Now happily married he returned with his wife to discuss the fear of losing a position he had enjoyed for thirty years. Wishing to see my client win—Uranus, the unpredictable, was the only planet making motion in the action of his horoscope—and knowing that Uranus can clear the air, I was sure he could win over the ouster. But no planet can be as perverse as Uranus, and he lost his position. When I met his wife days later, she said, "You wanted so to have him keep his place that you predicted that he could beat the unpredictability into a winning, but Uranus can destroy as well as progressively improve."

How right she was! But though I did not want to plant this possibility into his consciousness, it would have been better to tell him that a loss was in the making as well as an improvement. This experience taught me a lesson I shall never forget. It supplied ample proof of the dangers in optimistic readings, even though this is what most people want.

Another time I telephoned a client to tell him that his marriage was in trouble—a marriage that I had arranged for him. He was curt and rude, which discouraged me. I soon got off the telephone without disclosing the information.

A week later, he called to ask that I meet him for a cocktail. When we met, he asked very anxiously, "Why did you call me?" I told him that he had a loss coming and that I wanted to warn him in time. It didn't surprise me when he said that his wife had just put him out.

There are two ideas involved here. First, the fact that I telephoned a client to tell him that trouble was coming. This is a situation that most astrologers face and which requires action. Second, the response of the client to a warning.

Solving a problem is ethical and right for the astrologer who is concerned with both the potential of his work and with the client who has shown faith in the ability of astrology. I combined both in this decision, giving him a chance to avoid sorrow and giving the science the chance to prove that, with a correct application, it can, and in fact does, work for man.

The man's rejection of my telephone call proved that the very thing that had brought him happiness was now being dismissed as of no further use, for he believed he was safe in his position. This is a further example of giving in to the atmosphere that the client creates. It usually ends in failure!

Astrology fails when the client suffers; the astrologer also fails when he is afraid to take action. By refusing to take the stand that astrology deserves, he fails to establish its potential and thus assure its position in the world.

Most astrologers are in this position. A decision must be made by the astrologer; the client should be consulted, or appraised and asked how much he can take of the adverse information as well as the good news. There is no such thing as a perfect chart. There is such a thing as good and bad aspects occurring at the same time. The *map of destiny* may show the loss of a loved one at the same time that it shows an increase in income. One is adverse, Saturnine; the other, a good Jupiter expanding financial luck—the windfall of Jupiter, the benefactor, combined with a karmic lesson.

The man I telephoned experienced calamity. His wife finally divorced him, which was a very great sorrow for both. She needed to succeed in marriage (this was her third). He too required the assurance of a peaceful home life, for he was in the kind of business that creates insecurity; but a good and satisfactory marriage might have offset it. Later, he lost a very good job which perhaps he would not have lost had his marriage lasted. A whole chain of events followed this one aspect. Knowing what this aspect could effect, I also knew that these mishaps could have been avoided. Not giving my telephone call the hearing it deserved (his false vanity cut him off) contributed to disaster.

A few years ago, the mother of a girl, whose chart she wished me to forecast, came to me. When told of a disillusionment that was on its way to her daughter from the man to whom the girl was now engaged, the mother exclaimed, "But I could never tell her that."

"No," I replied, "let her be run over by the oncoming train." The mother stared at me, shocked.

When the blow fell, the daughter had to be hospitalized. The whole thing could have been avoided by a little preparation from the mother. Time was on their side; but the purpose of coming to an astrolger was completely lost to the mother, who was looking for a happily-ever-after ending. Happiness was not on the clock of destiny at the time of interpretation; but the girl did have a beautiful marriage-horoscope which, in time, would work out.

I have often asked clients which kind of a forecast they prefer. That is, as they naturally come to hear good things, would they also want me to apprise them of the danger spots? Those who want to know the bad as well as the good have been the clients that have been coming to me year after year. With the advice that nothing is ever lost and that, with patience, we can always avoid an obstacle if such should be the fare at that time, the client will usually accept this and create the atmosphere for final success. However, the astrologer must be allowed to practice the kind of astrology that the client really needs, not the one that gives a light, glowing account of all the areas in his life.

A producer brought to me the chart of an actress he hoped to sign for a production. After he had obtained his objective, I warned him that on opening in another town, she would be so difficult that he would be in despair, wishing that I had never agreed to signing her. She did just that and behaved with such difficulty that he thought he would have to replace her. But when they opened in New York, she changed completely. Her behavior had to do with her Sun-sign (her birthday); it was in total disagreement with the city in which the production opened. Knowing that she would feel this pull, I cautioned for patience; and she was fine when they got to the city that agreed with her Sun-sign. They enjoyed a full and successful run.

A optimistic attitude should be taken to all first forecasts, giving everyone a chance to see how great astrology can be. The client should be tested for susceptibility to the kind of information he can digest. His chart will show his nature, and the astrologer should approach the client from that point of view. The client should not hold against the astrologer any adverse information (it may prevent his making an error in judgment) any more than he would resent the doctor stating that a lung is infected, if indeed it is. He does not go to the doctor to be placated and flattered. Astrologers, then, should be seen in this same light and allowed to practice on the same level, instead of on the basis that the science is one of magic and mystery.

People have been surprised by the calculations that precede the forecasting. They have asked, "But aren't you psychic?" When the answer is, "Astrology is a science requiring calculations by logarithms to ascertain the position of each planet (if the birth hour is known) and not fortune-telling or psychic feelings," they remain untouched and many times are disappointed. They *want* it to be fortune-telling. They prefer the gamble, the mysterious.

A forecast should take at least an hour. First, the client should be given time to enter into the spirit of the reading. A brief rundown should be made on what kind of personality he is, particularly if it is his first reading. The client should acquaint himself with the language of astrology, for astrology *is* a language. How it is explained is also very important.

An outline of the kind of destiny to expect is demonstrated; the phraseology of the science is made familiar; the good and so-called bad are explained, as well as their uses for advantage; the kind of character toward which one is inclined, with a clue to one's health, is given. This clears the air for the real prediction, which should be given last, after the client has had a chance to get acquainted with his horoscope. An objective point of view from an outsider (whose business it is to study character) is in itself worth the time and money spent for the experience.

A psychiatrist is not expected to get more than a mere part of the general history of each patient on the first visit. Why must an astrologer be expected to pull rabbits out of his hat in ten or fifteen minutes? He must be allowed to practice honestly on a high level.

Consulting an astrologer should not be a life and death experience. If the astrologer does not say exactly what you came to hear, it should not make you condemn the science any more than going to a clumsy dentist would make you condemn dentistry.

All astrologers are not good, any more than are all doctors. In selecting an astrologer, recommendations should be examined exactly as a doctor's might be.

Each astrologer has a different form of reading. I know an astrologer who persists in telling his clients to leave one part of the country and go to another. He should be a mundane astrologer and analyze the destinies of countries. I can see the advisability of this advice only if the client is ill or doing badly in the city in which he lives.

Another astrologer may be interested only in lifting the client into a more spiritual way of life. The astrologer I have in mind preaches self-denial. This may be good advice, but it is hardly acceptable, especially if the client is faced with a marital problem that requires an immediate solution. He wants and comes for practical answers.

Finally, in case the astrologer has not covered the problem the client is being harassed with, time should be left free and the client encouraged to ask the main question puzzling him. An answering period of about fifteen minutes should be set aside to discuss the immediate problem. This would then give the client the feeling that he had participated to some degree in the venture and that he had received the aid he sought.

2

Here's How

There are those who need only a plan to make the right moves *at the ripe time*. Planning or aiding in a destiny is particularly fascinating to me and can be most satisfactory when the results are seen. The client's cooperation in bringing about the desired results leads to the most exciting chapter in astrology. Some signs help you to aid clients, but other signs fight to the bitter end for disaster to overtake your clients.

There are many aspects to define in the horoscope; the more important ones can be explained by the astrologer. He should be eager to explain them because the more the client knows about himself the easier it is to accomplish what is hoped for. The intelligent client enjoys knowing about himself, and the astrologer finds forecasting more pleasurable since the client's attention is completely enlisted and undivided.

We now come to the part of astrology that is boundless in its fascination: Interpretation.

Every sign behaves and acts differently from the heart, which is the Sun-sign, or your birthday. Each individual chart has the Moon placed in one of the twelve signs. This luminary represents the consciousness or mentality that will show your thoughts or desires. Twins born minutes apart will have a different degree for both the Moon's position and the rising sign, possibly even a different rising sign. This will change their personalties and slant their thinking, making them different.

Many years ago a man sent me to the home of his two sisters-in-law to give forecasts. They were twins, yet they did not resemble each other very much: one woman had gray hair; the other had black. They were born exactly fifteen minutes apart. I found that the first sister I read for showed a happy marriage that should then be in effect. She said nothing, but there was a very curious smile on her face. She left the room and sent in her dark-haired sister, whose chart showed a tragic end to a marriage, and I said so. She too sat silent and did not offer any comment. I was completely bewildered, for I knew what I had seen.

After the forecasts, luncheon was served, and I was seated beside their mother. Knowing that something was wrong, I asked the mother the birth times again. The gray-haired sister had the later birth time; it was she who had had the tragedy. Her husband had committed suicide. Therefore, the first woman I had read to had the unhappy marriage; the second sister, who was born first, was happily wed. I had read the charts right, but had taken them in the wrong order.

Years later, the sister who had the tragic chart again consulted me concerning a doctor in whom she was interested. After reviewing her chart, I recommended that she marry him at once *if* she wanted him. However, she delayed the marriage.

About two years later, while dining at her home, she mentioned that she thought she would marry the doctor then. I said, "No, you have gone past marriage-*time*." She laughed this off saying there was plenty of time.

A few months later she telephoned me and asked "How in the world did you know it was too late?"

When I asked why, she informed me that he had died of a heart attack. The pattern of tragedy, of losing her men through death came true, though her sister, born only fifteen minutes earlier, is still married to the same man. This is a very pointed example of the differences in a destiny when only minutes are involved.

How then can those born on the same day yet living in different cities—with the longitude and latitude to be taken into consideration as well as the different birth times entering into it—expect the same kind of lives? The answer is they definitely should not expect parallel lives.

That is another reason why the language of astrology is so very fascinating. The time difference that changed the rising signs gave these sisters different experiences; the time also changed the degree of the Moon. The Moon and the Sun are called the lights: one the mind and the other heart or individuality. What each says in the horoscope is very important.

When I am asked by people why they are not like someone they know born under the same sign, the answer is, "You were born at a different hour, in a different place, and are therefore not alike.

Let us now take a closer look at the meaning of the ten planets. The position of Venus, the planet that rules the social and erotic life, will show the loves that are to come into your life. How you will deal with them, or they with you, can be seen at once. If Venus is afflicted, you may have to change many times before the right person comes along. If Venus has no afflictions, you may stick to one love all of your life. In addition, if your Venus is backed up by strong planets, you will never have to worry about comfort or income; you will be well cared for. If it is afflicted, you may have to curb your appetites and watch the budget.

Mars is the planet of action, the start of every new adventure. If it is in a favorable position, everything you do will be successful. If it is afflicted, you may have to make many initial efforts before succeeding. You may go from job to job, for under such conditions it is always the job that is at fault. It never occurs to you that you are making the mistakes, and you may refuse to learn by each experience. If Mars is afflicted to sweet Venus, the planet of peace and harmony, the Mars interference will cancel out peace. Turbulent Mars will direct all of his warring nature toward the loved one and project his energy or guilt onto that person. The ensuing difficulties will give him the right to go on to another love, who will be blamed the same as the former.

When Mars is not afflicted and is trine Venus, Mars behaves like a lamb; the loved one can do no wrong. Then you will see a tiny girl handle a big, husky fellow quite well. He may seem like a bear to everyone but her, yet she twists him around her little finger. Girls will flock to a man with a good aspect of Venus to Mars; they see no wrong in him, and he is as gentle as a dove. A sweet Venus and a gentle Mars is a wondrous combination under the aspect called the trine.

Mars controls energy and the sex life. A strong Mars can work anyone to death, for the more energy he expends, the more he seems to have. Sex is energy, energy is work, and work is money; therefore a good Mars is a money-maker.

Mercury is the planet that will show you how to reason and express your practical ideas. If Mercury is afflicted to Venus, you may be a fault-finding lover, noticing only the mistakes your loved one makes, never being quite satisfied with a new hat, hair-do, or what she says, for Mercury rules the speech organs and the words one utters. If your Mercury is in good aspect to Venus, that is, in a trine or sextile state, you will always have a ready compliment for the loved one. You will remark on what a beautiful girl she is, even if she has a wart on her nose, for you will see only the sweetness in her—that is, *if* Mercury, who speaks, and your Venus, who loves, are in a happy state.

If Mercury is in a bad aspect with Mars, you will have heated discussions at the drop of a hat. In fact, you will be waiting for the remark that will justify an argument leading to tears or blows—depending upon how unfavorably your Mercury is afflicted to Mars, the bitter, sarcastic, vituperative, belittling demoralizer. If Mercury is afflicted by the most devastating planet, Uranus, there is nothing you will not say to inflict pain. An afflicted Mercury can devastate you with spoken words. Mercury in good aspect to Saturn has a photographic memory and can heal you with a perfectly comforting remark, knowing exactly what you need to hear at the right time. Saturn rules time and necessity. A complimentary comment resulting from this combination is not superficial; it is a thoughtful remark you deserve. It is sincerely made.

We come now to the best known planet, Jupiter, by Jove! Jupiter represents the best luck in the horoscope. Wherever it is found, there is luck. If you find this wonderful planet in the house of marriage you will attract a good and happy marriage. Your mate will find you. Here is an example:

A drab and unnoticed girl happened to live near a new road that was being built in a small town. One of the supervisors of the construction job came to her house for information. They became friends and eventually married. *He* found her. Jupiter did not appear in his chart as the good-luck planet in his marriage house, but her chart showed a good marriage.

During the war many manufacturers, men who had never before had money, came to consult me. One person in particular, a man who had never earned more than sixty dollars a week, became a millionaire! Jupiter was in his house of income. He needed only the right set of circumstances to achieve wealth, for with good Jupiter in the house of money, he would have to be rich someday.

Many authors will have Jupiter in the third house, which rules writing; that is one of the reasons why they become writers. They have many ideas to express; Jupiter in the third house, which is the house of thought and speech, is what makes an interesting writer. Whether through one's own efforts, marriage, or inheritance, Jupiter will tell the tale. His position will clearly put one's judgment or opinions squarely where they belong, identifying one's ideals or philosophy.

The position of Saturn in the chart will show the divine plan the intelligence has set up for final evolvement. Life can be planned without mishap with a good Saturn at the helm, but the rewards have to be earned.

At the mention of the fact that Saturn holds sway—either by transiting around the horoscope or by its position at birth—most people who know something of the science, or even astrologers, visualize and predict dark and gloomy times. I find that Saturn sobers and conditions one for a better plan. Wherever Saturn appears, serious attention must be given. If it is found in the sixth house of service or employment, the inclination will be to produce a serious work someday. The hardships that will have to be encountered in one's toils will bear rich fruit in time.

I am sure that Saturn appeared in Plato's sixth house of service; and that would account for his writing the *Republic*, a doctrine of law, for Saturn also rules political law. Saturn is factual and his rewards are absolute. You will get exactly what is due you under an active Saturn. The best way to get along with an apparent adversity—this merely seems so—is to agree with it. It will then cease to harm or discipline you. The tasks that Saturn demands are not glamorous; that is why they are looked upon with distaste. If it is found in the house of marriage, you may marry a reliable person older than you. Since Saturn rules time, you may not wed until you are very mature or older. If Saturn is in the house of income, you may not get your "big" money until late in life. If it is found in the tenth house, as it was in the charts of both Napoleon and Hitler, fame will surely be yours, but at a great price. Reputation, represented by the tenth house, will be tested again and again; in the end—for Saturn will have the final say—it will be the truth, not *maya* (illusion).

Uranus is the next in strength to the five history-making planets. Uranus arouses and changes. Its methods are shocking and disturbing. It means to shock and even destroy if it has to attract your attention.

Uranus does not employ subtle means, as Neptune does. The ways of each planet are different, for their purposes are different. They go about their business according to the nature of their purpose. Uranus is unmistakable in both action and purpose. If and when it destroys situations or circumstances (it rules divorce), it does so in order to make you rebuild them. The old molds were useless. It may seem cruel to the person having to suffer a blow from the so-called ruthless Uranus, but the time will come when its message is clear, revealing, and emancipating.

Uranus, when in a good state in the wheel of life, helps the greatest inventors, builders, originators. Men who dare to say and build new worlds (Uranus) are unafraid of criticism from the old (Saturn), who might hold them back, and who are jealous of new. Uranian ideas or innovations seem too radical or centric. Uranus is the planet that rules egocentrics.

Uranus makes very tall, lean men; the bone structure is emphasized. If not, it is afflicted and it will cut down the height. Hitler's chart had Uranus rising, but it was afflicted by both his Jupiter, another planet that influences height, and the Moon, which rules over the gland that controls height. Therefore, he was not as tall as he might have been. But he was unmistakably egocentric. Uranus makes a man high-strung, nervous, argumentative, and authoritative if it is on the ascendant. Uranus gives a man a dome-shaped head, such as it gave Franklin D. Roosevelt. The cranium seems to spread domelike over the head; the bone structure is emphasized, for Uranus eschews fat; and since there is little or no covering, the bone line is clear.

Uranus hates monotony or the past. A person with Uranus emphasized in the personality house, or near it, can be rocognized easily, for he refuses to look backward; he is always pursuing the future, running into *time*, or more exactly running *ahead* of time. That is why the function of Uranus is in direct opposition to Saturn, the planet that rules the past and tradition. When these two planets quarrel with each other in the horoscope, the screams circulate around the world. Uranus rules ether and the circulatory system. Uranus does not keep secrets; that is the function of subtle and sly Neptune. If Uranus meets with Saturn in your chart, the past is revealed in all its shabbiness, for Saturn rules the yesteryears. One may not like the past revealed, but one thing is clear—you will not return to it. Uranus will make progress impossible unless the past is sifted into more constructive channels.

Man is prone to doing the same things over and over, never understanding that he does not have a more interesting pattern in life because *he* will not change. He expects life to lead him by the hand into all sorts of interesting adventure. This can only come about through his own efforts, thoughts, or the force and drive of his conscious mind. Uranus is the planet that will force progress on one willy-nilly. Even under affliction, it can be a better friend to man (it rules the house of friendship) than man is to himself. It is a difficult planet, making personalities very complicated if emphasized on the ascendant. Once it is understood and reconciled, there is never a dull moment, for it is the planet of genius. An active Uranus can produce much excitement in the chart of a person or a country. If it is not afflicted, it can make celebrities or world figures overnight. A rising Uranus in his chart made Hitler a world figure. He might have left the world in a better state, had it not been for Saturn in the tenth house of reputation.

If you are ever in a group where one person takes a perverse or difficult stand on every subject introduced, you can be sure that he will have either a Uranus sign that is afflicted or Uranus in conjunction (that is, in the same sign) with Jupiter, the planet that rules judgment and opinion. If his Uranus is in conjunction with Venus or afflcted with Venus, he will be a social problem, a nonconformist who always finds people difficult to deal with; actually it is truly he who is odd.

No one can argue longer and more tenaciously than those with an afflicted Uranus. These people are the misfits. The strange thing about it is that the planet has a fascinating attraction. It makes those who have it emphasized very unusual. They will attract you against your will. They are difficult to get along with because, while they attract you, they do not necessarily find you as attractive as you find them. They cannot understand why you continue to desire them *after* they have "divorced" you, and divorce you they will once they have penetrated your interests; Uranus is afflicted when this is expressed. They are fighting for freedom from you. Let them go, for if they are kept against their will, there is no peace. The tyranny created from a forced association resulting from an afflicted Uranus is the most intolerable of all partnerships. Perversity is the key note.

I have two clients, a couple, living under this perverse Uranus vibration. The husband had Uranus afflicting his Sun. He will argue stubbornly against his wife until she is driven into the most desperate exhaustion. He refuses to release her. He will neither cease the harassments nor the impossible situation that he has created with another woman, knowing that it is destroying the marriage that he refuses to live up to. This is sadism in action. He is an egocentric whose stubborn defiance expresses soul torture.

Uranus is a soulless planet. All the inventions introduced into the home life while Uranus was transiting through Cancer, the sign that rules the home, have been cut to the bone of curves, embellishment, or spirituality.

Uranus is occult. That which is hidden is suddenly revealed. That which was wrapped in flowery encasement is exposed starkly, realistically. Cancer, the sign of the home life, is divorced of all but necessity. Gadgets of all sorts cut homework down to a minimum. Food is half-prepared by experts before it is brought home. Articles for the home are now constructed for utilitarian purposes rather than beauty alone. Even dining has become a thing of efficiency rather than a leisurely pleasure. Uranus has done it all.

Cancer is the sign of childhood; Uranus in Cancer has modernized it. The pregnant woman immediately enrolls at the clinic, and efficiency experts take over, instructing her on what to do both before and after childbirth. Almost nothing is left to nature: the experts know better.

Uranus introduced revolution and rebellion. If the child expresses himself in a rebellious manner, he is not considered an ill-mannered child. He may be a potential genius, so he is taken at once to a child specialist who translates his growing pains into a complex identified with mother failure or paternal tyranny, giving the child the right to practice psychological warfare to his heart's content. His selfishness and self-centeredness are allowed to flow beyond all proportion until the child becomes a dictator in the home. The parents are then afraid to take too strong a position for fear of criticism and of being called unfit. The child has supplanted the parent, and the child experts stand by ready to bolster his claim! This is true, especially in the United States, a country that is ruled by the sign of Cancer. During the transit of Uranus, the unusual planet, in the sign of Cancer, it made it almost impossible to remedy this situation until the planet changed signs at the end of 1955.

Of all the ten planets in the Sun's family, Neptune is the most spiritual. Neptune rules the sea; it is the old man coming up out of the sea with his three-pronged fork, or trident, with dreams to sell—the dreamiest fancies of lovers' blind eyes. I call Neptune the dream-maker man.

First, there is the dream. Neptune is the planet of mysterious ideas not yet understood. Neptune needs a strong Saturn to bring the dream down to a practical level, or a strong Uranus to make the dream a workable reality. If Neptune is rising in the destiny map, the individual can be the most mystical of all humans, feeling way ahead the events about to happen on earth. Those with Neptune on the ascendant have long spiritual fingers feeling the pressures of life through "vibrations." The antennae, the fingers, can pick up the event.

Such people are the visionaries. Abraham Lincoln had this planet rising; but Neptune was also accompanied by a practical Saturn that aided him in bringing his visions down to the practical level. He was truly a destiny individual, for Neptune has the say in spiritual evolvement. When Neptune makes a fortunate aspect in one's horoscope, something dreamed through the years can come true. The spiritual satisfaction that this planet can bring under good auspices is immense. It is precious and beautiful.

On the other hand, when Neptune is out of step with the wheel of destiny, the rug is pulled out from under one's feet (Neptune rules the feet). The adversities that come through its underminings are never seen. Neptune is a very subtle, silent watcher. When it strikes, you are completely unaware because first it creates an *illusion* which blinds you, preparing you for the denouement. It may bring you a love affair that has all the appearance of being the love of your life, but because you are in debt to the law of karma, it is swept away at the very peak of the happiest state. The disillusionment is deep and unabiding, for the unhappiness that a Neptunian reversal can bring is the more severe for having seen the beauty and happiness that *might* have been.

A very successful publisher came to me years ago. He wanted me to chart the right time for him to divorce his wife. Being more interested in how to make marriages work than in dissolving them, I tried to talk him into a compromise, indicating that the present marriage was coming to an end and that it was better to use *time* (resorting to my favorite planet, Saturn) as our best bet, for in due time he could have the girl he wanted to marry.

He rejected the more secure path to happiness, seeking a short cut. We picked the best day for what he wanted—a divorce—and a new date to espouse a beautiful and lovely Neptunian dream. I pointed out the nature of that aspect and warned him that it would be hard to handle.

But he was a business tycoon who had handled, as he put it, tougher things than a beautiful woman. Yet that is exactly how Neptune operates; it makes you overconfident. He came to me regularly, and I was in a position to follow the history of the new marriage. He always referred to it as "my baby." I continued to point out to him that though we had picked Jupiter, the planet of bloom, to make the marriage, Neptune was the buzzard in the fuel pile. He did not pay any heed.

He lived around the corner from me; and one New Year's Eve, as I was leaving my house, he came running toward me. He insisted that we return to my apartment for a consultation. Something had happened for at that moment a party was in progress in his home. He had to know the outcome of an incident. I told him that his happiness was being tested by a threat of the very planet against which I had warned him. I explained to him that, as big planets move very slowly, so does the good or evil that they bring. It does not come or go in a trice, but goes back and forth until the final denouement. It was the beginning of the end for his marriage.

A man brought by a friend to their New Year's Eve party fell in love with my client's wife. He had treated this marriage as he had the previous one, and his wife was ready for a man who would treat her differently. The first wife, who was ill at the time of the divorce, died soon after. Had he waited, he would have entered his new alliance more honorably. The second marriage was dissolved very unhappily, for his beautiful wife had gathered much information that made it prohibitive for him to fight for her. He did not even get the opportunity to do what any man who really loves has a right to do, fight for the thing that he loves. He had to let her go without a sound. Neptune silenced him.

He never recovered psychologically from the defeat. The day she was granted the divorce, he sat on my terrace asking over and over again, "Why?" Nothing consoled him, for he could not possibly accept the answer. Neptune had broken the illusion that it had created. Thus, an afflicted chart had come full cycle. The planet with a more austere method might have brought lasting happiness, *if* it had been properly handled.

But when in a good position, Neptune can return a lost love. When the man she loved married someone else, a woman who had married indifferently and gone to live in Paris came to ask if she would marry again. The Paris marriage had ended with her husband's death in the war. Neptune was making a beautiful trine to Saturn, showing that something from the past would return to her.

She was astounded because, as she remarked, she thought she would never see her former beau again. But she did see him again, and after twenty years of separation, they reconciled. He told her that he had never forgotten her and that he realized he had made a mistake. During the intervening years, he had consoled himself with work. He was now more successful than when he jilted her. Her waiting period rewarded her too. They are now living in New York.

Pluto was the last planet to be discovered in the Sun's family. There may be two more planets beyond Pluto to be assigned to the two signs that have to share rulers; but as yet this is unknown, so Pluto is the last addition. Pluto is a newly discovered member, and enough time has not passed to show all of the things this slow and powerful planet can do. It has been assigned to rulership over the powerful sign of Scorpio. This seems to be correct, for the drastic measures that it can bring about would certainly seem that it belongs to a strong sign.

Pluto does everything on a mass basis. It is too big and rigid to reduce to personal identifications. Pluto rules the *ists* and *isms* of politics. Pluto entered Leo in 1939. It brought in the political gangster during its transit through the sign of Leo. Leo is the sign of kings and queens. It is the sign of aristocracy and capitalism.

Pluto set about dethroning royalty everywhere. It brought in new political thinking: Fasc*ists* and Naz*ism;* gangster*ism* in politics—leaders more powerful than a king or queen. The power of the leader was underground. The ideas that made the leader powerful had no relationship to the ideals he said he was bringing to a people; they were separate and diverse, and had nothing in common; they were not meant to, and did not do so, until Pluto left the sign of the true authority, the sign of Leo, and entered Virgo, the sign of labor and service, in 1957.

Leo rules the youth of the world. Pluto, afflicted, is a gangster. Pluto has made dictators of the youth of the world. Pluto has made gangsters of teenagers. A modern youth wants to rule; and if he cannot, his frustration is so great that he tries to rid himself of this maniacal energy by committing crimes. Since Pluto is voracious when afflicted, there is no appeasing the youth of the world. The more you do to please him, like the *Golem,* the bigger he grows.

If Pluto rises on the ascendant of the horoscope, that personality is strong, powerful, and meant to rule. The strength of a person with this planet rising is magnetic, forceful, and felt at once. If it does so in a woman's chart, she is mannish. She is the virago who cannot reduce her force and is thought to be overbearing and difficult. If this force and power can be syphoned into creative action, it is then dispensed; those who have to deal with such persons do not have to meet this power. Otherwise, they exhaust everybody with whom they come in contact; many do not understand this, and even the person in question is unaware.

In 1882, Pluto entered the sign of Gemini, the writer's sign. It did not remain there for long however; it retrograded (or went backward) before it re-entered Gemini in May of 1884 and remained in the writer's sign until June of 1914—just about thirty years, which is its normal time to go through a sign. That thirty-year period produced great writing. Those born during that period and who are writers are having their say. They were born during the great literary era.

Pluto creates the strongest kind of atmosphere in whatever sign or house it is found in your horoscope. The events it brings are not subtle like Neptune's. They come and go suddenly like unusual Uranus. They are not factual and businesslike like Saturn's. Pluto is a wave flowing over everything. It covers all other events and reduces them to nothing; all other maneuvers are forgotten. Pluto's events demand immediate and undivided attention. You cannot think of anything other than what it has brought about. It entered Leo in 1939—starting World War II.

3

You Are More Than One Sign

There are twelve houses and twelve corresponding signs, each house representing one department of your life. The planets in a house, or those absent from it, translate how that house will affect that certain area of your life; the sign ruling that house will tell the nature of the influence.

Each astrologer or student interprets differently. The doctor translates differently from the described symptom. The many paths the client may take or choose to express at top level can be identified by the interpreter.

For example, a client in whose chart Venus, the planet of love and sociability, is very prominent asked how she could take advantage of this. I asked what her social plans were. She was invited to attend many important social affairs. I found that one day was astrologically special. I suggested that she plan to attend all the affairs on this particular day. She had been invited to one party which she preferred not to attend, for she said it would be noisy and boring (Venus likes tranquillity). I insisted that she go, but to arrive exactly at seven. I knew she would meet someone of great importance.

She showed little enthusiasm and preferred to go to another soirée. After much difficulty, I was able to persuade her to do as I suggested, although I knew she would carry out the program only to please me.

As she arrived at the party, a man who was leaving and who held the door open for her, mentioned that the party was a bore. He suggested a quiet place for a cocktail. She accepted his offer and thus started the most wonderful friendship of her life.

One planet may stand out in the horoscope with

such force as to obscure one's birth sign. That planet should be worked for all it is worth in order to derive the greatest possible advantage for the native. That planet will represent a talent that might not be recognized otherwise. A wonderful planet on the ascendant can change the destiny of the individual if properly handled and timed correctly—just as a weak planet or sign can be translated into a better life if controlled like an unwanted trait. A weakly aspected Sun-sign can show an unimportant individual; but if the sign rising is strong, or a fixed sign, the whole career can be recharged.

A weak personality sign, that is, a weakly aspected ascendant, may give an impression that the person is ineffectual and unimportant. But if the birth sign is strong, you are greatly deceived for then you have someone who only seems unproductive. The weak personality has seemed to underestimate the strength behind the strong and worthy Sun-sign.

In June, 1951, *Life* magazine ran an article entitled "What Manner of Morph Are You?" by Robert Coughlan, showing physical types. One's temperament could be more or less interpreted by appearance. The three types in the articles were the endomorph, the mesomorph, and the ectomorph, identified in astrology as the cardinal, fixed, and mutable types. Astrology identifies similarly so that each sign found in the *individual* chart is seen at a glance in his walk, speech, and action.

The Fixer Signs. The "big shots"—the first quadruplicate—of the zodiac are the fixed signs. The word *fixed* means exactly what it says. They are fixed in attitude, thought, and habit. They change momentarily just to please you or to get what they want, yet eventually return to their old habits. The reason for this is that they are most determined. The fixed signs are Taurus, Leo, Scorpio, and Aquarius. Not only are they strongly indicated in the world's history, but similarly they also show up importantly as destiny individuals.

During World War II, the four destiny individuals at the head of countries involved were fixed signs. Hitler was Taurus; Mussolini was Leo; Roosevelt was Aquarian—though Churchill was a Sagittarian, it was the emphasized Scorpio in his chart that associated him with the others. It is the prominent Scorpio in Churchill's chart that gives him *word*-power, for the Sagittarian is didactic and literary as well as oratorical. These men, regardless of how they expressed themselves, were destiny men put on earth to change world history. Their fixity of purpose will be clear in history. Only fixed signs follow through what they start out to accomplish.

The times then were suitable, for during World War II three of the epoch-making planets were in the same sign—Taurus. Taurus, ruling land and money, showed that these would be leading factors. Hitler said he wanted more *Lebensraum* for his people. Land was taken from peoples, becoming part of other countries. Astronomical action was evidenced in money matters, in which not millions but billions were involved. Two factors were prominent during the period: *money* and *planning,* both representative of the two planets that were then together, or conjunct. Saturn rules the divine plan; Jupiter rules big money. Saturn rules *time,* and the time was right. The time had come for world economy to be put to the test of human values. What better way to bring about this metamorphosis than through the planets that represent planning and values—Saturn and Jupiter? Who else could have carried it out but a Taurian Hitler and an Aquarian Roosevelt? There is no mistake in the clock of destiny; there is only man's failure to interpret and read the dial correctly.

The fixed signs are the winners for they *will* to win in different ways. Taurus is doggedly determined, since it is ruled by Venus, the planet which succeeds through charm and kindness rather than through reason. It never gives up and so attains success through patience and singleness of purpose. Taurians do not abandon desire for success until they achieve their goal. They make bankers and buyers of land; they like to buy things and resell them for profit. They are comparison buyers who instinctively know the value of everything, including people. People are kept in their lives depending on what value these people have for their intents and purposes. Remember that

Hitler banished anyone who opposed his views or did not approve completely of his plans.

Taurians are just as solid as they look, for they are as reliable as the lines upon which they are built. They are sentimental and they like affection. It upsets them to discover that they have incurred enmity; for the signs ruled by Venus are narcissistic types, and love is important to them. They are most reassured if they have material possessions. They prefer to live in the country or suburbs. They are wonderful gardeners and feel comfortable when they are surrounded by nature. This insures their interest in earth as a symbol of their material goals. The afflicted Taurian is greedy; he underestimates others deliberately, for in so doing he can use them to his advantage. His stubbornness serves him always in deals involving money, for he can outwait you. As he grows older, he becomes heavier in all things, both physical and mental, for he is not a thinker. Reading is too taxing. If he is intellectual at all, it is because Gemini is in his horoscope. Gemini follows the sign of Taurus, and very often Mercury or Venus is in the sign preceding one's Sun-sign. Such reading as Taurians do is for practical reasons and seldom for pleasure.

The second of the "big shot" signs is Leo, a fire sign. His perseverance will have an entirely different purpose in view than Taurus, whose aim is wealth and security. Leo is not so interested in earthly gains as he is in his will to dominate. Leo is a royal sign; so no matter where he finds himself, he expects to rule as a king should. If he cannot get you to be his subject willingly, then the lion roars you into submission, for the temper of Leo is violent. The redeeming feature about this fierceness is that when it subsides Leo goes right on being your friend, just as if the quarrel had never occurred. For this reason, he makes a good "enemy"; he forgets his anger afterwards. The key to this is that Leo rules the heart; generosity and sincerity reign supreme, which means he has to return to his royal self, his true state. Leo has great faith in what he does, says, and fights for. When he does win, it is the faith he had in the idea that is justified. That is the true reason he wills to dominate. Leo is always in love, for the sign rules youth, love, drama, sports, and pleasure. Leos are in love with a sport that is dramatic (racing horses) or an idea that can be presented dramatically. They are always acting, for they *are* the theater. Mussolini was always putting on a show; the ideas he expressed were only a backdrop for the show he was presenting—himself playing the lead.

The afflicted Leo (when enemy signs to Leo are emphasized), who may have Scorpio or Taurus in his horoscope, will be very stubborn. Perhaps the opposite sign, Aquarius (though the opposite sign is not as difficult as the square signs, Scorpio and Taurus), makes him perverse; the big heart will then be seen sporadically rather than continuously. Leo can then be spiteful, malicious, determined to win over you. He does not like to be defeated. Leo is the most willful of the four fixed signs. Taurus wants material gain; Scorpio wants power; and Aquarius wants internationality —but Leo wants to rule!

The third of these fixed signs is the notorious Scorpio. This sign has the worst reputation of all, and justifiably so. There are very few *evolved* Scorpians on earth. Scorpians get their reputation from loving power so much that they will ride rough-shod over anything or anyone to attain power. Their fixity of purpose never loses sight of the path to power, and no sign is more resourceful. If the situation seems impossible, it will only take a little longer for Scorpio to accomplish the task. The key to this is that he never forgets what he seeks.

Taurus may outwit you in a financial matter, but you will discover this and deal with him more cautiously next time. Leo may succeed in dominating your will at times, but in the next situation you will know how to handle him. But not so with Scorpio! His resourcefulness will attack or threaten you from an entirely different angle each time. It is impossible to know from which position he intends to outmaneuver you, or to anticipate his next move. He does not know from which angle he will strike you either. Scorpio is co-ruled by Mars; Mars strikes or acts on impulse. Scorpio has two rulers now. Since Pluto was discovered in 1930, many astrologers assign Pluto as ruler while many use Mars. Having two rulers may account for the drastic changes in the methods Scorpians use.

For example, when Scorpians first enter into a situation or an association, they are very ardent and devoted; they go all out for you. You may feel sure that you have met the love or friend of a lifetime. The promise seems great. They make vows that persuade you to believe that you have nothing to fear either in faithfulness, devotion, or friendship and that you can depend upon them. But their demands are exhaustive; any deviation from these demands or standards condemn you without trial or hearing of any sort. You are guilty as charged. There is no excuse. If you try to explain, Scorpio does not listen.

If you had known that he was so exacting, you might have been prepared to act accordingly. But he purposely smiles you into false security, letting you appear to get the better of him. But this tolerance is dishonest. He means to pay you back at the first justification; his reason for getting even with you does not exist. It may be the fact that you accepted him too easily that he is avenging. He baited you, and you fell for it. The truth about Scorpio is that he is born a detective and he was checking on you, testing your mettle. He found you out, and the relentlessness with which he pursues his planned revenge is the most calculated, mean, and cruel method that can be imagined. For with Mars being ruler, Scorpians are warriors. They understand turbulence; in fact, they enjoy it. It is always surprising to them that a little war is not part of one's program in life.

In *Les Misérables* by Victor Hugo, a detective named Javert relentlessly pursues Jean Valjean, convicted of a minor crime, even after Jean Valjean has become a useful citizen. Javert is the example of the continued hostility or revengefulness of Scorpio.

The Pluto-ruled Scorpio type especially expresses this hostility vividly. He quarrels with everyone. Always, humanity is stupid and difficult. If he becomes a criminal, and he can, for he refuses to understand any law but his own, it may be impossible to reform him.

I know of one Scorpian who served fifteen years for murder. It would seem that if a man had lost that much time in prison, he would surely see the light. However, this Scorpian, upon release, returned immediately to crime. He was proud of his cunning and told many colorful tales of his adventures in outwitting the so-called squares. He is now back in the penitentiary. The time he must serve may take the remainder of his life. He is not wrong, the breaks were against him. Scorpians are never wrong. They are ruled by the scorpion, the unevolved.

The most outstanding Scorpian personality of world fame was Mahatma Ghandi. He was born under the Sun-sign of Libra, but he had the powerful sign of Scorpio rising, giving him his personality. Scorpios like to fight, but in this case it was for a cause—the emancipation of his people. It was the Scorpio in his chart that made him want to fight and not the Libran Sun. Librans avoid anything disagreeable. Only Scorpio could have weathered the harassments that were his lot in the cause he chose. He was the *eagle* type of Scorpian, flying best in a storm. There are three types. The lowest is the *Scorpion*. The next is the *Eagle*, who flies out of sight and into the sun. The eagle roosts higher than any other bird, is the most wily, and lives in the mountains. The eagle is an exclusive bird, and so is Scorpio. They never let you get too close. The last type of Scorpio is the *Dove*. It was this type of man that Jesus spoke of when he said in Chapter 10 of St. Matthew: "Behold, I send you forth as sheep in the midst of wolves: be ye therefore wise as serpents (the first type, the Scorpion) and harmless as doves." The dovelike Scorpian is the wise priest or the wise philosopher like George Santayana, who lived out his final years in the quiet sanctuary of the church, but who thought his own thoughts and had his own say. His dovelike wisdom was not influenced by the atmosphere of religion. Rather, he quickened into speaking truth because he had passed to the final victory that is Scorpio's. Having passed come to rest in a dovelike peace, seeing the uselessness through the first two stages, the eagle of wisdom had of struggle.

Finally, there is no such thing as colorless fixed signs. In whatever way they seek to express themselves, they are never dull. The Scorpian can get quiet, but then he is gathering energy for the next storm. He is never, but never, wishy-washy. He knows what he wants and may postpone it, but he never cancels it out. Most astrologers run from these people, but they offer an interest that I find fascinating; they can handle a storm.

We come now to the last of the "big shot" fixed signs, Aquarius. Aquarius is a fixed air sign, so its drive to importance, though just as determined as its three brothers, is intellectual. Air is the medium of Aquarian expression: air waves, radio, television, all forms of communication that reach universal proportion. The Aquarian heads the list of famous people because of this very reason: he is an international person. His path is the widest, for he is unlimited.

The view of the Aquarian is kaleidoscopic, for he sees the whole rather than the immediate object. This is why he prefers, and is able to deal with, universal ideas and circulate them on a worldwide basis. The fact that Franklin D. Roosevelt was an Aquarian made him the appropriate destiny individual to guide part of the history of war, for he enjoyed his international role.

Aquarians are considered odd, difficult, more to the point in that they are egocentrics. They are either *pros* or *antis*. They do not move exactly in the times; they are ahead or behind. They refuse to conform, for they hate limitation or regimentation. That is why they are not understood. They can be counted on to do and say the unexpected, for this immediately takes them out of the regulated class, which they heartily detest. They may not always feel the irregular forms they express. Still, it takes them out of the everyday run-of-the-mill personality. The way they will express their oddness will depend on the sign position of the planet that is their ruler, Uranus. Each time we have had an Aquarian president, important history has been made. The Civil War president, Abraham Lincoln, was an Aquarian. He is a fine example of this sign that aided humanity through changes, *change* being their medium. That is why they take the perverse view; their not liking to leave things the way they find them seems to be a compulsion. This is perfectly fine *if* they bring about an improved state. But if you get a perverse Aquarian period, then the changes can be cruel.

The Cardinal Signs. We come now to the next quadruplicate, the cardinal signs. These are the doers. They carry the action of life. Nothing suits cardinal signs better than to be on a new active schedule. They keep the wheels of life moving.

Let us start with Aries, which is the first of the cardinals; in fact it is the first sign of the natural zodiac. Aries represents *fire* action; Aries starts everything. The Sun must be in Aries for spring to begin anew. Countries ruled by Aries start things. Germany is ruled by Aries. Mars, the war planet, is the ruler of Aries.

Aries, being a doer, prefers the new, which is why he likes to blaze trails. Aries is the bonfire, the rallier. He is splendid when presenting the new building, to being the new political candidate—anything that needs a fiery start. But do not expect him to finish or leave a tidy scene, for that is not his function. The details must be handed over to someone else. Having campaigned for the new idea, he goes on to conquer newer fields. He rejects boredom. Being a changeable sign, the cardinal Aries enjoys a change of pace, welcoming new endeavors. Aries likes to face and subdue new challenges. Aries moves faster than any of the twelve signs. Mars, its ruler, represents action motivated by impulse. Restraint of any sort foils him. It is a very masculine sign. Aries is uneasy in a sentimental scene. Therefore his brusque manner is meant to offset this and not to offend. As fire gives out warmth and stirs one, so can Aries be depended on to give, for he is generous (if not afflicted), especially in new situations. As the bonfire dies quickest, so does Aries. He must be re-enthused—that is to say, refired to keep his interest alive. Put him in another department for the moment, he gets bored, give him another title, change his atmosphere, and you continue to get the best out of him. Sameness is death and stagnation and makes the true Aries unhappy and unproductive.

The second of the cardinal signs is Cancer. Cancer differs greatly from the first of the cardinal signs, for it is as slow as Aries is fast. Cancer is a water cardinal sign; therefore, action in emotion. That is why Cancer people make fine actors and musicians. This emotional form of expression suits them perfectly. They are reflectors and project themselves into the part they play for the moment. The reason why Cancer is the slowest of the cardinal signs is that its people resent change. They are moody and take a while to accept new ideas; all of this slows them up, for they have to adjust themeslves emotionally. Once adapted to the new idea, they begin to reflect or mirror it. They cannot be hurried, as can be seen in their walking gait, which is of the poorest type. They have difficulty in lifting their feet from the ground; this produces a crablike gait, a sort of shuffling along, another indicator of their resistance to leave the past. The body and its expression tell much about one's character. Cancer is identified by baby-white skin, a sensitive nose, and a poor gait.

Cancer rules the common man—the masses. Cancer-ruled cities, such as New York, show the teeming mass of humanity at its heterogeneous height. Cancer controls the conscious mind, for its ruler, the Moon, has rule over the mentality. The conscious and unconscious states are the Moon's form of expression. That is why each New Moon changes the conscious expression of the world. For this reason Cancer natives deal admirably with the common man. They belong before the public, once they have adjusted to their sensitive and timid natures. They make the finest parents.

The third of the cardinal signs is Libra, an air sign. This sign likes action like the first two, but the action must be of the pleasurable type. Libra is ruled by the very social planet Venus, so Librans are at their best at social functions of all sorts. I call them the "marriagers." It is the sign of partnerships. Librans like to form alliances at once. That is why they marry so quickly and frequently. They do not seem to *work* until they have married. This may account for the fact that they do not like to be alone. The reason for Libra being the marriager is enigmatic: is it because he does not like to be alone, or because forming partnerships is his business? Libra women make marriage their career. The men do marry more than once, but that is because the sign is cardinal and likes change. Sameness bores all of the cardinal signs except Capricorn.

Libra is ruled by Venus, the planet of beauty, comfort, sociability, and love. Librans for that reason do well in esthetic fields. It is very unusual to see a Libran badly turned out. Instinctively they know more about clothes and how to wear them than any other sign. They give the very best parties, and they know what to expect at a social event; for that reason, they are expert hosts. However, this runs into money, which may account for the fact that Librans have money troubles. They are either experts at getting money (for they belong to the parasitical species) to entertain or they carry on the social feasts without thinking (Librans are not thinkers, they are doers) how the bill will be paid. This puts them in debt. Librans are noted for their lack of pride; that, no doubt, is why they do not care if they are indebted to the world. The last party one Libran gave had the world at his feet. Venus-ruled signs are narcissistic. He was loved and that is all that counts for him.

The last and fourth of the cardinal signs is Capricorn. This sign is not as popular as Libra, not as aggressive as Aries, and less emotional than Cancer. This is the only cardinal sign ruled by one of the five big history-making planets—Saturn.

The five planets of everyday circumstances are: the Sun, the Moon, Mars, Mercury, and Venus. Aries, the first cardinal, has Mars ruling; Cancer has the Moon for a ruler, and Libra has sweet Venus ruling. Capricorn has the second of the five heavier or "outer" planets for its ruler—Saturn. The other four are Jupiter, Uranus, Neptune, and Pluto. The stronger the ruling planet, the more important will be the destiny.

Capricorn is more serious than the former three because Saturn is an austere planet. Capricornians are born organizers. They like a plan. They enjoy pomp (England is ruled by Capricorn) and ceremony. They are like the background of the organized church where everything is recorded. Saturn rules time and the recording of "permanent" events—births, deaths, and marriages.

Capricornians like breeding; they are innately refined, and they carry themselves with quiet dignity. They dislike noise, for it seems common. Old China comes under the rulership of Cancer, and the Chinese love dramatic noise; their firecracker noise is their way of showing enthusiasm (fire).

Al Smith, a Capricornian, was born on New Year's Eve. His famous remark, "Let's look at the record," is a typical sense of time, and the record of time is ruled by Saturn. He was a prominent Catholic, having a church built in New Jersey in his name. England, where tradition is upheld and past records of history have been kept for centuries with a care toward posterity, is a Capricornian country. The crowning of royalty is the personification of this love of tradition carried out with pomp and ceremony—money spent for a tradition that is well planned, expressed with dignity in a religious atmosphere, exactly at noonday (with the Sun at its highest degree), precisely on time.

The Mutable Signs. The last of this series are common, or dual, signs: Gemini, Virgo, Sagittarius, and Pisces. These are the talkers, the writers, travelers, and advertisers. The mutables sell ideas. They are not interested in action like the cardinals, nor in things liked the fixed signs. They are interested in thinking, talking things over, traveling, writing their ideas, and selling them through the advertising route.

The first of the mutables is Gemini. Gemini is the middleman. He does the leg work for the boss (a fixed sign) or he represents the boss and speaks for him as his secretary. He answer letters and telephones. He likes to commute. Gemini rules the teenager: that is why those born under the sign seem so youthful. The Duchess of Windsor is of Gemini birth and always looks youthful in carriage. Gemini is a talker, sometimes just a chatterbox. But there have been highly evolved Geminians: Ralph Waldo Emerson, the poet; Queen Victoria of England, during whose reign more colonization was carried on than under any other British ruler.

Geminians are very versatile. They can carry on two different forms of service at once—to be at their best, they should. They do everything in twos and threes, like marrying more than once. Their duality shows up in that they understand perfectly the very thing they are against. Wishing to do two things at the same time presents a problem to them, for all thoughts come in twos. Separation and decision harass them continuously. This may be the reason why they defy age and are the perennial youths of the wheel of life. They seek new thoughts to wrestle with (the mental chase helps them preserve their looks). Tell them something new and their faces light up. It promises a new pursuit, a new reason to be young again, for Gemini is ruled by Mercury. Geminians have very trim figures, a light walk, and an easy manner. They are the lightweights. They ask for less, and consequently, they receive less. Their rub with life is casual.

The second of the mutable, or common, signs is Virgo. Virgo, too, is Mercury-ruled; but the second time that Mercury rules, it seems to have grown up. Now it is far more practical than its younger sister-sign who seemed too busy sowing wild oats to come to maturity. Virgo is a practical sign: he always thinks and talks with a purpose. Virgo has the same trim look, quick, alert gait, and youth of Gemini. But there is more sternness in his features than in Gemini's. Virgo is the sign of labor and service. Virgo is always working and thinking continuously in terms of toil. People born under this sign work everyone else too. Virgo finds social gatherings useless. He does not come off well in the living room, feeling more at home in the kitchen. Virgo rules food and the diet.

Virgo is the critic, the born analyst. His criticisms can be as scathing and sarcastic as Scorpio's are; in fact, he resembles Scorpio in his subtle remarks. Virgo is feared in social groups because he can make deep criticisms that are not constructive. He does not act for the literary reasons that Geminians do. All must have a practical return. His writing is cut to the bone for facts alone. It is the textbook form. One must talk about subjects that offer him something or Virgo will interrupt and dismiss the topic to get back to his work. He, too, does everything twice, marries again, splits his life's work, starts out as a nurse or doctor (the sign rules health) and winds up a writer! The moment your service is ended, he eliminates you. Queen Elizabeth I of England was famous for breaking off with those whose usefulness had come to an end (she was a Virgo). Here, again, there is a similarity to Scorpio! Both put the blame on the other person. They charge you with an accusation that seems true in order to discard you. The difference is that Scorpio will bait you into provoking him in order to create the breach. Virgo will find enough fault with you via the path of criticism. When this happens, you may be sure the last nugget of usefulness has been mined from you.

The third mutable sign is Sagittarius. The common signs are the talkers; naturally, they talk for different reasons on different levels, just as the fixed signs are determined in different ways and the cardinals act in different ways. The mutable signs think, talk, and write for varied reasons.

Sagittarius is not ruled by the first five planets of everyday circumstances, but by the first of the big five, Jupiter. Therefore this third mutable has picked up speed and importance, being in higher company, and wants to say greater things.

Sagittarius does not talk happily about little things, like Gemini. Nor does Sagittarius dwell on the merits of his work, excluding all other subjects, like Virgo. Sagittarius is a traveler, so he goes as far as any thought can take him. His is the longest thighbone; in fact, whatever height that Sagittarius has will be seen in the thigh. Nature does not usually make mistakes. Gulliver must have been a Sagittarian, for Sagittarians plan to travel; nature has provided them with the limb that covers the space. Sagittarius rules sports, and most athletes have notably long thighbones! Notice the beautifully developed thighs of runners at the track or the race horse who carries all of his gracefulness in the thigh line. One of the exceptions to this rule was Sir Winston Churchill, who was not tall, having the shortening influence of Scorpio rising (the rising sign controls the physical body). But it can be noted that he had a very short waist, showing that whatever height he did carry was in the thigh.

Ruled by Jupiter, Sagittarians are expert with ideas. Jupiter rules philosophy, law, and politics. He prefers to think and talk. The poet Milton, who was a Sagittarian, uses a philosophical subject in his epical poem *Paradise Lost,* showing the waging of war by Satan against law (God). The simplest tale by a Sagittarian writer or orator becomes Jupiterian.

The last sign of the zodiac and the last mutable of the common signs is Pisces. Of all the mutables, this sign is the most indecisive: two fishes tied together with the band of limitation, the fishes pointing in opposite directions; one fish flows upstream and the other, downstream; and so, it seems, do Pisceans.

Pisces is a dual water sign showing the emotions, like the tides—a continuous ebb and flow. The sign is not easily described. Pisces deals with spiritual ideas. Pisceans think and speak beyond man's practical understanding. The ideas of Pisceans are tied up with feeling, sympathy, sorrow, self-effacement, and renunciation. They are the "divine discontents," for they aspire to great heights and find that bringing their dream down to a practical level is so far away that they seem to be chasing a jack-o'-lantern.

4
The Importance of Each Sign

Each sign has special destinies to perform. Aries are the "starters." Taurians have custody over the world's possessions. Geminians are the middlemen, salesmen, and the go-betweens. Cancerians are the homemakers. Leo is the head, the boss (someone has to be king or president). Virgo is the employee (someone has to keep the records straight and serve the executives). Librans run the cocktail parties and keep the marriage marts in operation. Scorpio has to inspect and detect trouble or else there would be no FBI. Sagittarians have to keep the law operating. Capricornians have to organize and plan to put the divine laws into effect. Aquarians are the club-makers or group workers. Where would friendship be but for humanitarian ideas? Pisceans are the good samaritans looking after those who need help.

The combinations of the other signs in conjunction with the Sun-sign under which one is born will make the difference in how destinies are carried out. We are living in a highly specialized time. All things are given a greater degree of attention for performance in the highest degree of efficiency. This is as it should be, for when Uranus, the planet that rules specialization, was in the sign of Cancer, which rules the home, all sorts of new gadgets were invented for home use. Cancer rules the masses, or common man, so that everyone might have access to modern improvements and specialties which are planned and priced within his range. This is another reason why astrology should be given every chance to prove its value. It stresses the advantages that can be had by consulting the destiny clock.

Man should consult his own personal destiny clock and have time for everything. He should keep his appointments with destiny intelligently, not as a hit or miss idea—but as a perfect plan, according to startime, and not make a mistake that has to be adjusted at the cost of time and money (energy).

There is another advantage to the use of astrology, namely, in analysis. The professional psychologist or psychiatrist can derive much help from a horoscope. Jung identifies its potential in the famous observation that "Whatever is born or done this moment of time has the qualities of this moment of time."

The analyst is dependent on the material that the patient or client gives in his history. Not so for the astrologer. If the client knows his hour, day, month, year, and place of birth, the astrologer, without the aid of history from the client, can see exactly his kind of personality, individuality, and destiny.

The position of the planets in their relationship with one another will show how a person will succeed in society or in love. Those who are successful in love are certainly less likely to welcome disease than those who find their love urges unrequited. Everyone knows today that illnesses are wonderful clothes hangers for the frustrated and unloved to use as coverups. Illness is brought out and paraded like a new dress. It makes conversation and keeps the inquirer too busy to notice the one thing the ill one is trying to hide—failure in love. This is kept from reaching the surface by talking about current topics. Sick people have the right to extenuating circumstances; they are not expected to succeed; illness keeps them back. All sorts of maladies are crutched upon these illnesses, but they are seen by the astrologer.

If Mercury is afflicted, showing biased reasoning, this can come through in illogical ideas. In the case of Mercury being afflicted to Mars, the fighting planet, speech can be explosive. How could the loved one's voice be alluring or melodious when a love vow comes out like a blast? If Venus, who rules the larynx, is afflicted and the love urges are biased, would the lover be able to woo the loved one into ecstasy?

Many years ago a client was disturbed over the fact that I predicted two marriages. "It's impossible," she explained, "for I am Catholic and cannot divorce my husband." But I knew that at that very moment, her husband was having trouble with the arterial blood stream, for he was born with two very obvious squares (afflictions—one to Jupiter, which rules the large blood system, and the Sun to the Moon, which rules the life force, the conscious and unconscious life). A year or so later, she came to me with the statement that her husband had bruises that he could not account for on his legs and arms all of the time. I saw the beginning of the end was at hand. He died of cancer a few months later.

The Moon, being in trouble, showed that he was a worrier. When he was in physical trouble, his mentality could not be depended upon to withstand the trial induced by the afflicted Jupiter.

Naturally, an optimistic chart has a better chance of weathering storms than the pessimistic chart. Jupiter is the optimist; Saturn is the pessimist. If Jupiter is afflicted, one cannot be expected to be hopeful; but if Saturn is in good condition, then discord is less likely to be the main theme. If both planets are afflicted, there is slim hope, for the dark side of the nature is bolstered by hopelessness. It is also true that these two planets have to do with money and planning; but if money is gotten the hard way, it will affect the plan. If plans are continuously frustrated, the body will reflect it; this is an example of the wheel within the wheel. The mental and physical life are clear to the astrologer, for the planets will tell the tale, notwithstanding what the client thinks. The stars will reveal facts of which the client is completely unaware. Many times I have confounded clients upon telling them of a condition that might occur in the charts of their children or mates. The were able to identify such conditions, but had not been able to interpret them.

But the importance of each sign and what it can do is the core of the matter. If an Aries type is put to work at a dull and monotonous task, he cannot and will not give his best. He is not living at the full energy-point of his ability any more than a Geminian is if he is hidden away with his background of potentials snowed under files of papers and catalog work; this would be against the best in the sign, thwarting it to the point of suffocation.

Part Two

5

The Career Potential of Each Sign

ARIES

Give a man a job he enjoys and in which he is happy, and he will give it his best, reaching the highest level of his capacity to fulfill his destiny. The signs that are enthusiastic about what they believe and think should stimulate others to act. But to do this, one must have something with which to arouse or excite another. This is what the fire signs can do best. But how can that be if the fire sign has no reason to fire another? Fire warms one and excites another. Whether it is a bonfire (Aries), a fixed fire in the furnace (Leo), or a log fire in the fireplace (Sagittarius), where a wonderful idea can be born, jobs of this kind belong to the fire signs.

The bonfire can be the rabble-rouser who rails against the injustices done to his fellow man, or it can be the fire that kindles the idea that you should join his outfit and see the world. He has started you on a new path, and that is the business of Aries.

He must be involved in work that does not curb his enthusiasm, and every new start keeps him going. For no blaze is as spontaneous as a bonfire. The best of it is in the start. The clue to the first fire sign is that it gives its best to the start. He must be accepted on that basis, taken at his flood tide, and not allowed to wane until his idea is put into motion, for his is the impulse idea.

TAURUS

How very contrary is Taurus in comparison with Aries! Taurians are not thinkers on the wing; theirs is a slow process. They must be given time, and the idea must be practical. If it involves money, so much the better to suit Taurians. They are not starters. That, no doubt, is why they are slow to become interested in the new idea. Spading soil, one would think, should be perfect for them, for they have the green thumb. But someone (Aries) has to start the action before Taurians, who are very persevering and who enjoy routine, will carry it out profitably. A Taurian will give long hours and patience seeing that the ledger is balanced to show profit. He is interested in results, being an earth sign, and he wants to see the fruit of his labor. Just as he can grow the green things, he wants the investment to grow, or he will abandon it. The clue to getting the best from him is to outline the idea (done by Aries), let him mull over it, and never, but never, hurry him (you are suspected if you do). When he feels his time is ripe, he will put the idea in operation. In this way, his particular type of action is at its working best.

GEMINI

Gemini is a wonderful talker. Geminians are chatterboxes when they wish to talk but have nothing to say. If a Geminian is aroused by an Aries idea that Taurus has proven workable, Gemini can sell it. If you take too long to get this idea, Aries will be very impatient and may insult you. It might be better if Gemini were present to explain the idea to slow Taurus. The brusqueness of Aries can frighten Taurus, who likes quiet and harmony. Gemini, then, is the one to show Taurus the wisdom of the idea—Gemini will capture the attention of the buyer. He likes moving about on short journeys, telephoning, and writing letters. He is the one who contacts the outside sources. He will enjoy the legwork. He must be given new ideas to talk about, for monotony stymies him. To get the best from him he must be allowed to move about talking and reselling the idea in different ways, through all practical forms of communication. Then you will have Gemini working excitedly at his best, performing in a way that he enjoys.

CANCER

Who will buy the idea initiated by Aries, priced by Taurus, and promoted by Gemini? The man in every walk of life, of course—Cancer. Cancer must be convinced that he likes something; he must like it or he will not want any part of it. It will not excite him, as it will Aries. Cancer must feel he wants it, and this is what advertising Gemini must do for every man. Cancer wants to know that everyone else will like it, or it will not be popular with him. So it must not be too exclusive, too highly specialized, in that he must cultivate a taste for it or learn to like it. Cancer is a very lazy sign; if energy has to go into enjoyment, you have lost him.

It must be something he can feel he wants that will give him emotional satisfaction. If struggle or time is involved, he will find an immediate substitute. His is the common man's need; he can be depended on to supply it, for his main interest is bringing results that will assuage his craving for physical comforts, food, and drink. Cancer is a great eater; he will feed you for the sheer joy of having an excuse to eat. Eating, of course, is an emotional satisfaction. So Cancer will read all of the advertisements for food and drink. He enjoys reading about food or that which gives him enjoyment emotionally. He enjoys his home so thoroughly that he can marry just to make his home dream come true.

LEO

Leo is the dramatic sign that understands the trail that Aries is blazing and that Taurus finds valuable for its results. Gemini has communicated its importance to Leo. Cancer has been stimulated to buy. Leo would then like to head the company that manufactures the article. He would make a wonderful president, composing high-sounding phrases and powerful slogans to dramatize the principles and sincerity of the company's love for the common man's needs. He would put heart in the matter, making you love the idea.

I am reminded of an experience I had buying a suit years ago from what I am sure was a Leo saleslady. It was a dark green suit trimmed with black fox. I thought the suit was very dramatic, but was afraid of so daring an outfit. The lines appealed to me, but not the color. I was trying to get out of purchasing it when this very dramatic salesgirl said, "But don't you see that this suit ceases to be a purchase? It is an investment because the lines alone show your figure off to great advantage." I bought the suit. Who could resist the very great appeal that this dramatic idea created? This is true Leo acting.

VIRGO

After Leo has dramatically opened the establishment with great fanfare, the details of running the place efficiently will have to be turned over to shrewd, businesslike Virgo. Virgo will hire the help, for he is a supervisor and instinctively knows how to use a man. He will feel nothing when he has to fire an inefficient fellow worker. In fact it will give release to his critical nature. Everyone must be on time. All must be neat and clean. No detail that has gone amiss escapes his quick relentless scrutiny. Nor will he shy away from pointing it out to the secretary as well as the president himself. His part of the operation is indispensable, and he knows it. Therefore, he will be seen in companies or establishments where the boss talks low to him. The boss knows he is needed, for Virgo has made himself invaluable. Someday, who knows, he may be the president!

LIBRA

Libra will serve best as the front man making excuses for the boss who forgot the appointment he did not intend to keep in the first place.

Libra has wonderful manners; he is well groomed and tactful. Librans hate unpleasantness so that even when those who are leveled against complain justly, Librans are quick to say something placating to restore peace. You might say they balance the scales. Ruled by Venus, Librans want harmony at any price. Libra will provoke a quarrel, but be dismayed when ire is aroused. He can never understand that he brought it about. For this reason, he can honestly defend his employer; he cannot understand why his superior should not be allowed the right to err.

Libra can give the office party or take care of the cocktail party when the convention has its big meeting in Washington. Libra can be the ambassador of good will for the policy of the company, sit in on the board meeting, and reinterpret for the boss when the latter offends executives from other companies. His suave manner, good clothes, and quiet voice tones down all the anxiety caused by blustering Aries, the overbearing attitude implied by the Leo president, the overbidding of money-wise Taurus, as well as the support given by the talkative advertising man (Gemini). Libra calms them all down with assurance.

SCORPIO

Scorpio sits back and secretly notes all the ideas introduced, puts his mental microscope on both views and persons, and supplies the answers about the reliability of either persons or ideas. Scorpios are born detectives; if what they see is wrong, they will investigate although they may not see how it can be corrected. They are valuable in pointing out defects. This is often not understood since their destructive criticism is hard to take and they almost never offer substitutions. That criticism may be inspired by envy or jealousy. Many times it is just plain jealousy. Nevertheless, they may be called the "tighteners," for they can see the weak link every time. Theirs is an "emergency" insight. They look for the vulnerable spot and use it as a weapon to discourage you. Their resourcefulness can make no argument work.

Scorpio understands power so well that he would know whether the outfit was running in powerful channels or not. Detecting is in his nature; to keep him at his highest level, he should be given ample opportunity to express his gifts. Instead of ideas, he uses energy to demoralize people, and this energy can make everyone who is in daily contact with him cringe. If his energy is channeled into a constructive force, he is free of hurting. The force has found an outlet to build power, which he loves, instead of building enmity and accumulating karma, the law of retribution, which is the end result of misdirected invective.

SAGITTARIUS

Sagittarius is the vice president, for he does not want the heavier responsibility of being the president; he wants to be the "lightweight" executive. Mutable signs always want to enter through two doors, but want only one for exit. His is a similar position to the Libra executive, who actually gives the office party. The Sagittarian is the fellow who shakes your hand and says how glad he is to see you, making you feel that if you had not come to the party it would have been a complete failure. He remembers you told him about your fishing trip, so he mentions it, which flatters you no end. That is his purpose. He is the one person who understands everyone at the party. He is the perfect person to spread good will for the company he represents in other countries. There is no rebellion in him; so if there are any differences to be ironed out with a foreign source that no one else can manage, he is your man. He will come up with a philosophical compromise or consolation that will appease the most difficult complainer. There will be a great warmth and kindness in his attitude. Sagittarians are at their best when they can express interest in a problem which their fellow man has faced alone. They honestly like people next best to ideas. But what good are ideas if they cannot be put to work for man? That is the end for which Sagittarian is aiming. He is delighted if an idea can solve the problem of a troubled soul—his idea, of course.

CAPRICORN

The Capricornian will not envy the Sagittarian, for he is not a backslapper. He will not envy the Scorpian, for he does not like to dig behind things or motives; he hopes they are what they seem. Nor will he take Libra's social touch under advisement. He would be wrecked if he had to take notes and watch details as Virgo likes to do. He understands the Leo president perfectly and is at home with him, for he has to stand behind him and keep him organized. He even understands Cancer. Though Cancer is opposite him in the zodiac, he is in sympathy with his mass-oriented mind. Gemini talks too much, so he will find an excuse to leave the scene. Taurus is a necessity. His practical mind and Taurus see eye to eye. Aries is a bit too boisterous for his dignified conservatism, but one must start somewhere so that he can abide it until all ideas have been presented.

Capricornians are the organizers. They like to see that the records are in order for posterity. They like to feel that the policy a Sagittarian promoted is a fact on record in the vaults. The company name is something that must be upheld. They must keep the records straight. Talk is one thing, but facts are truths. They like to follow plans. It may take time to get the company or establishment in perfect working order, but what does it matter as long as the record of the company is clear and kept according to the original plan? This can be brought about only through vigilance, time, patient effort, organization, and everyone doing his duty. Capricorn likes to do his duty. The rightness of it suits his nature. He is therefore at his best when these, his best traits, are being utilized.

Capricorn's ability to organize—whether it be a company, the church, a mate, children, or an institution—is displayed with agility.

AQUARIUS

Aquarians find a big organization their particular cup of tea. Nothing suits this universal sign more than to spread its genius all over the world. Nowhere is there a better chance to accomplish this than in an organization or company. In spite of all the humanitarian things said about Aquarian, I find that he is the least concerned with the individual. The job is too small and limiting for his wide-lens view.

Just as he rebels against limitation, his Capricornian colleague understands it, and they can complement each other when working in companies. Before Uranus, ruler of Aquarius was discovered, Saturn was assigned to rule Aquarius. Having had the same ruler could be the reason that they work well together. Capricorn cannot understand the casual attitude that Aquarius takes toward his fellow worker, but he recognizes that it is a better attitude than he can practice. Capricorn finds this useful when working with the freedom that Aquarius can bring to an atmosphere; then Capricorn can put it into motion.

Aquarians, being airy, do not let things disturb them personally. Their concern is with the over-all. Circulating any idea on a universal plane is their finest aim. They seem to do this subconsciously. In group work they get the best out of this trait, for they never let the crowd catch up to them. This is truly the secret of their success. The moment they are personalized, the illusion of their greatness seems to be dispelled. As long as they are allowed to remain aloof and work freely, they create, invent, and circulate on a manifold basis. If the idea can be limitless, they can bring it to fruition. The Leo president must stand toe to toe with Aquarius, for Aquarius understands him; but being an employee does not satisfy Aquarius. He is not frightened by such titles as president, king, or boss. He has outgrown all such designations and moved into a wider, universal circle.

PISCES

The last of the twelve signs is Pisces. Pisceans are the emotional mutables. Among people they respond on the emotional level. Thoughts must have emotional appeal. They would work well with those who are maladjusted in an organization. They are troubleshooters. The mutables talk, but here this talking sign is combined with feeling, for it is a dual sign. Sorrow, misunderstanding, trials, and a need for sympathy are their department. The Piscean troubleshooter would be able to handle delinquents. In a medium in which they can express sympathy or give help, they function at their best. There is a reason for this.

If Pisces is in a field that provides emotional satisfaction, similar to his little brother Cancer, he is a visionary. If he has not found his proper niche, he is very sad and dissatisfied. I call Pisceans the divine discontents when they have not found their path.

They are not satisfied where they are. Put differently, wherever they are they would rather be somewhere else.

In any form their lack of clear aim or seeming state of indecision rests on the feeling, or love, they may have for the job. Theirs is an emotional idea, which is very difficult to bring down to a practical level. All fields of psychological approach would suit them. They would make good mental doctors, for they would be dealing with emotional entanglements that require thought. They are able to put their long spiritual finger on the heart of the matter without any effort at all.

In addition to the meaning of the twelve zodiacal signs just discussed, there are ten planets to be found and identified in every chart. A fast-moving planet like the Moon changes signs very frequently; others take longer. The influences are different for each birthday because of the difference of the time and place of birth. This is why astrology is the most ponderable phenomenon. It has great possibilities and can be most satisfactory. If utilized for right purposes, it has more to give and is the widest field for expressing oneself. You can pick the profession in which you would do best. You can ascertain the state of your health and the dangers to be avoided. You can see which are the best years, and you can idle the motor on the slow years. The year that the right person will come along is unmistakable.

Astrology is not all prediction. There are many other sides to its usefulness that are far more rewarding. The astrologer can give you the type of astrology that fits and suits your need. Knowing your Sun-sign and your personality-sign can be the threshold to freedom and happiness.

6

Characteristics of Each Sign

ARIES—THE RAM
March 21-April 19

Aries is the first cardinal fire-sign: cardinal for action, fire for romance. Arians give the best to the start, moving faster than the other eleven signs. They are egoists (not egotists); they prefer action to theory, struggling to gain a position to appease their self-conscious ego. Their masculinity spurns sentiment, which embarrasses them. Generous, though brusque, they are natural athletes, for this gives them the opportunity to express physical prowess.

PERSONALITY: They are enthusiastic, humorous, bold starters, giving of themselves without hesitation, for starting anything arouses their optimism. The idea must show promise quickly or they lose interest and turn in a new direction. Challenge should be present in every undertaking.

IN LOVE: They give the best initially to the love affair. Then they are kind, generous, and protective. Once avowed, they see no need for further declaration.

IN BUSINESS: They are pioneers and prefer a business that helps them express themselves in a new way. They may change the present interpretation of an established idea. Being self-centered, they persist until they find what satisfies them. Detail bores them; it represents limitation, which they cannot stand. They must be allowed to move on if you want to get the best from them.

IN MARRIAGE: Having given all of the excitement to courting, Aries settles down to marriage and takes it for granted that his love for the mate is an established fact. He is surprised if this is questioned.

TAURUS—THE BULL
April 20-May 20

Taurus is the first fixed earth-sign: fixed for determination, earth for practicality. Taurians have beautiful eyes, full and round. Their most important feature is their short neck. They are sweet and sentimental in manner. The substantial impression they give is quite genuine for they represent security and money. Taurians are the slowest of the twelve signs. They are difficult to convince, but once aroused they are staunch and faithful.

PERSONALITY: Taurians are gentle, agreeable, and sentimental, but they are stubborn and resistant. They weigh you quietly, for values enter into all their ideas. If they seem stubborn, it is because they need more time to "get into" the idea; they feel it out, but they do not think it through.

IN LOVE: They are very kind and attentive to the loved one, catering in all ways to the security and comfort of the beloved. If love is rejected, they are downcast and silent; their love needs response or it wilts.

IN BUSINESS: Taurians drive on steadily; if they are hurried, they blunder and lose their true worth. They can be depended on in evaluating any business idea, for handling money is their specialty, and they treat all financial matters seriously.

IN MARRIAGE: Taurians enter into this state after much quiet deliberation. Once married, they stubbornly try to make it work, giving it constant and patient effort, for change is frightening. They abhor change. Theirs is the most enduring and lasting of partnerships.

GEMINI—THE TWINS
May 21-June 21

Gemini is the first mutable (common) air-sign: mutable for adaptability, air for intellect. Geminians are the easiest to meet, but the hardest to hold or keep. Their easy and ready smile is their best feature. They are talkative, gifted conversationalists. Their teenage or youthful appearance makes them eternally young; their inquisitive nature sends them in pursuit of new ideas and helps keep them young.

IN PERSONALITY: Geminians are versatile and adept in winning affection. They are interested in almost everything; they make friends at once, for they never seem to remain a stranger. They travel lightly, not wishing to clutter up their lives with the responsibility of things or people. They are not prepared to give much of the self.

IN LOVE: Gemini, being of divided interests, is undecided. Geminians wish to reserve some portion of the self for other pursuits. They must be accepted on this level or they leave the scene. The less you expect from them, the more they yield. They prefer two loves —for comparison.

IN BUSINESS: Geminians have many abilities; they do best in two or more endeavors. They need a hobby to turn to when their business bores them. Someone else—Taurus, for example—must take care of the money end.

IN MARRIAGE: Geminians are never given credit for loving as deeply as they can. They are not demonstrative, for their divided interests seem to take up all their time. But they love you in their minds.

CANCER—THE CRAB
June 22-July 22

Cancer is the second cardinal and first water-sign: cardinal for action, water for emotion. Cancer is the slowest of the active cardinal signs. Pale, shy, and hesitating to express for fear of being rebuffed, he is very sensitive. He has the poorest-shaped mouth and a crablike shuffling gait. His fine acting ability stems from the fact that he becomes the character he plays, reflecting, mirrorlike, his emotions.

PERSONALITY: Cancer is passive, gentle, plastic, and very home-loving. Domestic life is a must. Cancerians do not resist through stubbornness or indecisiveness, but only because they fear that making the wrong move can lead to failure. Like all water signs, they are complainers fretting over imagined injuries that render them helpless and powerless to defend themselves.

IN LOVE: Their clinging devotion is the key to how much they love. They become moody and inconsolable when love fails them. Still, they will always give the lover another chance. They love to return to the past.

IN BUSINESS: Cancerians understand what the public wants and are good business people, for they can change with the needs of the public, adjusting to a new demand and catering to it.

IN MARRIAGE: Cancer's devotion to the home and children is his main source of inspiration. This makes him want to feed the family, for Cancerians are very fond of food. They make the best mates. If there are children, the marriage remains safe.

LEO—THE LION
July 23-August 22

Leo is the second fixed fire-sign: fixed for wilfulness, fire for romance. Leos have beautifully shaped heads, high from temple to crown, and high-bridged noses—a symbol of their pride, haughtiness, and imposing nature. They are always in love with ideas or people and fight hard to keep them. Leo is generous to a fault and very forgiving, but resentful if his generous heart is not appreciated.

IN PERSONALITY: Leo is beaming, dramatic, forceful, and excitable, wishing to arouse everyone into the faith and enthusiasm of love. Leos are the banked fire wishing to consolidate you with people or ideas. They are potential speculators wishing to excite you in the drama of life.

IN LOVE: Leo dramatizes love into a thing of beauty and wants the whole world to love as ardently as he does, for he is always in love. He has no enthusiasm for life when he has nothing to love.

IN BUSINESS: The faith Leos have in their own ability insures and excites others to work with them. However, their overbearing self-confidence arouses resentment and irritates others. They are always honest and sincere.

IN MARRIAGE: They rule the roost like a medieval lord, again arousing resentment. Unless this is forgiven, the marriage often ends in the divorce court.

VIRGO—THE VIRGIN
August 23-September 22

Virgo is the second mutable (common) earth-sign: mutable for adaptability, earth for practicality. Virgo is the hardest of workers, for work and he are one. He is lost without a job and never ceases to talk about work. He resembles his mutable sister Gemini. His trim, neat look comes from his cleansing quality. His long upper lip establishes the practical talker, for he talks only for a purpose. His long, wedgelike nose indicates severity.

IN PERSONALITY: Virgo is very critical, practical in attitude, and a detailed talker. He seems always about his business, which cuts him off from being pleasant socially. Virgo does not come off well in society. He gives the impression of always analyzing everything.

IN LOVE: Virgo analyzes and examines the beloved too much, cutting down the response of the loved one. That makes him even more critical. He does not realize that his fault-finding keeps him from attaining the love he seeks. Virgo women are the proverbial old maids.

IN BUSINESS: His concentration is too continuous. He carries his business everywhere. He is best at supervision, but makes a better servant than master.

IN MARRIAGE: Virgo expects perfection. If he marries a practical mate (Taurus or Capricorn), he is safe; otherwise, his chaste attitude makes it difficult for the mate to live up to expectations.

LIBRA—THE SCALES
September 23-October 23

Libra is the third cardinal and second air-sign. Being air, Librans are intelligently weighing everything. They are the most beautiful of the zodiac and are the best-dressed people of all the twelve signs. Marriage and social life are what they live for; consequently, they make the best hosts. They love to give parties, which they do well. They are spendthrifts and have many financial difficulties.

IN PERSONALITY: Librans are charming, gentle, and well-dressed. They are society. They are always seeking mates, for marriage is their goal in life. For this reason they give the impression of possessive pleasing natures and well-bred manners. They are dismayed in coarse or noisy atmospheres. They are popular socially, for they dress up any party.

IN LOVE: They happily hope that love will lead to marriage. But they will not tolerate a long-drawn-out courtship. If this occurs, they move off to a new prospect. They miss their best chances because of this "quick-win" trait. They are parasitical, and they want results.

IN BUSINESS: Librans do better in partnerships than on their own. They are not good at handling money and require another who is capable. Although they are comparison buyers, they should be free to express creatively. They are artistic.

IN MARRIAGE: They give the best to the start

of the marriage. If the mate expects the initial status to be maintained, trouble ensues. Librans must be aroused anew, which means a new mate is in order.

SCORPIO—THE SCORPION
October 24-November 21

Scorpio is the third fixed and second water-sign: fixed for invincibility, water for emotion. The fixed signs are the "big shots," and Scorpio is the most power-loving of the fixed signs. Scorpio has the worst reputation because his intense, relentless drive never accepts defeat. This makes him troublesome and attracts resentment. The heavy beetle-brow, the beak-like nose, and the oriental eyelid best describe Scorpio. They have scanty hair, even tend to baldness.

IN PERSONALITY: Scorpios are magnetic, intense, secretive; they seem very attractive at first. They will dispute passage with anyone if their importance is challenged or underestimated. If they have cast lots with you, they will be loyal; if you do not bend to their domineering demands, they turn against you with hate.

IN LOVE: Scorpio makes the heaviest demand on the loved one, requiring complete and constant attention, effecting all kind of ruses to get that attention. If you fail in these demands, he is contemptuous of you in a heartless, remorseless, unforgiving way.

IN BUSINESS: Scorpio is resourceful. A job, impossible to others, takes him only a little longer. Scorpio is powerful and thorough in any business deal, for he likes to outwit others. He is in such complete control of his emotions that he seems heartless. That is why Scorpios make good surgeons.

IN MARRIAGE: He is devoted and attentive, but sex is his conflict, driving him to infidelity, no matter how much he loves his mate. If she is weak and does not command respect, the marriage fails.

SAGITTARIUS—THE CENTAUR
November 22-December 21

Sagittarius is the third mutable fire-sign: mutable for amenity, first for romance. Sagittarius, like all mutable signs, likes to talk, but for different reasons than the others. Sagittarius talks to consolidate and compile ideas, which are his true love. Sagittarians are bachelor-born students and scholars. They are tall and easy-flowing; they have large teeth, long noses, and narrow heads. There is no rebellion in them. They are hopeful; their demands are easily satisfied.

IN PERSONALITY: Sagittarius is good-natured, hopeful, and optimistic. The higher types are generous and helpful benefactors. They will travel for an idea or to put one into circulation. They prefer to associate with those who offer challenging ideas. Being alert for this, they burrow into an idea instinctively.

IN LOVE: It is love at first sight, then indecisiveness. Sagittarians know that they cannot live up to the responsibility of consolidating love. Nor do they make heavy demands on the beloved; this insures them with the lover.

IN BUSINESS: Sagittarians are very expansive. They gamble; if their judgment is neither ripe nor right and they fail, they are not dismayed. They hope for better luck next gamble, for they believe in the promise. With new hope, they start again.

IN MARRIAGE: They fall in love easily, marrying before their judgment has reassured them, finding out all the wrong things too late, and thus wed more than once. Better luck next marriage!

CAPRICORN—THE GOAT
December 22-January 20

Capricorn is the last cardinal earth-sign: earth for practicality, cardinal for action. The most quiet and dignified of the cardinals, he is more concerned with his reputation than the others. His is a deeply quiet ambition, seriously sought and often mistaken for melancholia. His penetrating eyes have a deep furrow between the brows. His small bones show in the dainty ankle; the smile is warm and sincere, and he shows it only when he feels it.

IN PERSONALITY: Capricorn is formal, dignified, courteous, yet concessive. Manners and breeding mean much to him, and he inspires it. Capricornians' disciplined carriage stems from the fact that they mean to get diplomatically whatever they can out of every situation.

IN LOVE: They are very cautious; they prefer well-to-do lovers. They require respect in love, for they are prepared to show reverence to those they love. Once firmly in love, no sacrifice is too dear. They respond to warmth and goodness; theirs is an enduring love.

IN BUSINESS: They are persistent, plodding, reliably pushing on for fame and honor. Time does not daunt their ambitions; time is a factor they laud. They are great organizers, preferring to organize large groups or companies.

IN MARRIAGE: If the mate is satisfactory, they are devoted without demonstrating it. If not, they are gloomy, depressed, and all is futile. They are not given to dual marriages and often wait for widowhood before remarrying.

AQUARIUS—THE WATER BEARER
January 21-February 18

Aquarius is the last fixed air-sign: fixed for resistance, air for intellect. This is the Hall-of-Fame sign. Aquarians like to circulate their ideas and themselves universally. Friendship is the clue to their success. They are joiners of clubs and group causes. They are better friends than mates, being too impersonal for lasting emotions. Aquarians are tall, lanky, and large-boned;

they have dome-shaped heads and wavy lines in the brow.

IN PERSONALITY: Aquarians are impersonal, breezy, detached, but kind, which makes them fascinating. They belong to the Declaration-of-Independence idea. The evolved inspire noble thoughts. The negatives are eccentric, odd, always disagreeing to change the atmosphere; evenness stunts them.

IN LOVE: Aquarians, being very perverse, are the most difficult in love. Attachments are binding, and they hate limitation. Pin them down and you have lost them; remain cool, and the Aquarian is secured. They are not emotional, yet rather intellectual. You must be the idea in the person they would love. Their real love is humanity. Fail their idea of love, and they divorce you.

IN BUSINESS: Aquarians give sudden spurts of ability. They cannot give a sustained performance. Being anchored in the same work is too limiting.

IN MARRIAGE: Once Aquarians have come to an understanding of what the association is to be, the erratic attitude disappears. Still, they require handling to prevent alienation.

PISCES—THE FISHES
February 19-March 20

Pisces is the last of the mutable water-signs; mutable for amiability, water for emotion. This is the mutable of uncertain emotions. Pisceans are pastel in coloring, have nondescript noses and full cheeks. They are "jowly." They are self-effacing because they are shy; shy, because they are always unsure. The evolved are visionary. Their indecisiveness makes them vague in outlines, body, and personal expression. They come alive only when spiritually inspired.

IN PERSONALITY: Pisceans are supersensitive to criticism and easily discouraged from expressing what they feel if there is the slightest doubt. They sympathize with sorrow and understand it more than any of the twelve signs. They are introverts and like to feel needed. Helping those in need gives them a chance to express their abundant emotion.

IN LOVE: Pisceans like to comfort and inspire their loved ones. They enjoy the sacrifice that may be required and are inspired to succeed in love. When not in love, they lose their direction. They drift, unable to feel their need for success.

IN BUSINESS: They succeed only when in complete sympathy with the idea or work. Otherwise, they do the job disinterestedly. Working with others is best for them. They do not make good bosses.

IN MARRIAGE: Pisceans must be sure of having chosen the right mate, for indecision is ruinous to them. It shatters their peace of mind or well-being. If their tranquillity is disturbed, they become completely disorganized.

The Big Wheel

The blank wheel, or the natal horoscope, on the opposite page emphasizes the importance of the map of destiny with which astrologers deal in detail. The ascendant, or the rising sign, is located on the first-house cusp and is the most important point. This is the part of the horoscope that describes your personality and your appearance. The ascendant is the sign that was passing over the eastern horizon at the time of your birth.

This will explain why you do not look exactly as the textbooks or manuals say that a person of your Sun-sign should look. You would have to be born at sunrise, or within an hour either way, for your birth sign to be rising and thus expressing its own personality and appearance, you would then have a double-sign influence. If you were born at another time of the day, the exact time of your birth places a different sign on the ascendant, and it will change both your appearance and the attitude with which you approach life.

Once you have identified your personality and your appearance according to the hour of your birth, you will have a better idea of your basic trait. Simply combine the sign under which you were born with your ascendant.

For example, an active cardinal-sign (either Aries, Libra, Cancer, or Capricorn) will slow down its activity if a fixed sign was rising. If such is the case, instead of dashing full-speed-ahead with projects, you will stubbornly consider every move until all the practical consequences are taken into view.

If you were born under one of the fixed signs (Taurus, Scorpio, Leo, or Aquarius) and your birth hour places one of the active cardinal-signs on the physical first house (the ascendant), this will change the basic behavior, manner, and appearance of your Sun-sign. (The active signs are Aries, Cancer, Libra, and Capricorn.) You will then be more inclined to go into motion and act more quickly, without pondering the advisability of making a motion. This is in contradiction to fixed signs, who do not enter into anything without forethought.

If you were born under a mutable or common sign (Gemini, Virgo, Sagittarius, or Pisces), your Sun-sign might indicate that you may never get through trying to resolve the wisdom of a decision or move. Many times, you may want to act both ways without singling out a particular path; this is really your problem—duality. However, if you have a fixed sign on the house of personality (the ascendant), indecision disappears; the fixed sign will slant such persons in one direction or another. The tyranny of which to choose is over.

A fixed personality on the ascendant is a good influence on mutable signs. A mutable Sun-sign combined with a fixed personality (a fixed rising sign) eases up the excessive singleness of purpose of the fixed attitude.

A cardinal sign will be less impulsive if a fixed sign guides the personality. Fixed personalities without the leavening of the mutables is too heavy. Mutable personalities have no fixity of purpose without the anchorage of the fixed sign. The combination of what you have for a personality plus the sign of your birthday will be shown in the turning of the wheel of destiny in the chart at the end of this book. Thus you will get a better idea of why you act and look as you do.

Part Three

In the following chapters descriptions are given of each Zodiac sign. After each description, the time span and meaning of each personality sign (or rising sign) is given. However, please keep in mind that the calculating of the rising sign is a very exact procedure, and that only the approximate time span can be given here.

Therefore, if your time of birth falls at the beginning of a certain time span, read the sign that precedes the one given. If your time of birth comes at the end of a certain time span, read the sign that follows the one given. This will also apply to the "wheel" charts that appear with each sign.

The personality (referring to your *time* of birth) or rising-sign charts will give you a general illustration of how the twelve zodiacal signs complete one revolution each day; their relationship to the position of the Sun at any given time is also shown. Yet it must be kept in mind that calculating an individual rising-sign, or natal, horoscope is a very exact procedure.

It is necessary in these charts, for the sake of simplicity, to give approximate time-spans for each sign that rises on the eastern horizon point (i.e. two hours). This is done because the actual periods of time relating to each sign rising are quite inconsistent and would be impossible to show on these charts.

Therefore, please refer to the rising sign that correlates with your time of birth; but in addition you must also consider the signs both preceding and following the sign indicated, especially if it does not express your personality and physical characteristics correctly.

ARIES: The First Sign
March 21 to April 19

When Aries persons consult textbooks and astrological magazines to see what is happening to their sign or what is said about them, they read that Aries is a pioneer, a trail-blazer, a starter of all kinds of new ventures, and a promoter of new ideas.

Aries is the sign ruled by Mars. Mars, a touch-and-go planet, rules energy, impulse, reality, and actuality. Thus Arians carry out all programs of action. That is why both Aries and Mars rule the first spring month when life springs into action.

Aries types are really warriors; hence they make wonderful army men, shouting orders and commanding action. The vanity of Aries expressed through braggadocio is not true vanity like the vanity of Libra or Taurus; it is more an egoism, for they are not really egotistical. The pride of Aries is the consciousness centered into male attitudes. Even the female Aries tends to be masculine because of her aggressiveness. Mars rules sex, so Aries must show masculinity in the way he expresses energy, in the games he plays and in feats of conquest. Challenge suits him because it gives him an opportunity to excel and prove his prowess.

If an Arian should have a Libran personality, or ascendant, he will be a sly type. His bravado will be held well in check, with a sweet, unassuming approach. His manner will be better than average, for Arians are not known for finesse. The Aries-Libra combination is ever on the track of a new group. This one is sociable, which is rare for Aries. If the new group does not go along with what he wants, this Arian will say it is because people are so difficult, people are always making you quarrel with them.

With the Aries-Libra influence, money troubles are

constant. There is never enough, and debts pile up. When a new business venture is begun with newly found associates, there is a great rush, making the end seem fantastic. The enthusiasm of Aries, the rally to get this idea going progresses by leaps and bounds. Like a bonfire, it never goes anywhere. The start was all there was. It dies at the initial stage unless Taurus or some other fixed sign is present to guarantee continued interest.

I have an Aries client with a Libra personality, or rising sign. The many and varied opportunities that came his way were miraculous, yet he never succeeded with one. It is almost as if he were annoyed that others had to give him the opportunities. In order to fail, he would start telling lies about those involved, projecting what he planned to do, or what he had done to others, and enjoying the discomfort caused those who offered him the opportunity, thus appeasing his quarrelsome vanity.

Arians are doers, not talkers. They welcome every opportunity to go into action; and thus they expend much energy, of which they have plenty. They can be very bragging talkers when their hands are empty; for this is their only available channel to rid themselves of irrepressible energy. All fire signs are generous. Aries is an impulsive giver. Aries people are very outgoing and give of themselves as well as their possessions.

If an Aries type has Mars afflicted to Mercury, the ruler of speech, contracts, and promises, he will be a quarrelsome Aries who breaks his word and will not fulfill contracts. He will start well but will wait for the first opportunity to start a row. If Mars is in good aspect to Mercury, the speaker can arouse and inspire others. His ideas will be exciting. All acts will work for a practical good.

When Mars is afflicted to Venus, the planet of love, there is a continued changing of loves, running from one love to another—the Don Juan complex—eversearching for the love who will not quarrel. But there is no such creature, for the quarrel is within. The Aries type whose Mars is in good aspect to Venus will offer love that is strong, courageous, and loyal as well as tender, gentle, and considerate.

When Mars is afflicted to Jupiter, judgment suffers. Aries's opinion differs then with everyone else's for the sake of winning. When Mars is in good aspect to Jupiter, the planet of opinion and judgment, Aries's ideas, judgment, and opinion are wise and magnanimous.

I am reminded of a very fine Aries widow who had Mars afflicted to Mercury, the planet of speech. When a friend called on her and showed her affection (Mercury afflicted to Mars turns the thinking to sex), she scolded and made the most scathing remarks, especially if it was a male. When she saw that her vituperative accusations had had an effect, she would sit back in high glee, relishing the fact that she had completely shattered someone by this behavior. Her negative energy was released through abusive speech.

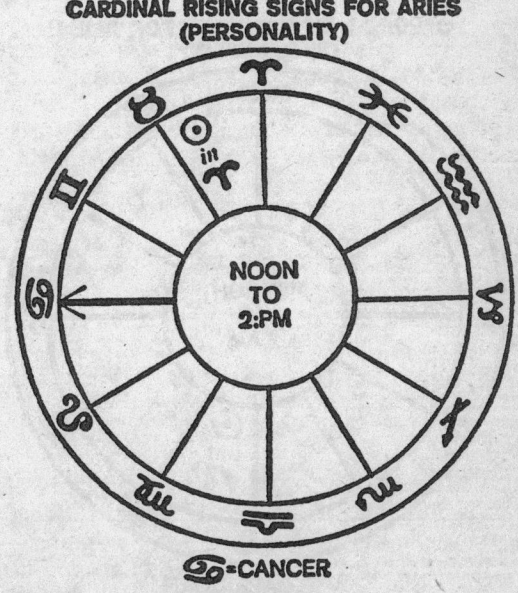

Noon–2 PM. The Aries type born at noon would have Cancer for personality. He would be entirely different from the courageous type of Aries. Cancer would cancel all of what the textbooks say. Cancer is shy and sensitive. Aries is noisy, busy, and pushy. The conflict here would be force subdued, an emotional person trying not to come to a boil.

Aries is red; Cancer is pale, white. This combination would give a very fair redhead or golden coloring—quiet and boisterous by turns. The scene of the struggle would be the home. Aries would want to be head man in the family. Otherwise, he would rebel, and the mother especially would be held responsible.

There would be a constant change of public or audience. Persons dealing with an Aries type born at noon would encounter a continual battle for general attention. One such type I know shows pictures of different members of his family when he is in bars, and forces everyone to praise the imagined good looks of his family.

CARDINAL RISING SIGNS FOR ARIES (PERSONALITY)

♑=CAPRICORN

MIDNIGHT–2 AM. Aries born at midnight with Capricorn for personality; he will probably be the most quiet Aries you will ever meet. For Capricorn is dignified, a stickler for conventional behavior. Tie this to the active, bustling Aries, and it will certainly tone him down.

Aries's reddish coloring will be darkened. His flat and broad features will be less spreading, and his head will not be wide. The forehead will be narrower, the eyes more serious. The jokes of this Aries will have an ironical catch in them. All actions will be studied, planned, and purposeful. Aries will be the master in the home; but the generosity to those in the home will be real, for that is where this Aries's heart is—at home.

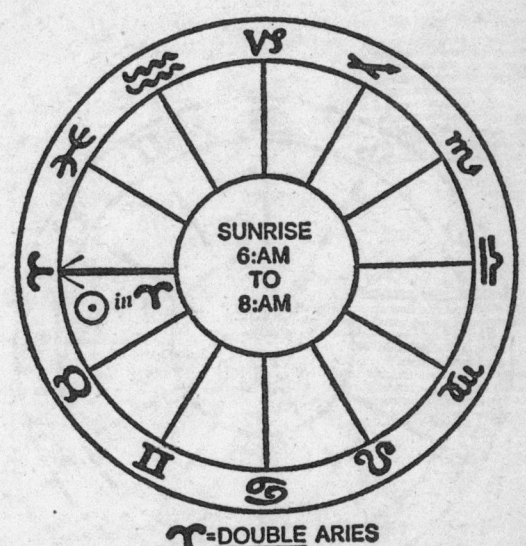

♈=DOUBLE ARIES

6 AM–8 AM. An Aries type born with his own sign for personality. He is a true type, for the individuality and personality are the same. This could be the flaming redhead. His double cardinality makes for much physical expression; his body enjoys action. The planes in his face are flat; his nose is large and spreading; his mouth is very wide with a large lip-line development. Aries people love a good joke, espe-

cially at the expense of others. They are always poking fun.

As comedians, they go for slapstick. They are not subtle and cannot understand subtlety. They like to find their way out of trouble; they are fearless and filled with courage to live life to the full. Their action and heart for the drive through life would be in harmony and banked on the self.

If there is nothing to love but life, then this Aries will be consumed with the importance of the self, flexing his muscles—either physical or mental—being the hero of every story he tells.

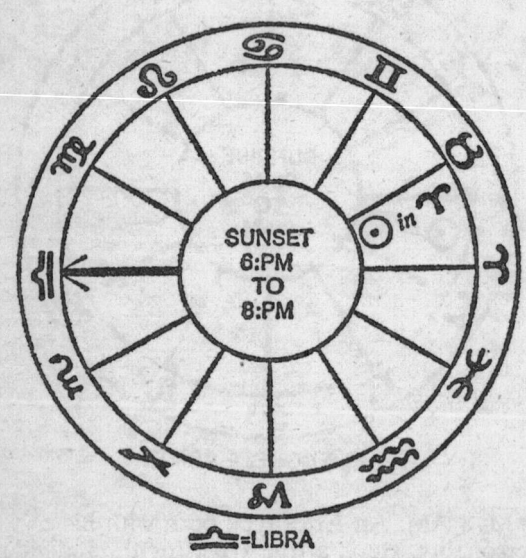

♎=LIBRA

6 PM–8 PM. Aries born at sunset has Libra, the sign opposite his birth sign for personality. This will be a bragging, vain Aries. His quarrel will always be with associates or the mate. This Aries will fight against the self and against his best interests.

FIXED RISING SIGNS FOR ARIES
(PERSONALITY)

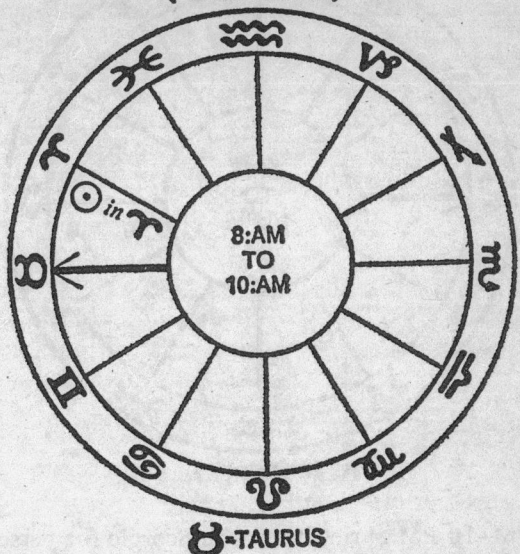

♉-TAURUS

8 AM–10 AM. Aries born in the morning will have Taurus for personality. This is the sentimental Arian, a very stubborn one too, who moves and acts with more deliberation than Aries is thought to have. Aries will now be interested in money and possessions. The brusqueness will have disappeared, giving way to better manners and greater sedateness. Aries with a Taurian personality is more considerate; his bragging will center on possessions.

Taurus will make Aries shorter, better looking, heavier, and less interested in games; for Taurus likes to be comfortable. Action is centered on the gain of money and material things. This Aries will not flirt to show how good he is with the opposite sex. His mate will be sought out in secret and mainly for practical reasons. This will be the only secretive Aries, for the sign is generally very forthright.

FIXED RISING SIGNS FOR ARIES
(PERSONALITY)

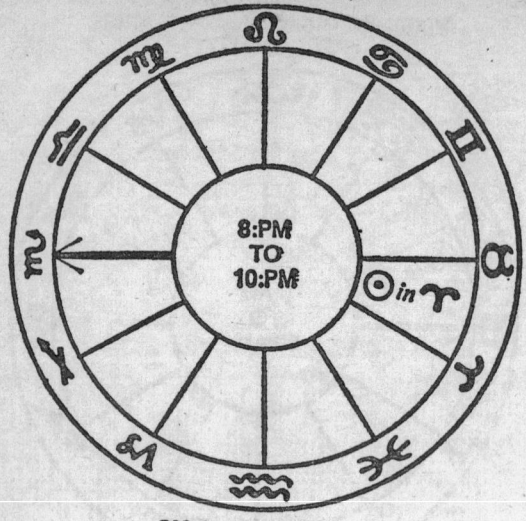

♏ = SCORPIO

8 PM–10 PM. Aries born with Scorpio for personality is the slickest type. Both of these signs are ruled by Mars. This time, the Mars of Scorpio has gained power and is cleverer. Action is combined with the desire for power.

This will be the strongest power-loving Aries you will ever see. It is also the first light, fair Scorpio personality. It is a very difficult combination, for this Aries is working everyone for the rise to power. Scheming Scorpio plus rough-shod Aries ride over everyone's head to get the prize. The double-strength Mars (Mars ruling both signs) will stop at nothing to win. The flat planes in the Aries face will be stilled and controlled, the generosity gone. The humor will be spiteful. There will be cruelty directed toward everyone who works for this Aries or toward those in the same service unless Mars is very well aspected in the chart. Health will be a problem with this combination.

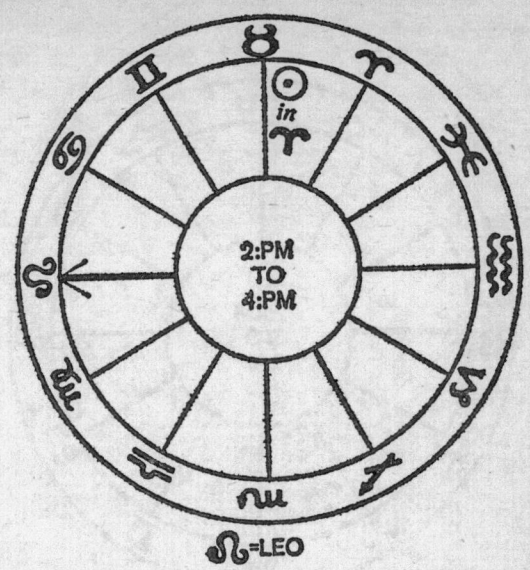

♌ = LEO

2 PM–4 PM. Aries born with the fixed sign of Leo rising is at least a kindred type. Both are fire signs and their like elements complement each other. Aries and Leo get on very well. Aries is romantic, but this Aries will be the most loving. An Aries with the birth-sun so high in his horoscope will be quite an involved person and better educated, for he will aspire to learning.

The face will have better construction. The nose will be higher-bridged, but still the coloring will be a very light gold with fair or ruddy skin. The native will command respect, and the generosity will be genuine, the manner superior. He will be less noisy. Aries with Leo for personality will always be in love with ideas as well as people. His personality will be warm; his individuality will have ideals. This will be one of the richest Aries, for the gamble with ideas will pay off.

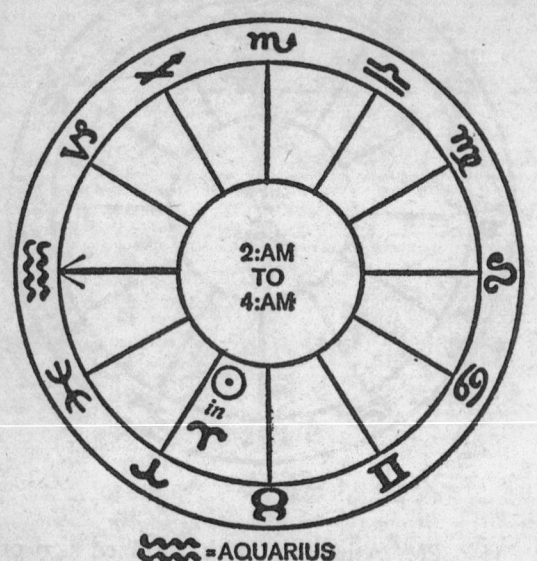

≈ = AQUARIUS

2 AM–4 PM. Aries born at this hour has Aquarius, the last fixed sign, for a personality. Fixed signs are good to Aries, for they steady him and relieve some of the useless action. The combination of Aries, a fire sign, with Aquarius, or air sign, could produce a "hot-air" talker. But, it also could be an enthusiastic talker with new, modern ideas.

Aries combined with Aquarius will be the tallest, easiest, and most modest type, but perhaps too indifferent. The brag will be there, but it will be modified and used only if something new and unusual has to be said. A writer with this combination will write in a new style or about a very odd subject.

All such types are not tall, dark, and handsome, but they are exciting and harmonious within, where many fires burn, love being the main one. A new love, a new fire, over and over again.

MUTABLE RISING SIGNS FOR ARIES
(PERSONALITY)

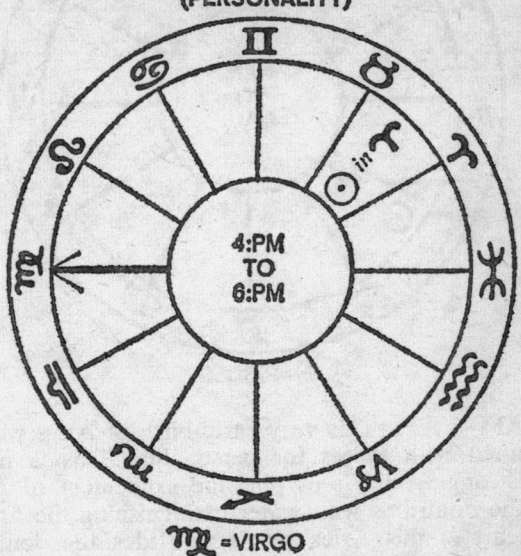

♍ =VIRGO

4 PM–6 PM. Aries born with the earth sign of Virgo for a personality is indeed unfortunate, for now all of the excitement and life he seeks and enjoys is bogged down into the practical, hard-working Virgo, who is not happy without work. The fire and desire for adventure are smoldering somewhere in the background of this Aries, but they are being postponed. If you encounter a small Aries whose features are not flat and he is neither humorous nor generous, you can be sure he is a Virgo personality. He is businesslike, always bustling about his affairs with scarcely a moment to spare, importuning everyone to work a deal in his behalf. This is the least exciting Aries.

MUTABLE RISING SIGNS FOR ARIES
(PERSONALITY)

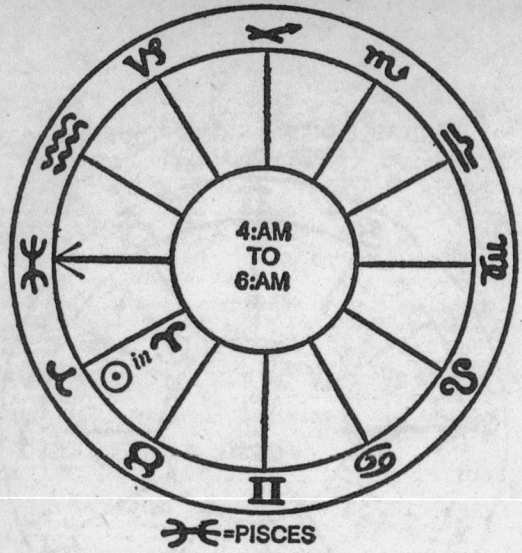

♓=PISCES

4 AM–6 AM. This very early birth of Aries will be combined with Pisces for personality. This is not a very strong type. Pisces plus the excitement of Aries into the doldrums with water extinguishing the fire. If the heart of this Aries gets a new idea the doubting Pisces may blight it.

In time this will change, but this Aries will be a late starter. The confusion of Pisces keeps direct Aries in a state of hesitation. The purpose of life for the fire signs must be clear, or at least he must think it is. The duality of Pisces, a common sign who sees both sides of the argument, has to contend with a situation out of his depth, since the cardinal fire sign will want to go right to the core of the matter.

Aries will be well thought of in his own community, or be the kingpin in the family, or the member of the family who is just coming home or going away. He will have a fast romance ending in marriage. After a few years have passed his mate is married, but this Aries is still single.

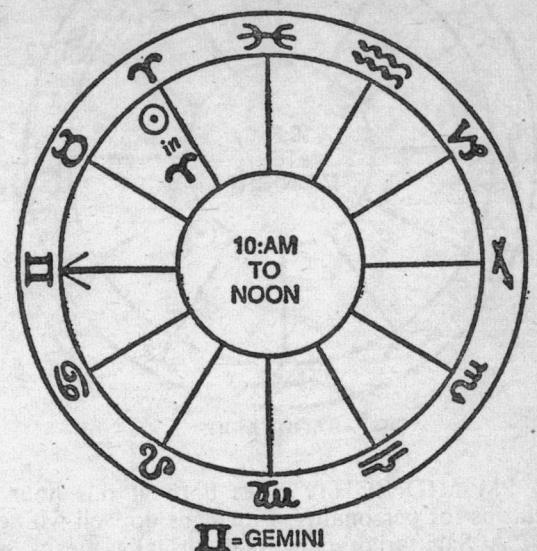

♊ = GEMINI

10 AM–NOON. Aries born at this hour has Gemini for personality; again, a fire and air combination. Talk here is always for a new hope or wish, or about relatives, especially sisters and brothers; the younger brother bragging about what a great guy his older brother is.

Aries combined with youthful Gemini is the perennial type that never stops attending the old Alma Mater games and keeps up with friends they chummed with in their college days. This Aries is a great talker; his friends are the best. Aries combined with Gemini marries the school sweetheart, but remembers all the loves of his youth.

This is the good-looking Aries who will always seem the same—and he is. He has no rebellion or meanness. He changes friends, yes; but he doesn't forget old friends.

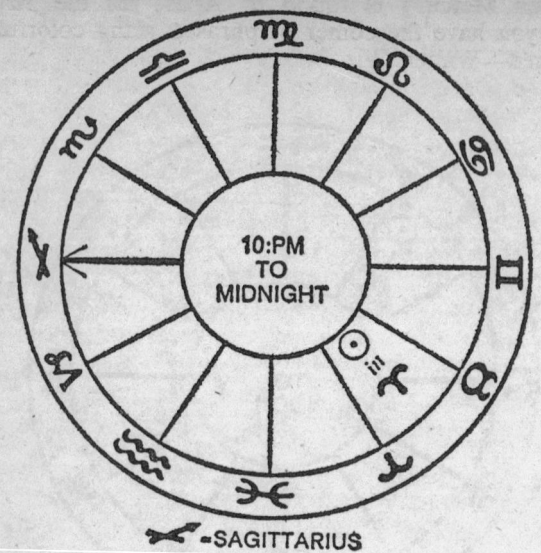

✎-SAGITTARIUS

10 PM–MIDNIGHT. Aries born at this hour has Sagittarius for personality. Fire signs do well with each other. A Sagittarian personality usually means gambling with ideas. Aries likes life to be a game; so this would be a gambler who bets on anything, especially games of all sorts. The challenge to his judgment makes the game romantic.

This Aries, who likes nothing better than action, will travel continuously on long journeys. On his return he may write about it because the trip was a gamble; everything encountered was romantic. It aroused the ideals of this Aries, for this is the better-educated type, whose love of ideas is consolidated.

The coloring is not real red, but rather muted. The features are not only flat but also soft. They may be quite heavy instead of muscular. These Aries choose mates who are inferior to them or to what they had planned, for the ego of Aries is strong even if he has not succeeded. He still thinks egotistically about the self, the hero that he is— "the Secret Life of Walter Mitty."

When Mercury is found in Aries, for the Aries born, you have the coiner of phrases, slang colorfully arranged—Walter Winchell has this planetary placement. However, he can be bullied and brow-beaten a bit too with this combination. This is the warrior who uses speech and words as his weapons.

The most historical Aries who lived up to the coloring of Aries was Thomas Jefferson. He was a true starter who began things and stayed for the finish. He had Sagittarius for a personality; this sign made him tall and scholarly, the student and writer of statesman quality, whose generosity was seen in his love for his country.

TAURUS: The Second Sign
April 20 to May 20

If you are a Taurian, the textbooks will say, you are slow, plodding, and stubbornly bent on making money; you might be a banker, financier, or anything that covers handling money. Taurus, the books add, loves green things, has a green thumb, prefers the country to the city. You are square in build, solid, with a very short neck, a *retroussé* nose, and lovely wide eyes. That is all true; but it must be kept in mind that there is no such thing as an all-Taurus chart.

Taurus is the pretty face that gets all he wants in life by his sweetness and charm, attracting what he needs, for Venus, the planet that rules Taurus, is the planet of wealth, comfort, and love. It attracts people and possessions for the native.

But if you meet a Taurian who does not come up to these specifications, do not be daunted, for the time of day has everything to do with it! A Taurian born at noon will look like Leo. A Taurian born at midnight will be tall like Aquarius. Combine the known birth hour with the Taurus birthday, then see what you have.

For all the reputation that Taurus has for kindness and sweetness, Hitler contradicted this textbook fable. If Venus, the planet that rules Taurus, is afflicted, no matter how wonderful Taurus is supposed to be, it will not be so. This famous Taurian had an affliction to his Venus from Saturn (a bargainer). There is no affection for anyone if sweet Venus is cut to the bone of feeling, restricted by Saturn. The kindness or goodness of Venus is reversed when under pressure of cold planets such as Saturn or Uranus. Instead of giving or being charitable, such Taurians demand in place of giving; they take instead of doing good. Their nature becomes parasitical, feeding on all of their fellow men.

A greedy Taurian is represented by the siren who beguiles you, seduces you, and then proceeds to strip you bare of all your worldly goods, abandoning you the moment your pockets are empty.

If Venus is afflicted to the sex planet Mars, you may have the golddigger who makes love his business. This Taurian uses sex to take you. He weds for money, repeating the marriages on a wholesale basis. However, as in all the readings given here that involve bad aspects, please keep in mind that other aspects can modify these influences.

If sweet Venus in Taurus has to contend with merciless Saturn in affliction, who is never satisfied no matter how sweet the talk, this Taurian will be heartless, straining for the last particle, each victory arousing a new appetite. Hitler, the tyrant, continually demanded more land after each siege. Venus's greed when afflicted was clearly depicted when Mephistopheles (Saturn) offered the world (Taurus is earth) to Faust, who was in love (Venus), for the soul is the utmost man has to give. This is the symbolic parable of Venus afflicted by Saturn.

A Taurian with Aquarius on the ascendant will be more humanitarian. This means that if intellect (Gemini, Libra, and Aquarius—Air), is strong in the Taurian chart, there is a chance that Taurus's craving for possessions will diminish and he will use intelligence to ease out of an impasse. Taurus rules the neck and voice. A student who has Taurus for her Sun-sign and Libra for personality will be more active and brusque. Taurus is a blunderer with a loud voice. Behind all of this Taurian coarseness (and Taurus can be boorish) would be the sweet voice of Taurus coupled with the suave manners of Libra. These Taurians have lovely voices (Uranus): they can sing; they can get what they want from life because of the quiet, gracious self-control of Libra and the charm and sweetness of Taurus. At times, aggressiveness is tantamount to failure for them, driving away from them the very thing their affectionate natures crave.

Taurians are not thinkers; they are feelers. An idea

must be repeated over and over again until they feel *en rapport* with the idea. Taurus is a very slow sign that must not be hurried lest he stumble or blunder.

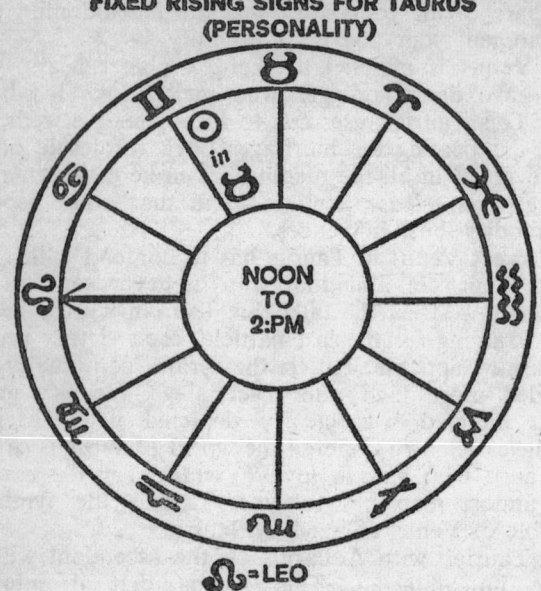

FIXED RISING SIGNS FOR TAURUS (PERSONALITY)

♌ = LEO

NOON–2 PM. Taurus born with the personality of Leo, at midday, is a much more determined person, for this brings two fixed signs into operation. Leo is persistent; Taurus is determined. This tough background is a heavy load for anyone to carry without being overbearing. Taurus stubbornly presses on; Leo wilfully perseveres to a dramatic conclusion.

Here, Taurus wants the limelight, with Leo fronting for him; this combination cancels the stay-at-home-for-comfort Taurian. This is the big shot in finance, the big realtor. Taurus-Leo can produce a very fine actor. The pride and fine presence of Leo combined with the beauty of Taurus is striking, and this person would deeply need love. Yet, neither sign being weak, you will have your hands full in a clinch with them. Leo is the king or queen, so don't take the light away. Taurus has a quiet vanity that is not flaunted like the other Venus-ruled sign, Libra.

FIXED RISING SIGNS FOR TAURUS (PERSONALITY)

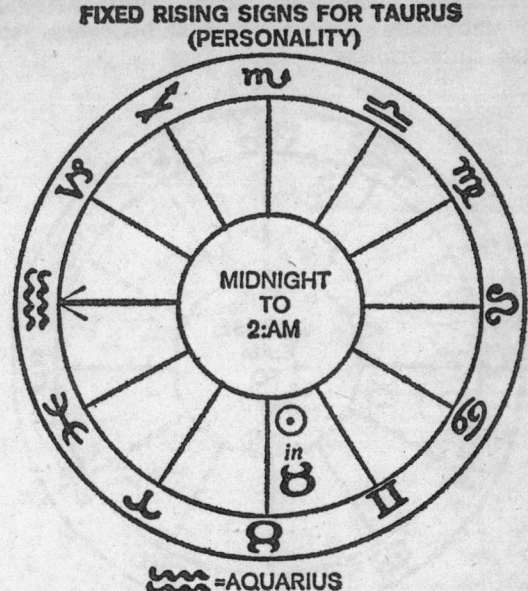

≋ =AQUARIUS

MIDNIGHT–2 AM. The Taurian born at midnight, with the Sun at the bottom of the wheel, or horoscope chart, may not hit the limelight until after middle life. This person will have the air sign Aquarius for a personality. Taurus will combine stubbornness with perversity. Aquarius can give the first impression of being airy, casual, and easy to do business with; but don't let that fool you. Aquarius is fanning the air to sound you out for practical reasons too. The Taurian with an air sign will want to circulate all over to sell to the world; yet he will want to come home someday and settle in the suburbs.

This Taurian will not be short, but tall or odd in build. One of my clients with this combination has a very odd nose. The knob at the end of the nose is grotesque. Part of the body is too thin for the other half. Friends get the better side of Taurians with Aquarius for personality. Taurus is a tyrant when afflicted, and this type is perverse and difficult with the family; he is the stubborn I-know-it-all type who perversely must dominate. He is a very quarrelsome Taurian. Aquarian argumentativeness plus Taurian stubbornness spells perverse stubbornness.

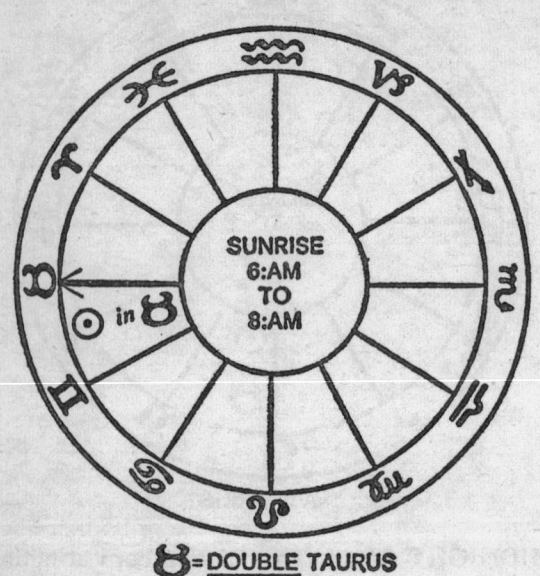

♉ = DOUBLE TAURUS

6 AM–8 AM. This time produces a double Taurian, for now both the Sun-sign and the personality is Taurus. The appearance is of the very round, compact head, the short neck; the heavy shoulders seem to move up closer to the head later in life. The eyes are large and have a curious surprised look. The nose is pert, *retroussé*. If Venus, the planet that rules Taurus, is afflicted, then the nose has a little bulb at the end.

The voice is good, soft, and low—a comforting tone. The personality is warm, affectionate; the smile, very sweet—peace at any price. Money and the person are one. There are all kinds of discussions that resolve values. Money will always be spent for comfort and food.

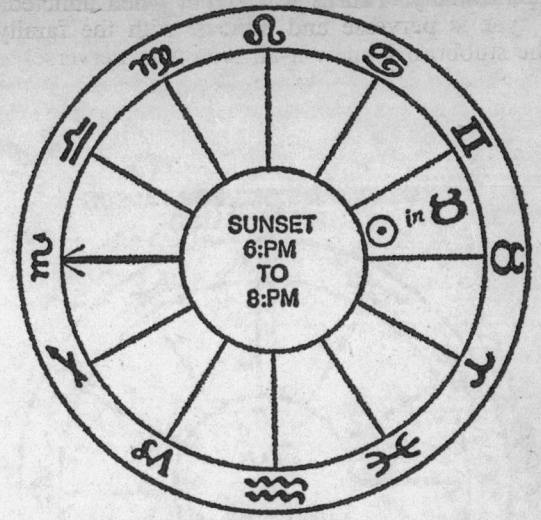

♏ =SCORPIO

6 PM-8 PM. Here Taurus has its opposite sign, Scorpio, for a personality; it is one of the toughest combinations. In fact, it will give the perverse Aquarian-Taurian a run for the money.

Taurus will not be seen in the appearance at all. Scorpio will completely obscure Taurian traits. Taurian stubbornness combined with the invincible Scorpio can wreck saints. Taurus is a heavy sign so that now he will have powerful shoulders; he will be intense in mien, aloof, secretive, and all the sweetness will be gone. The head seems to be sitting down on the chest, the shoulders riding up from behind. The hair is thin, getting ready to bald.

The quarrelsomeness of Scorpio routs the peace-loving Taurian. You would never believe he could be Taurian. The meanness of Scorpio is always in the foreground, delighting in caustic remarks. So when the textbooks tell you of the lovely Taurina, do not think of the Taurus whose rising sign on the personality first-house is Scorpio. The amazing rub to this type is that he has no consciousness of being offensive.

CARDINAL SIGNS FOR TAURUS (PERSONALITY)

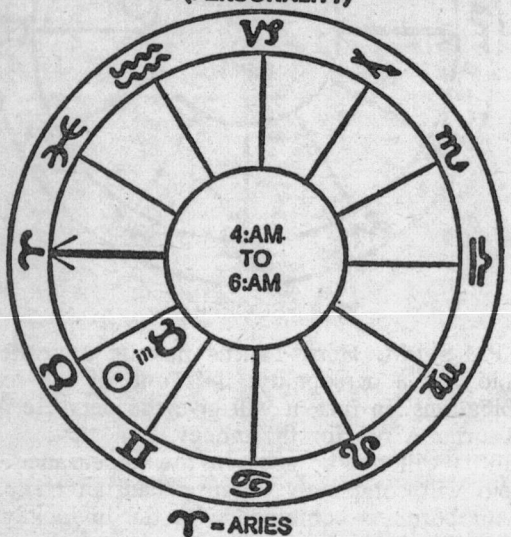

♈ = ARIES

4 AM–6 AM. The Taurus born with the first cardinal sign, Aries, for a personality would give Taurus a more active and aggressive initial attitude. Taurus will move more readily and willingly into action with far less resistance. Taurus will want to stay; Aries will want to move on—so this Taurian will not be the slow, plodding type at all.

Taurus is brown. Aries will put red in the color and make the features larger (for Taurus has delicate features), taking away the small, dainty nose. This Taurian will not be so beautiful. The fixed look will be replaced by a more outgoing, generous countenance. However, every move will be made for money.

CARDINAL SIGNS FOR TAURUS
(PERSONALITY)

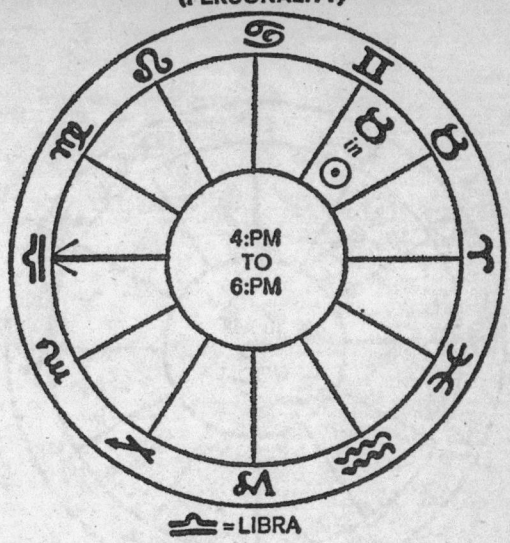

≏ = LIBRA

4 PM–6 PM. The Taurus born with the sign of Libra for a personality will have a double Venus setup. Venus, the planet of beauty and love, rules Taurus and Libra. This will be a real beauty. Taurus will dress much better with the Libra personality, choosing clothes with an eye for line and color. Taurians like fine clothes, but Libra will give a style that's different!

This Taurian has lovely manners and has dropped the blundering ways. Libra dresses up any party. This will not be a stubborn type in marriage, for Taurus insists on fulfilling the marriage vows. However, Taurus will change mates. In the end, money must be acquired through marriage, or the race is on.

You will be won with charm, good manners, good clothes, and many forms of entertainment; this fellow rushes a girl by taking her to every smart restaurant in town. Money is involved one way or another. With this emphasis, Taurus is now slimmer, goes out more, is lighter in color and disposition. Their eyes are the most beautiful you will ever see.

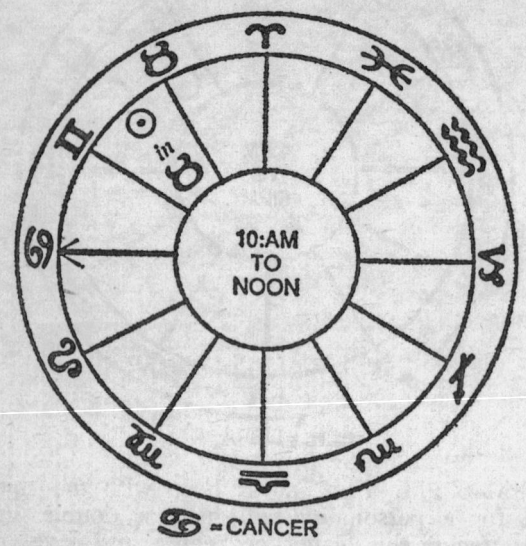

♋ = CANCER

10 AM–NOON. Taurus with the soft, shy water sign of Cancer for a personality will combine the love of family with possessions—the family *is* the possession. This is the mother who is cooking for the children, stuffing them and herself, sitting with a box of chocolates when you visit in the home.

Weight must be watched here, for the body is short and covered with fat. The personality exudes a sweetness. The country house is best; it is not easy for them to leave (Cancer likes to stay at home) and go to the city. A suggestion about weight is useless. Cancer does not care how it looks as long as its emotional life is satisfactory. If there is no family to worship cloyingly, money will take the place of people. Taurus combined with Cancer will mother possessions or holdings, giving away only one thing—food.

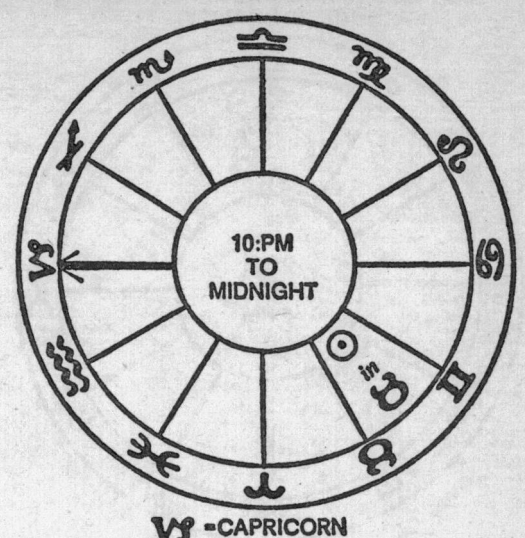

♑ =CAPRICORN

10 PM–MIDNIGHT. Taurus born with the earth sign Capricorn for a personality has now found a kindred spirit. Both being earth signs, they work very well together in the trine (trinity) or harmonious state. They speak the same language. Taurus wants possessions; Capricorn wants name or fame.

Obesity is absent. Capricorn hates gluttony or gourmandism. The bones are smaller and the manner more serious, somber, and orderly. The clear coloring that Taurus is known for is toned down into a definite brunette. The nose is not as small.

The youthful look of Taurus has fled to make room for the more mature and capable Capricornian. Taurus is now very peaceful; for earning money, he has the organized personality to make it all possible in time. Time is not wasted. Taurus is not blundering or allowing sentiment to flag him down. Planning and acquisition are harmoniously united.

MUTABLE RISING SIGNS FOR TAURUS
(PERSONALITY)

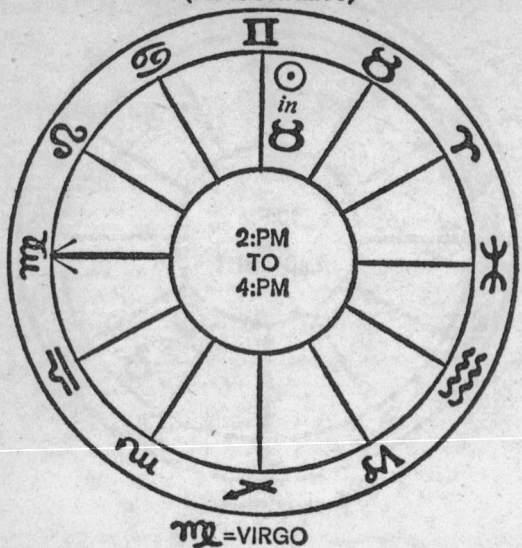

♍ =VIRGO

2 PM–4 PM. Taurus is again lucky to have the earth sign of Virgo for personality. Virgo has less charm than the sister sign Gemini. Taurus likes money; Virgo likes work. This is the most hard-working Taurian, who will socialize with employers and co-workers. Taurus people born with Virgo for a personality will be the most studious, wanting to go to college. Taurians are not good students. Whatever is learned (it must be useful) is used for monetary purposes, and work is the prime motive for a Taurian combined with Virgo. Taurus, with Virgo, is busy with his work, and he is always telling you about it. He evaluates progress by the paycheck.

The features are not soft, but have a strictness. The nose is longer and wedged; the mouth is not curved ready to smile, as is usual with Taurus; and the eyes are busy for investigative reasons. The whole manner is more critical.

MUTABLE RISING SIGNS FOR TAURUS
(PERSONALITY)

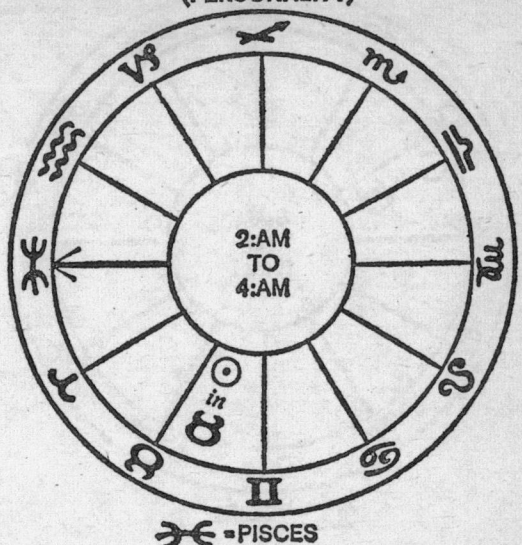

♓ =PISCES

2 AM–4 AM. A Taurus born early in the morning has a Piscean personality that gives the least determined Taurian. Stubbornness has completely disappeared. Many initial attempts are made to earn money. When states of indecision are finally resolved, Taurus with Pisces for a personality becomes a pillar in the community, taking an active part in civic affairs. He may be the banker in a small town, or even the realtor working in new settlements, promoting a new community.

The mutable signs—Gemini, Virgo, Sagittarius, and Pisces—help the Taurian to listen to the other point of view and accept it, for Taurians are notorious in that they listen without understanding. A mutable Taurian is like a leavened cake that is delicious, but not heavy, for it did rise.

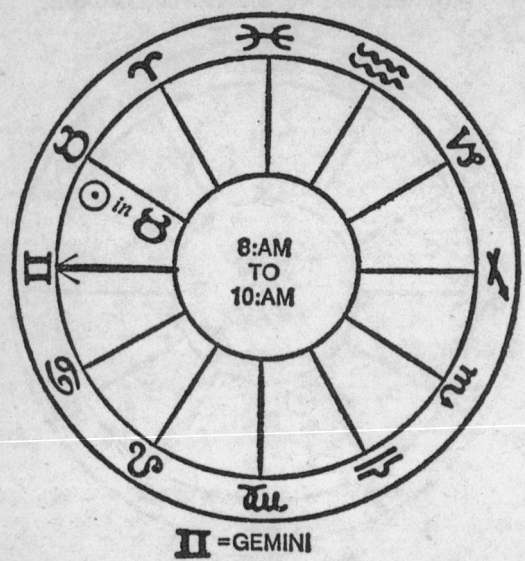

Ⅱ =GEMINI

8 AM–10 AM. Taurus born with the first mutable air sign, Gemini, for a personality, is another very good-looking Taurus, the very, very-little-girl type. Geminians talk all the time; combined with Taurus, their talk will concern possessions, clothes, or new things they are going to buy. They are always visiting one relative or another. One client, a Taurian with Gemini for a personality, is continually going from the home of one brother to another.

This type is not heavy; the neck is not short; the gait is neither slow nor plodding. Taurus with a Gemini personality is very attractive. The self-centeredness of Taurus is transferred to the brothers, sisters, and the community. The easy manner of Gemini, who likes money, combined with the sweet Venusian individuality, will talk for it by selling, teaching—or through a hobby such as writing.

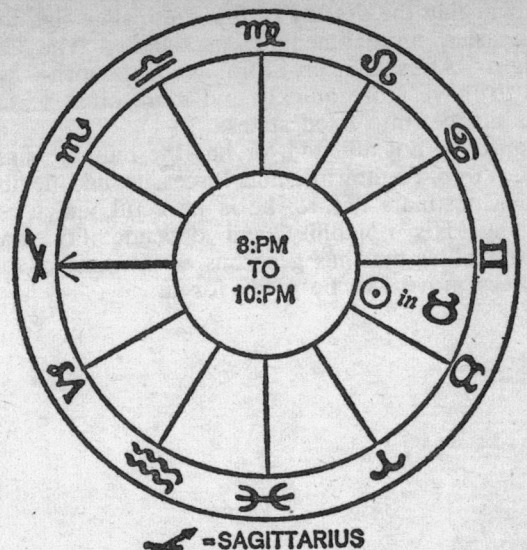

⚹=SAGITTARIUS

8 PM–10 PM. The Taurian with Sagittarius for his personality is the promoter. He always has a new gamble. You will do most of the work—he will just give you the ideas, put everyone to work, then travel around inspiring everyone with his hail-fellow-well-done attitude to make money. This is a tall Taurian, laughing you into joining his deal.

It is hard to resist the gamble, for charm combines with faith. All fixed signs resist people. Taurus is the first fixed sign; his resistance is directed at possessions and money.

The afflicted Taurian has either Leo, Scorpio, or Aquarius rising for personality. They are difficult to deal with, for Taurus may listen to what you say without understanding you. Every word must be phrased to arouse him to feel that it can end in a profitable way.

Taurus will manifest his resistance through lack of agility in his gait. But with Sagittarius for a personality, his gait has quickened. He has cultivated the mind and eliminated stagnation. He thinks at top speed, changing the destiny of the fixed, slow sign to a lighter, easier, more amenable personality. The Cardinal signs—Aries, Cancer, Libra, and Capricorn—help Taurus to move more quickly and more often so that he does not get into fixed states.

If Taurus is not afflicted, or has the mutable signs, Gemini, Virgo, Sagittarius, and Pisces, to add flexibility to his obstinate nature, he is peaceful, quiet, and comforting. His reliability and dependability make him a soft pillar that has generous countenance. However, every move will be made for money.

GEMINI: The Third Sign
May 21 to June 21

Gemini is the first air sign. It is also the first mutable sign. Gemini is perennial youth, the teenager sign. Gemini is the the easiest sign to get to know, but the hardest sign to keep interested. Gemini smiles constantly, making the laugh lines on the side of the nose deepen with age. Geminians smile in and out of every situation in life.

Gemini is the quickest walker, physically moving faster than the other eleven signs. Geminians think on their feet and are as mentally agile as they are physically swift. Their little-girl look retains the youthful hairline of the adolescent, the unruly curling hair at the temples seeming to fringe out and away from the temples in a wind-blown effect. The general facial expression is open, as if ready for speech.

The body remains slender and trim throughout their lives. The walking gait is quick and precisely spaced.

Even in later years Gemini makes mothers look almost as young as their daughters. Geminians have a childlike inquisitive interest in everything. They never tire of seeking a new mental interest. This sign is ruled by Mercury, the planet of youth, winged Mercury, the symbol of mental travel. That is exactly what Geminians do: they travel into a new set of ideas that keeps them young for practical purposes.

Having a dual sign, Geminians do everything twofold—marry twice, give birth to twins, have two homes, two professions, or make their hobby a form of service.

It is not that these persons are too lazy to decide on one thing; in fact, you would be flattered if you knew to what extent they have deliberated over you. Resolving anything is Gemini's great problem.

The indecision that rides the Geminian can be costly. Either he waits too long and misses the opportunity or he moves too fast, precipating failure. Seldom do Geminians arrive on cue. They harass themselves for having missed out, harangue others until their will is carried out, or worry until the job is done.

If Gemini's ruling planet, Mercury, is harmoniously placed it will create a type versatile enough to do almost everything—act, sing, dance, write plays, play an instrument.

If Mercury is in good aspect to Mars, speech and action are harmonious; nice thinking is combined with brave deeds. If Mercury is afflicted to Venus, it will be another Geminian rushing from one social group to another or from one lover to another.

Mercury in good aspect to Jupiter will make a writer, journalist, or reporter in love with ideas; this type loves to think. Should Mercury be afflicted to Jupiter, no one can depend on this Geminian, a professional promiser or liar—the psychological liar who is capable of being a demagog has this. When Mercury is in good aspect to Saturn, Gemini will have a wonderful memory, will be a serious student, and will be extremely reliable in any transaction. A Mercury in bad aspect to Saturn means a depressed, gloomy pessimist. Fear rides this person. This Geminian will exact the last bit of strength from everyone.

When Mercury is in good aspect to Uranus, a lightninglike thinker emerges: his ideas come and go in flashes. If Mercury is in bad aspect to Uranus, the most perverse, contrary person alive results; he would not agree with the gods. Gemini with Mercury in trouble with Uranus will argue meanly, nastily and maliciously for hours.

Geminians who look exactly the way textbooks say they look would be born at sunrise. The Geminian born at midnight carries weight or is even fat. Gemini born at sunset will be very tall, for that would be the Sagittarius personality. The Geminian born at noon will be prominent: he is destined to fulfill a public life and will work very hard to get there since he has hard-working Virgo for personality.

Years ago, a Geminian came to me in a great state

of anxiety. He had lost his girl via the indecisive route, and only then did he realize how much he cared. He had had two marriages. The first was to a childhood sweetheart he was too young to manage. The second marriage had been to the fixed sign Aquarius, and the first marriage had been to a Leo. Being a Geminian, his marriage to the first fixed sign showed that he had unfinished business as far as marriage and relationships were concerned. Geminians like to get things accomplished. It was clear that in the second marriage he wanted to resolve the mistakes he had made in the first—therefore, the attraction to another fixed type. He had not learned much from his first marriage, and his aim was to beat down these fixed barriers. His premise was wrong to start with; therefore he could not win. Geminians imitate others. He imitated his first wife (Leo) by trying to impose his will on the second (Aquarius).

A Geminian should avoid, as he should have avoided, a fixed type—Taurus, Leo, Scorpio, or Aquarius—until he has gathered enough strength to map out a plan to deal with all the habits of a fixed sign. Instead, he plunged right in. The need to win was imperative in him, and he failed himself because of the immediacy of his desire to win at last. His goal was to finish a problem that had overwhelmed him. There is nothing wrong with wanting to win or prove to the self that one can stand up in given situations. If all sides are treated fairly, the moral victory, for that is what he sought, should not leave ruin.

The favorite stunt of mutable Gemini is to let you go as far as you like before he stops you. His first state is of indecision. The reason for this is that he has not decided how much he wants you. If Geminians do not want you, they feel free to give you the AIR because they never pressure you. Gemini is an air sign. The fixed types know they want you and set their sights on you. The second wife of this Geminian did this. He thought he had nothing to worry about. This time he would show these fixed signs—always forcing their will on people! So he gave her, in the parlance of the day, a bad time. At first she placated and appeesed him, which, as I have said, fixed signs will do when they have to be humble to win you. Their behavior is decisive.

This completely undermined the Geminian; he pulled out all the stops and did everything he wanted to avenge himself of the first marriage and the new second marriage. But the fixed signs return to their old fixed point of view. The fixed-sign wife had to be reckoned with when she saw what was happening. He had forgotten that you do not change fixed signs. When the honeymoon was over for her, she stopped him cold— *Out! Out! Out!*

If a mutable sign gives you the air, it is not serious —Gemini may take you back. Being dual, he may find he now wants you: he has made a decision. If fixed air gives you the air that is another matter, for just as he knew that he wanted you, he also knows when he does not want you.

Aquarians are unpredictable. They will turn on you for odd reasons. Gemini can get along with such elements like himself as Libra and Aquarius. But fixed air is different from changeable air and must be treated on its own level. In the case I referred to, the very fact that both were air signs made it possible for the marriage to be compatible. The neurosis of this Geminian was to pay back old debts to the wrong person. He is a Geminian who could not make up his mind about how to win; the fixed sign knew how to win and did.

When his second wife ended their relationship, he was devastated. The defeat was the greater because this time he had been lulled into a false security. He could not believe it. He did what Gemini does, he wrote letter after letter. He tried to talk her out of her decision, something you never do with fixed signs; a decision must not be forced. He needed this lesson to evolve strength. We attract to us the very cross we have to shoulder to free ourselves. We attract what our destinies indicate—in order to progress to higher levels of consciousness.

I worked out a plan with this Geminian. It took great vigilance and hard work to keep him on schedule, for he was prone to repeat his mistakes again and again—this is one of the unfortunate traits of the mutable signs. It is not stubbornness; it is rather that a new path cannot be decided upon. The fixed signs would not want to try new paths: you must take them "as is." Seeing that the mistakes he was making produced no solution, he returned to my program.

The surest way to convince his fixed-sign wife to return was to agree with her view that a separation was necessary.

Fixed signs do not give up anything without a struggle. They cannot understand the failure to fight for what is wanted. When he stopped trying, as I had instructed him, her interest was reawakened. She wondered. Had she been provoked into ending an affair that the other person really wanted no part of?

I then counseled him to court her again during this phase of her curiosity. Had he changed? she thought. At least he appeared to have been chastened. His original scheme with her had failed, and this made him think as he followed the schedule that I set up for him. He won in a blaze of glory and put the ring on again. Since he had what he wanted, he thought, why not go back to getting even, the very original program? Well, that is exactly what he did.

He had remarried in May, while all of the planets were in fixed signs. This put her in the driver's seat, for she was fixed. The power was suitable to her maneuverings, her fixed strength. All of the planets of everyday circumstances came into opposition to the May marriage. He was so busy with his original plan that he was unaware of it. The first wrong move he made, she put him out, and this time he stayed out, for then she realized he was only playing a game. Being Geminian, he could not possibly beat a fixed sign.

MUTABLE RISING SIGNS FOR GEMINI (PERSONALITY)

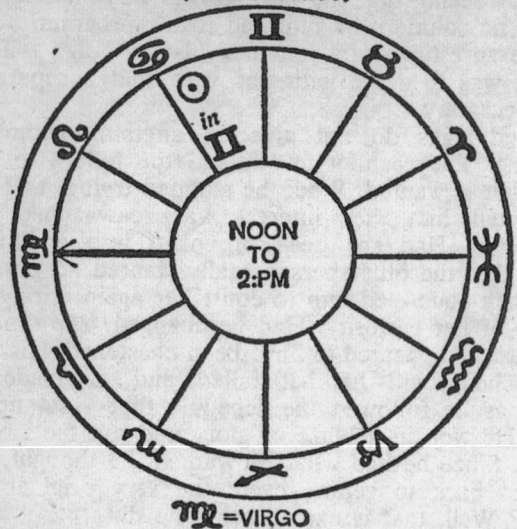

♍ =VIRGO

NOON–2 PM. Gemini born at the prominent hour of noon will have the earth sign of Virgo for a personality. This will be the hardest-working Geminian to keep or get the prominent position. Gemini is a good talker, but with Virgo for personality, conversation will be informative and instructive with a fine choice of exact phrasing. Economy is one of Virgo's traits, so there will be exactness and no wasting of words. Geminians will go right to the point.

The youthful look of Gemini will be a bit more mature, and certainly he will have a more practical attitude toward life. Trim and neat, Virgo will tone down Gemini's fluttering from idea to idea.

A client who has this combination runs two first-rate businesses and is very successful. Two homes and two men. One of these men, a Virgo, is needed to help her run the farm; the other, a Geminian, helps her to run her home.

MUTABLE RISING SIGNS FOR GEMINI
(PERSONALITY)

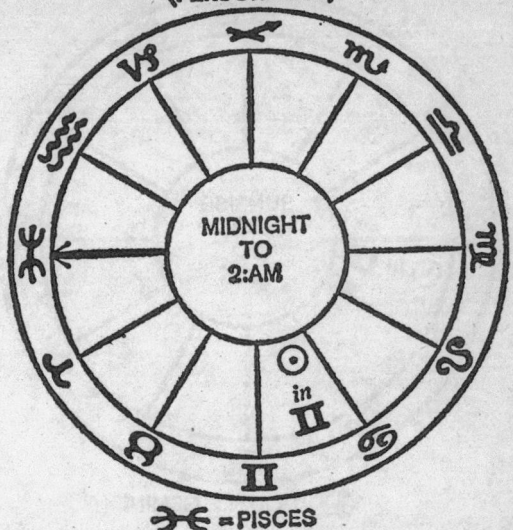

MIDNIGHT–2 AM. A Gemini born at midnight will have the mutable water sign, Pisces, for a personality. This is not as important a birth hour as the noon birth, for the rulers of the personality and the Sun-sign are very different and not compatible.

Gemini with Pisces can never decide which way to go. The discontent and the indecisiveness are too much. Gemini, being air, and Pisces, water, are different elements trying to adjust. Each sign should be allowed to fulfill itself on its own level. That is the only way to reconcile these alien elements. Gemini traits should be expressed in the home, Pisces attitudes in the outer life.

This can be an ethereal type of beauty—dreamy, girlish, yet soft, sweet, and pliable. But it can be very hard to mold, slipping either through the fingers or off into an *Alice in Wonderland* world.

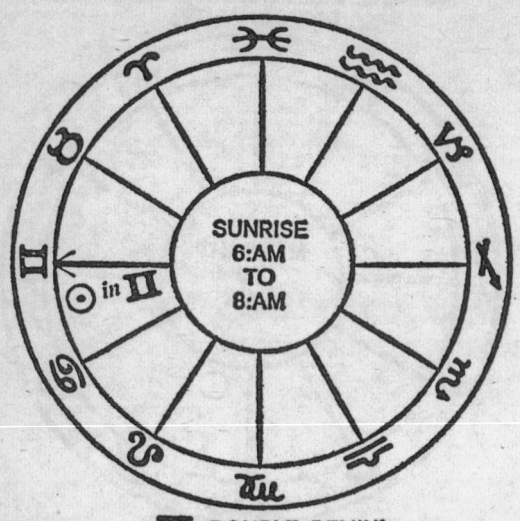

♊=DOUBLE GEMINI

6 AM–8 AM. The Gemini born at sunrise has Gemini for a personality and the Sun-sign for individuality. A double Gemini makes the type that loves learning. Bookish, the eternal scholar, Gemini is an inquisitive sign, so he will pursue some sort of subject that will fulfill the versatility for which the sign is known. A Gemini client of mine writes plays, is an actor, plays an instrument, works in night clubs, and writes lyrics for a composer—there is almost nothing he cannot do in the theater.

The more interests Geminians have, or the more talents they express, the greater and happier they will be, for Gemini born with Gemini for personality is self-centered. The thoughts and heart focused on the self make the narcissistic person that Gemini is known to be; he talks constantly about the self's abilities, what he has and what he can accomplish.

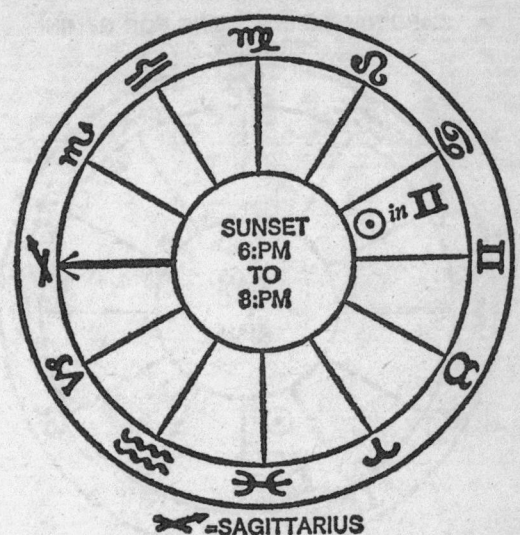

⚹=SAGITTARIUS

6 PM–8 PM. Gemini born at this time in the evening will have the mutable fire sign, Sagittarius, for a personality. Sagittarius makes Gemini very tall. Sagittarians are serious students. Combine this with the bookish Gemini, and you have a talker who will tell you of his travels, the books he reads, and his many literary talents.

The most entertaining Geminian of all has Sagittarius for a personality. He seems to know everything, for Gemini speaks many languages and Sagittarius knows many subjects. You must want to hear about these things, or you are in for it. To stop Gemini from talking when he has something to say would be a loss.

This Geminian will be the youthful student type; he is tall, easy-going, smiling; he may seem to be going nowhere, but he could be a great writer, traveling all over the world in pursuit of ideas.

CARDINAL RISING SIGNS FOR GEMINI
(PERSONALITY)

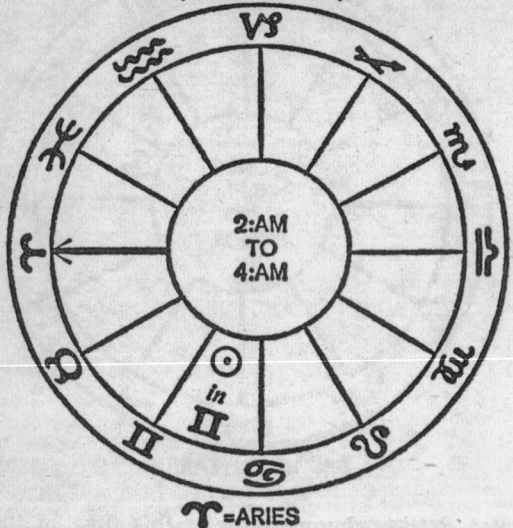

♈ =ARIES

2 AM–4 AM. Here Gemini is born with the first fire sign Aries for his personality. He is very exciting, for the activity of Aries plus the enthusiasm of fire makes this Gemini very alive and vital.

Gemini starts everything right, with the head. The sign at this time is in its very own house, the third house, and Gemini will look exactly as it ought to look. For once the text books are right! The enthusiasm for writing would pay off. Gemini with Aries for personality might write a humorous book in the Ogden Nash style.

There may be two marriages, however, but by choice and not because of trouble with the mate. Gemini is neither rebellious nor malicious, so partings are always friendly.

CARDINAL RISING SIGNS FOR GEMINI
(PERSONALITY)

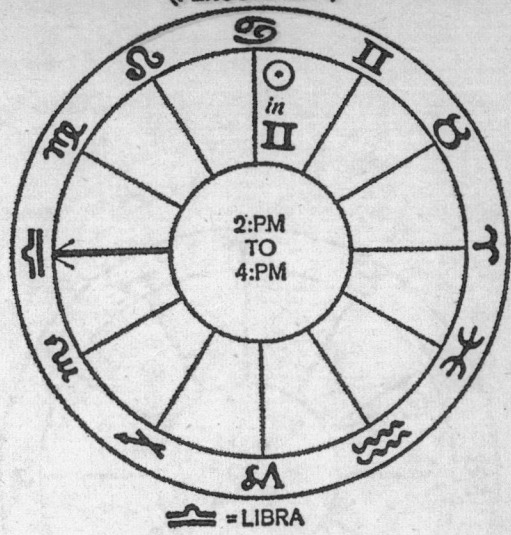

⎯ = LIBRA

2 PM–4 PM. Gemini born with the cardinal air sign Libra for a personality is another very fortunate Geminian. Libra is air, and Gemini is air. Libra weighs the matter; Gemini discusses the idea. The lawyer interested in civic affairs or the civil rights of man in everyday life would be an example of this type.

Libra is the second sign ruled by the planet Venus and gives one beautiful eyes, fine bone construction, and lovely manners. Combine this with the youthful, easy, smiling Geminian and—*"Oh, what loveliness!"*

Another example of this combination is a very well-dressed creature who is a party-goer and attends every smart event of the season. She belongs to the international set and shines more in Europe than at home.

An importer of beautiful clothes copies (Gemini imitates) originals to sell at popular prices (Libra is civic-minded). This client, who sews very well, buys originals in Paris. At home she makes exact copies and spends the money she saves to decorate her home.

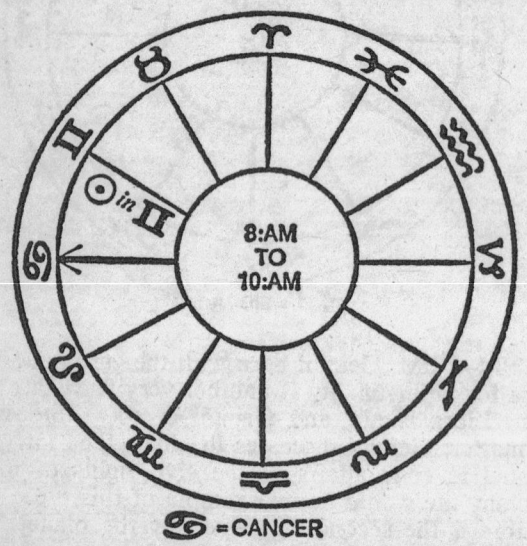

♋ = CANCER

8 AM–10 AM. The Gemini born with the sign of Cancer, the second cardinal sign, for his personality is very emotional. The emotional trials will not center on the family. Rather, they will center on the persons they work with. Gemini will act like a baby (Cancer rules babies). So the childish Geminian will be complaining about someone.

Gemini will change jobs many times. It would be best if there were two forms of service—one to offset the other. Then there would be less to be discontent about. This combination would make a splendid imitator, doing sketches of famous people.

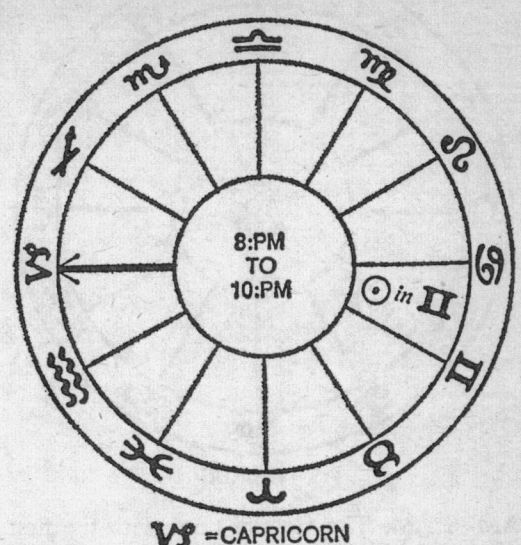

♑ =CAPRICORN

8 PM–10 PM. Gemini born with the last cardinal earth sign, Capricorn, for a personality will be the most practical Geminian. Geminians with Capricorn will give most of their attention to the form of service that will lead to fame, for the sign is more name-conscious than Capricorn.

This Geminian is very small and dark, with dignity and good manners; the native is nevertheless very gay and vivacious. Her youthfulness is combined with the serious, somber Capricorn—the very young girl with an old head on her shoulders. There is melancholia blending with the gaiety—the serious, enigmatic smile.

Gemini with Capricorn may not arrive at the desired goal until late in life. The earlier years were spent finding the form of service that would be suitable to lead to inner satisfaction, the work appropriate to the intelligence of Gemini, and the integrity the path must vouchsafe.

FIXED RISING SIGNS FOR GEMINI
(PERSONALITY)

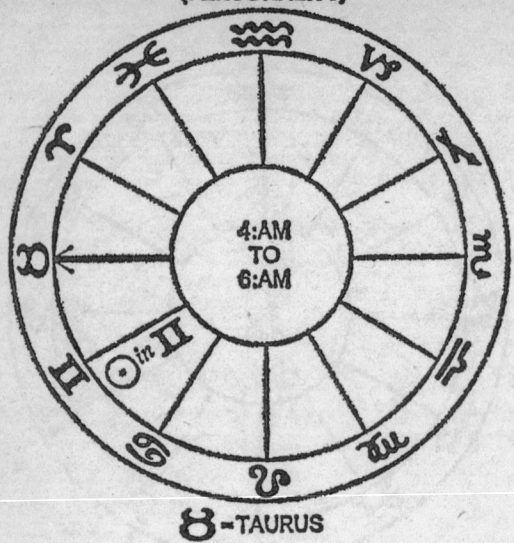

♉ -TAURUS

4 AM–6 AM. The Gemini born with the first fixed sign, Taurus, for a personality should be very good-looking. Taurian beauty blended with the youthful look of Gemini is a very fortunate combination of large, expressive eyes, a quick, spontaneous, sweet smile, and a firm chin that shows determination. The over-all nature is a desire to please and to be gracious.

Gemini, whose dual character wishes two things at the same time, makes decisions easily now that it has a fixed sign for a personality. Its interests will concern possessions, something of value. Marriage this time will be treated patiently with a stubborn determination to make it work.

One Taurus personality with this setup has had three marriages. The Gemini aspects brought the divorces, yet she worked hard in each case to make her marriage work. The clue is that since Gemini rules youth, she chose two men that were much younger than she was. The heavy Taurus practicality insisted on a material point of view which the youthful man could not live up to.

FIXED RISING SIGNS FOR GEMINI
(PERSONALITY)

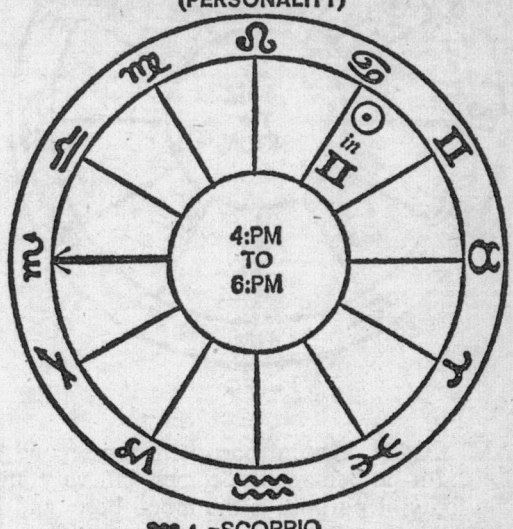

♏ =SCORPIO

4 PM–6 PM. Gemini born with the third fixed water sign, Scorpio, for a personality does not have as easy a time of it as it did with Taurus. Air is too intelligent and casual for the deep emotions of invincible Scorpio, who does not want anything to be treated lightly.

When Gemini is so far from the appearance-and-personality ascendant, it will not show at all. The heavy, imposing Scorpio will change the appearance; the hair will be scanty. The smile will neither come easily nor will it be a complete smile—it always has a reservation with Scorpio here. Scorpio is a very exclusive sign and is not willing to offer friendship quickly.

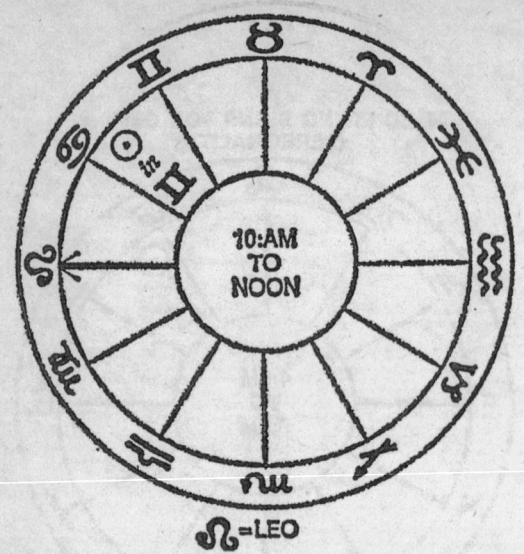

♌ =LEO

10 AM–NOON. Gemini born with the second fixed sign, Leo, for a personality comes off very nicely. First, the fixity of purpose is the mood here, and he is determined to consolidate through friends. The native has a teenage look with a quality of pride and carriage; he moves with greater presence and is not so hurried. The coloring is light; the strength of expression is in the warm, kind, immediate smile.

Friends are the valuable idea for Gemini with Leo for a personality. Friends are loved. Each new friend brings new hope. In fact Gemini may neglect the mate for a friend in later years. The Gemini-Leo personality might wind up marrying a friend.

Gemini will be faithful to promises as well as a strong, reliable person in matters concerning reputation in business, and he is a power at home. The generosity this Gemini expresses is genuine, for love is behind it. In fact, this Geminian will delight in meeting new people to love.

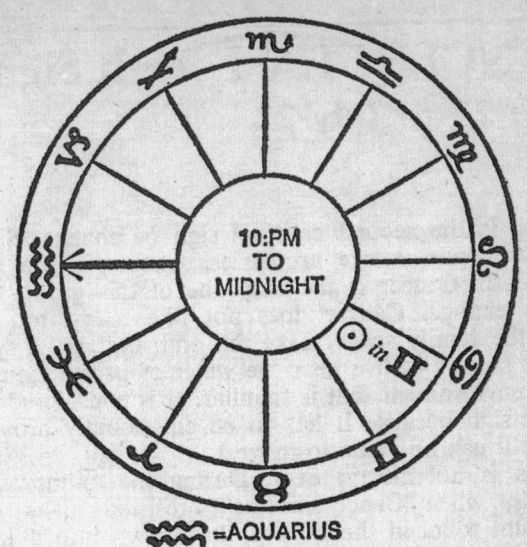

♒ =AQUARIUS

10 PM–MIDNIGHT. The Gemini born with the last fixed sign, Aquarius, for a personality is very fortunate. Air Aquarius and air Gemini, being the same element, complement each other.

Gemini is now very tall. The little girl is now a very chic model with stunningly slim bone structure and a very unusual face. Hers is the charm of the casual beauty who is too friendly to be tied up conceitedly in the self like the Venus-ruled signs, Taurus and Libra.

Gemini with Aquarius for a personality should get an early start in the theater, for Gemini rules youth. Later in life, Gemini, who still looks young, can play the part of sophisticated ladies of the international set, for Aquarius is universal; Gemini is the in-the-know individuality.

An actress client who has this combination is always given ingenue parts and is turned down for parts for older characterizations because she looks too young, though she is ancient.

11
CANCER: The Fourth Sign
June 22 to July 22

Cancer is the second cardinal sign of change. Signs that welcome change are Aries, Cancer, Libra and Capricorn. Cancer is the only one of this group that resists change. Cancer does not like to go too far from the family scene. Like the crab that is its symbol, it prefers to live near the water of its emotions—in an environment that is familiar. It is considered the laziest sign because it has to be emotionally aroused before it can be made to move.

This is not always easy. During the unimpressed periods, when Cancerians have resisted ideas that have not touched them, they slow down into a lethargy. Stir them emotionally, and you have them on the run. They act out their emotions, which is very good for them, for then they are able to expend their tremendous emotional energy. The energy of Cancer is all stored in his emotional urges.

The ideas that arouse Cancer must be practical. Cancerians love food that is emotionally appeasing. Cancer businessmen will surely take you to lunch or dinner to work out a business deal. China is a Cancer country. The office buildings in Shanghai used to supply kitchens as part of the office unit. Tea was served during business appointments and during the transactions, many inviting dishes were served. The Chinese believe a man is more vulnerable if he is well fed. They soften him: a hungry man is nervous and difficult.

All countries that come under the sign of Cancer are food-conscious. During my trip to Europe right after World War II, I found that Holland, a Cancer country, had recovered quickly and was able to provide plenty of good food. I was glad to arrive in Amsterdam, for I was really hungry after spending two weeks in England, where there was a food shortage. England is a Capricorn country, the sign opposite to Cancer.

Cancer births are the most sensitive, shy, and most easily hurt of the cardinal signs. Cancer rules babyhood. Cancer never quite gives up being the child and always wants to be babied.

In reading for Cancer persons, the first thing to do is to find out what kind of home life they have—in order to help the sign out of any emotional difficulties. If the home life is unsatisfactory, they are failures in business. Cancer's problems are always emotional. The fellow cardinal-sign, Libra, wants affection; otherwise his hunger for it sets up complexes. Librans are not ashamed of their vanities, but Cancer is the vain introvert.

Cancer is emotionally vain. He likes to own things. Like the crab, once Cancer gets his claws around anything, he makes it very difficult for the object to pry itself free. Cancer is very possessive of people; cloyingly attentive, he cannot seem to release what he owns—everything belongs to him. Cancer hesitates to share family and friends. He likes to keep his mate and children in the background. These are private possessions that must not be approachable. For example, the Chinese family-system isolates the family to the back of the house; visitors never see the wife. This may account for feeding the business associate in the office; the home is kept unsullied and free from outside interference.

If you know a Cancer type that does not do this, you may be sure that another sign, like Leo, is strongly emphasized. Leo likes to show the loved ones off, to contradict the Cancer trait of keeping strict watch and providing a protective wing. Cancer is the sign that rules mothers; like the mother, he is jealous of his offspring to a smothering degree. That is called the mother complex, which is a problem of all Cancerians.

The Cancer actor is one of the finest on the stage because he reflects his part like the child who is playing a make-believe game. He is the part, the chameleon becoming the characterization in a mirrorlike manner.

This ability to imitate makes it important in dealing with Cancer types to express the correct emotion or feeling toward them—in keeping with the good responses you wish—the earlier the better, for Cancer rules children.

A Cancerian is very easy to detect. First, he has a very pale complexion and baby-white skin, even in adulthood. Next, he never loses the infant forehead; there is a "baby look" about the brow. Whether or not the sign is afflicted, Cancer types have very poor one-sided mouths. The teeth are never seen or are a sickly color. Very often they have protruding teeth that keep the lips from closing. Invariably, the mouth droops at the corners, for, being complainers, they are always discontented.

All the water signs are complainers. Cancer and Scorpio are the worst. Cancer demands comforts; Scorpios complain to make everyone insecure, for they are very insecure. Pisces is just not satisfied—nor content. It is almost impossible to please the water signs.

The moodiness of Cancer persons blights all possible associations. They will close up against you, and there is no prying them out of their moodiness until it has run its course. They do what the crab does: when a footstep is heard, the crab scuttles back into the sea to avoid contact. The ocean (emotion) is the safest retreat. They nurse a hurt until it reaches the proportion of a storm. The other difficulty is that you never *know* what you have said or done to hurt them. Hence, placating them is impossible.

Catering to their sensitive natures is a full-time job, for no sooner is one problem settled than you have done something else that requires another peace conference. Therefore the water signs are very tiresome, taking all your energy, tact, and patience to stay out of rough waters and keep the ship running on an even keel. The truth of the matter is that Cancer types are "injustice-collectors" scheming and planning to get continual attention. They harbor grudges; this puts you at a disadvantage: you have to make extra motions to win them back.

The fire signs, the most generous of all, forget what you said if they did not like it. The earth signs are too practical to give words space to live in their consciousness. The air signs just give the words, and you, the air.

The water signs nurse every grudge, dropping it down into their subconscious for further use. Being collectors, they cannot bring themselves to forget. Cancer saves it, for he may have use for it later when he needs you. Scorpio keeps it, for it makes good blackmail material. Pisces keeps it, for years later it may serve to put his visions into a state of realization.

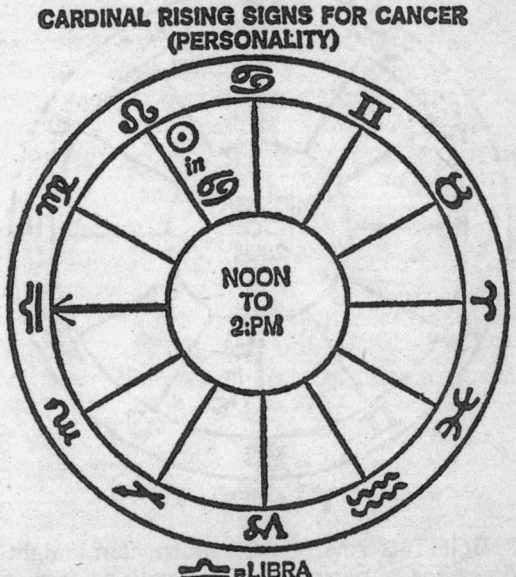

CARDINAL RISING SIGNS FOR CANCER (PERSONALITY)

NOON TO 2:PM

♎ =LIBRA

NOON–2 PM. The Cancerian born around noon will have Libra for a personality. This reduces his sensitivity. In exchange, you will get vanity—people who are not ashamed to admit they are beautiful and who want many luxuries. Cancer loves money; Libra likes to marry. So Cancer marries for a lovely home.

The noon-birth Cancerian makes the home a public meeting-place for business reasons. His partners in all ventures are asked to this showplace of a home.

A Cancer client, who is vain of his looks, is always in shorts when you arrive at his Connecticut home. There he sees a chance to express vanity of the body beautiful. This is his home, so both home and body are shown off. He is a beauty too! He loves his body and exercises to make it beautiful: he swims, dances, exercises. Vain Libra frees him of shyness. The preoccupation with the self is introversion paraded via a beauty-conscious self and a beauty-conscious home.

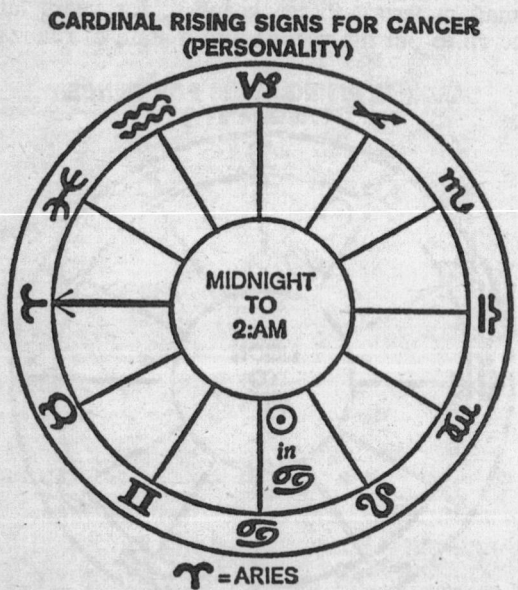

CARDINAL RISING SIGNS FOR CANCER (PERSONALITY)

MIDNIGHT TO 2:AM

♈ = ARIES

MIDNIGHT–2 AM. Cancer born at midnight will have Aries for a personality. He will be very satisfactory. Cancer rules the fourth house, the home area, and that is where it will fall in this person's chart—on the cusp of the fourth house where it belongs. This is a normal Cancer, or as normal as Cancer can be. Aries moves in a touch-and-go motion. Cancer with Aries for personality will be less sensitive and will fight all of the traits that keep Cancer back. Aries will give color to the pale skin. The mouth will not pout or droop quite as much; the nose will be larger; the teeth will go back in the arch line; and the rolling gait will be less pronounced.

The inner vanity of Cancer will be combined with the personal brag expressed by Aries, a game player who is proud of the fans he has collected or the cups or trophies he has won. The hero who is a big wheel in his little home-town forgets this when visiting another city; he cannot understand why he isn't noticed.

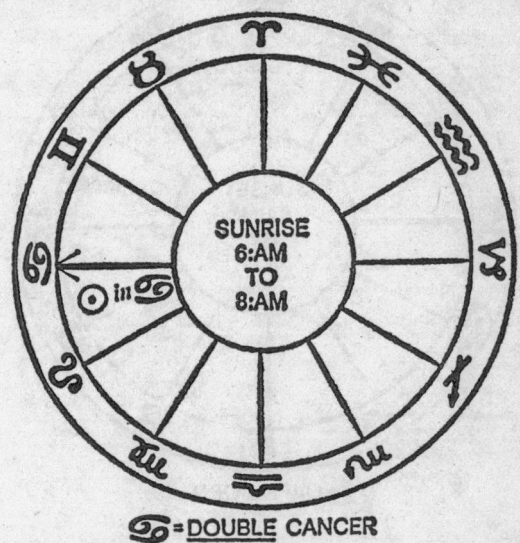

♋ = DOUBLE CANCER

6 AM–8 AM. Cancer types born at sunrise have their very own sign for personality; they are double Cancerians. This Cancer will just roll when he walks; he will have trouble getting his feet off the floor, for the feet seem to be turned in on the self. The stumbling walk will make this the poorest walker of all the twelve signs.

The nose is delicately molded, with thin nares that keep the childish lines of the baby. The mouth is still poor, and the coloring is very pale; the hair is silky and fine and seems to cling dampishly to the scalp.

The body seems always moist. The very odd thing about Cancer types is their odor. There is an aura of moldish smells about them, such as damp places have mustiness. The closet or room of a Cancer person seems always to need airing.

A doctor client with Cancer for a personality mothers his patients. Once I heard him tell a patient to let him worry about the illness—the patient was told to forget the illness!

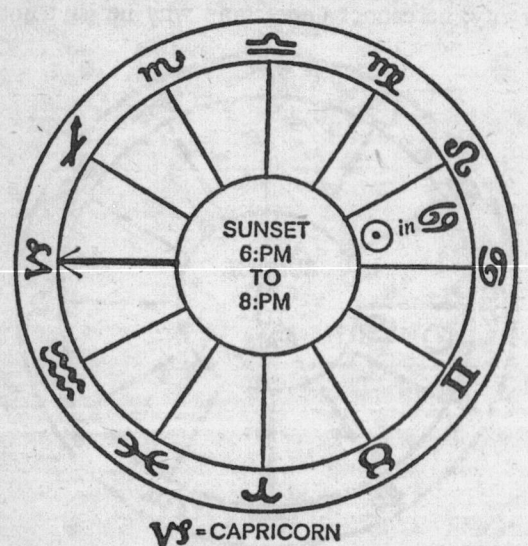

♑ = CAPRICORN

6 PM–8 PM. A Cancerian born at sunset will have Capricorn for a personality. This will be the least complaining Cancer, for Capricorn is too dignified to tell you his troubles. This Cancer type will contradict all of the pale skin, sensitive nose, and poor mouth types. The personality of Capricorn will darken the skin, broaden the nose, even give the stumbling gait more control.

Capricorn will make this Cancer investigate all of the histories of his ancestors or forefathers. Relatives will be disciplined into making names and reputations or collecting honors for Cancer to record. The whole trend will be toward a well-do-do life, amassing friends whose background alone recommends them.

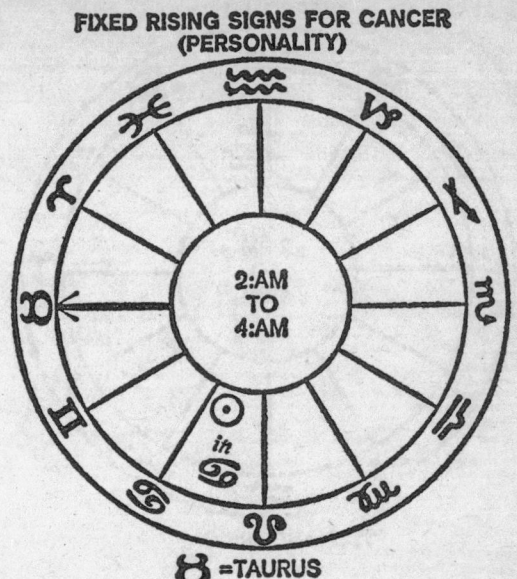

FIXED RISING SIGNS FOR CANCER (PERSONALITY)

2 AM–4 AM. Cancer born with the first fixed sign, Taurus, for a personality is a stubborn collector of things, instead of people, for Taurus is the personality. Taurus rules money. This would be a very rich Cancer, for he loves money, and now his personality attracts it.

Water and earth do very well together. There is no conflict; one feeds on the other. The emotions are tied up in money or earth. The home for Cancer is the safety zone; the house for Taurus represents earning ability. This is the banker whose house is the talk of the town. To be invited there is a great honor.

This is a beautiful Cancerian type too, with a firm step, the features of the face tightened, the mouth finely formed, and the nose delicate in construction as well as sensitive.

FIXED RISING SIGNS FOR CANCER (PERSONALITY)

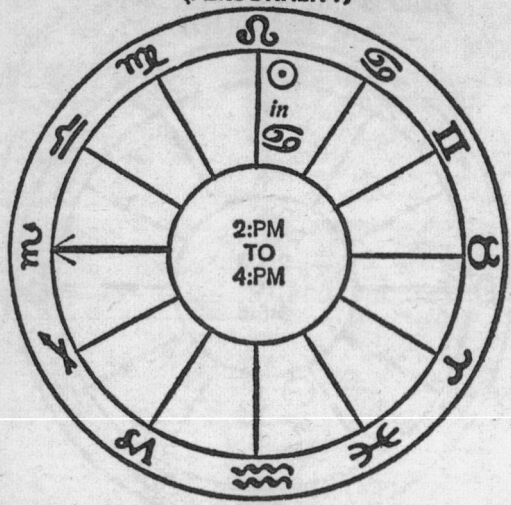

♏ = SCORPIO

2 PM–4 PM. Cancer born with Scorpio as the personality travels to other countries to investigate how others live or to find out the conditions of their home life. Cancer with Scorpio is a wonderful combination. Harmony on the emotional level is the mode. This could also be a very lazy person, completely happy within, self-satisfied and making no effort to improve life.

One of my clients, who falls into this category, is the mother of two children. They are the subject of all her conversations, and she makes no secret about their being the sole reason for her existence. In front of others, she seldom refrains from kissing and fondling the rather grown-up youngsters until even she is embarrassed. Aside from the drudgery to which this woman subjects herself for the sake of her children, she lives in an emotional swamp.

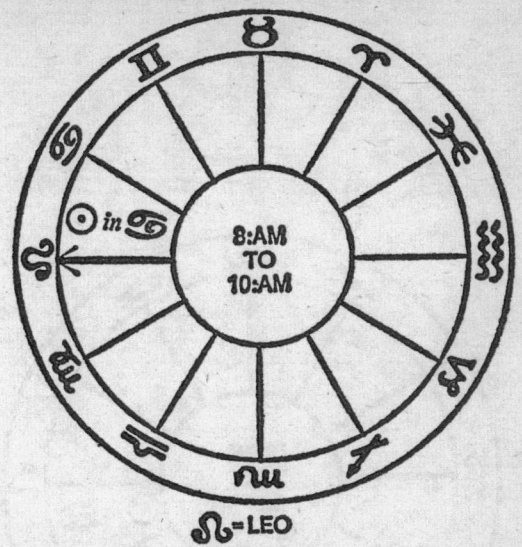

♌ = LEO

8 AM–10 AM. The Cancer native born with the sign of Leo for personality is more proud, for Cancer is a common type of person. Cancer rules mass, not class. The Leo influence picks up Cancer persons and gives them greater presence. They are less sloppy and ordinary in this combination.

The warmth in the emotions is not selfish; they flow out toward people, instead of in, on the self. Water signs are only interested in themselves. The extrovert sign of Leo cuts this down.

The coloring of this native is not as pale; the nose has more of a bridge. The mouth does not droop, for pride in the lips prevents this. The carriage of Leo will give Cancer a better walk. The emotions that are expressed can be trusted, for they are more controlled; they are not the self-seeking satisfactions that motivate the pure Cancer type. The Leo personality wants the other person to get something out of it too.

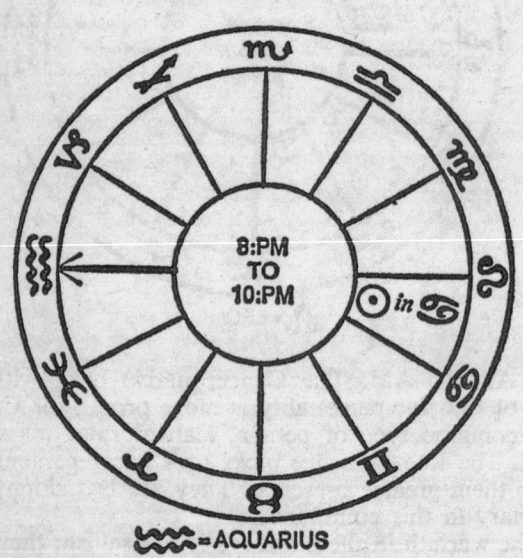

≈≈ = AQUARIUS

8 PM–10 PM. The Cancer native born with the air sign of Aquarius for a personality will not be all emotion. Air won't let it happen. Air is intellect. Cancer will be more intelligent this time around. Cancer will now take the feeling away from the self and think more about his neighbor, the world, and affairs all around him instead of thinking continually about the self. This will be the first really tall Cancer. Cancer is usually a very short sign. Now at last he will leave the home and family.

MUTABLE RISING SIGNS FOR CANCER
(PERSONALITY)

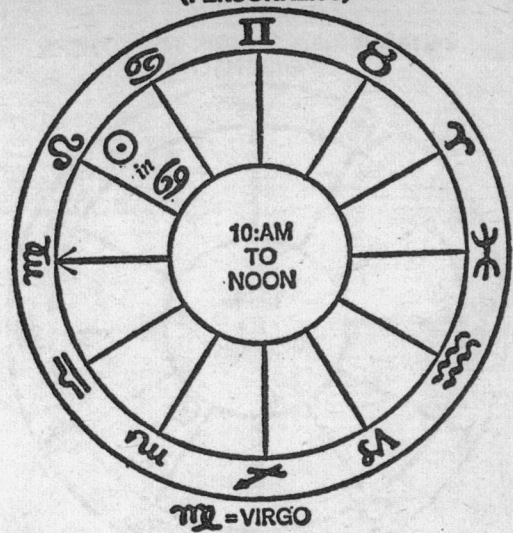

♍ = VIRGO

10 AM–NOON. The Cancerian born with the sign of Virgo for a personality will be the most practical one because the combination of earth and water means controlled emotions; the feelings are held in check when the stakes are high.

Virgo has even and classical features; so Cancer will be very good looking if he is born at this hour—a trim, neat Cancer, home-loving and true. The home will be immaculate. But now the family will have to work—every one of them. No drones in this family! The only expression of charity this Cancer has is for the family, and he will work everyone else for the family's benefit.

Another of my clients, a Virgo personality with Cancer, supplies chickens to a food company that makes chicken soup. At another time she sold eggs and butter to dairies. Food was made her profession. Virgo rules work; Cancer is food.

Though this Cancer will feed you when you visit his home, do not expect to be entertained, for Virgo is too busy, and Cancer is working for his own selfish ends. You are sacrificed.

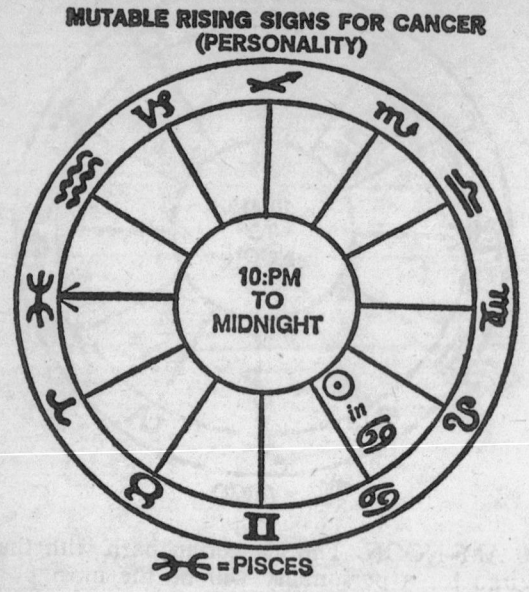

MUTABLE RISING SIGNS FOR CANCER (PERSONALITY)

10 PM–MIDNIGHT. The Cancer person with Pisces for a personality is another home-loving Cancer who gives all of his attention to those he loves. The children are doted on. This could be a great actor giving all of his love to the theater.

This influence gives another tall Cancerian. The nose is not delicate; indeed, it is a very large nose. The build, although tall, will be uneven in line, and the whole body will seem to be coming apart or lacking in coordination. His rolling gait combined with a not very direct stride makes him a poor walker. The confusion of Pisces combined with the self-love of Cancer could keep him living in a dream-world that satisfies him enough to prevent growth, progress, or attainment—living in the swamp of self-content, dreaming of what might be.

Cancer this time may have to give the world something worldwide. John D. Rockefeller, whose foundations were distributed all over the world for the common man's benefit, typifies this combination.

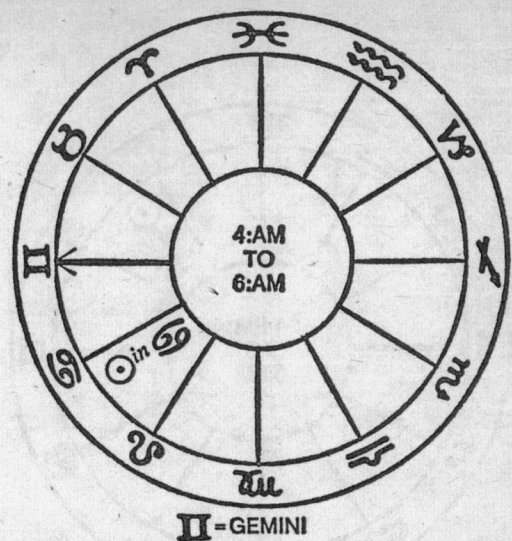

Ⅱ = GEMINI

4 AM–6 AM. A Cancerian born with Gemini for a personality has the baby sign combined with the youthful teenage sign. There would be no way in the world to guess this person's age. A personality being that flexible could act like a baby one day, a girl or boy the next. Good-looking too, he will have clear skin and a pert nose. He will be quick instead of slow and have no fat at all. This Cancer could eat all he likes without worrying about weight.

This Cancer type would never stop talking about the family. Each member would be a book in itself. The family might get all of Cancer's money, for it has generous Gemini for a personality. This time Cancer would feel as if the families of sisters and brothers were just as important as his own home. The mother would be the object of much attention, as if she were a possession to be taken care of. One client with this combination supports his mother and has bought her a home even though the mother has remarried.

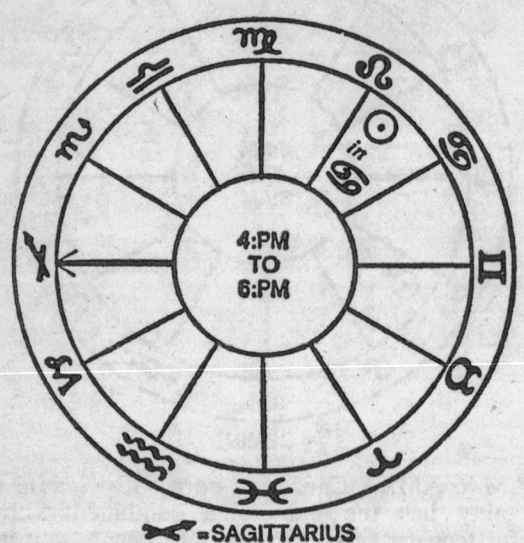

↙ =SAGITTARIUS

4 PM–6 PM. Cancer persons born with the fire sign Sagittarius rising will have more enthusiasm for the ideas of the people they meet. Introverted Cancer is now going to be talkative, complaining only of the in-laws and how they throw their money away. This Cancer would also be very wealthy, having inherited an income from the mother's line of the family.

You would never find this Cancer at home. He has a home in a tropical country, a home away from home. Cancer with Sagittarius could settle, like Sir Harry Oakes, in another country and make the adopted country a better place by giving it improvements that could be shared by all.

This will be a tall, dark, and handsome Cancerian, warm, but not too clinging.

LEO: The Fifth Sign
July 23 to August 22

Leo is the second fire sign and the second fixed sign. The first fixed sign was Taurus. The first fire sign was Aries. Leo is the most determined of the fire signs. The first fire sign, Aries, is cardinal and therefore changeable. The third fire sign is Sagittarius, which is mutable, amenable, adaptable. It is not stubbornly determined to reach the goal; the fixed sign Leo is.

Aries is the bonfire of the fire signs. Leo is the consolidated fire of the furnace. Sagittarius is the log fire. There are three ways of expressing enthusiasm: the bonfire that rallies or arouses, starting you off with enthusiasm for a new idea (Aries); the fire that the rallier started, consolidated into a determined idea, pinned down, fixed until the idea becomes a reality (Leo); the final fire of the idea can now be put into a book as a theory for practical uses—for example, the textbook that measures ideas, or the philosophy written about for the forum, the Supreme Court, or the lecture hall of wisdom (Sagittarius).

The Leo-fires wish more than anything else in the world to excite you with their new loves. Leo rules love and the loved ones. Leo is the lover in love with love. Leo is always in love with something, for Leo is the sign of the heart, youth, amusement, games, and speculation. What more lovely way to speculate than with the heart? Since the heart interests are uppermost in the atmosphere of the Leo-born, Leo is the most reliable lover and the most constant lover of the romantic fire-signs.

The first fire sign, Aries, being a cardinal or changeable sign, will change loves. Leo, being fixed, will not want to change loves. Once Leos decide that they have found a satisfactory lover, it takes a great deal to divorce them. Though the loved one may leave them, they remain steadfast even if faithfulness is only a state of consciousness. Their flame burns steady and constant.

It takes the furnace fire a long time to cool. It is a gradual dying out, taking time until the last ember has burned to ash. The bonfire of Aries makes the most exciting blaze, but it is a hollow fire; examination will make one wonder what made it burn at all once it has run its course. A faddish love and a faddish friendship is typical of Aries.

The deep and lasting fire of Leo, which wants everything to last, can be too much for the lighter loves who fear the binding tie. If the loved one is air (shallow) he will give the Leo lover the air. The air type cannot stand the concentrated warmth and domination (the Leo fire) which their air fanned into action.

The water signs are devastated and seek relief with earth or other water signs, since they cannot stand to be boiled up into a dramatic pitch. It is water that is too subtle and sly for an honest, sincere fire sign to manipulate.

The earth signs are a match for Leo, for their practicality makes Leo ashamed of giving so much to so transient an endeavor as love. Leo will resist earth as long as he can, dramatizing his love. Fire signs need air to intellectualize. Fire needs earth to give purpose to its enthusiasms; otherwise they never become fact.

Cancer, or any water sign, has the common touch; fire signs have class; Leo represents royalty. If you have to have an enemy, Leo is your best bet. He is too superior to stoop to harboring a grudge, too royal to be mean in the final struggle. You are forgiven and returned to your original position as friend or lover.

Like the lion, Leo can go into a rage and roar, bellowing out all the anger his energy can support until he is worn out. Then he retreats to the lair and recuperates the losses (much energy was spent). Perhaps this is why Leos are the least repressed of all the twelve signs. Nothing is buried; rather, it is brought up and burned out, the anger completely dissipated.

Having fixed you in their consciousness at the start, you remain a fixed habit. They need not reinstate you, for you were never out. You were just suspended, to be returned to your original position after the heat of the storm.

This hauteur, or superior attitude, of the lord of the signs (Leo is the sign the Sun rules) gets Leo into trouble. He is not understood. Leos are following through; they are trying to be the shining Sun. Playing the role (they are very dramatic) means playing royalty to the hilt. It must not be forgotten that the sun always shines. We may not see it shine from our section of the earth, but it shines on nonetheless. The Sun is king in the celestial heavens. Leo can no more help wishing to shine in any atmosphere than the flowers can stop growing.

It is odd how a common trait is forgiven and an inferior habit readily tolerated, but for a Leo to behave in an uppish manner is considered conceit. The least admired trait in Leo is his desire to dominate others. Kings dominate their realms; Leo sets up his court. In the family he is the star. Among friends he runs the show. If you refuse to play subject, there is trouble. Leo is the boss. If Leo has nothing to boss or dominate, he is lost and everyone is victim to his wrath.

I have always suggested to my Leo clients that they become authorities on some one thing and become masters at it. If Leos can talk with authority on a subject that they have mastered, their native energy has been channeled into an idea and not on people.

In class the Leo student will yell out, volunteering the many ways I should explain an aspect, telling me how to teach what he has come to learn. One student with a Leo Sun talked so much that the other students complained, asking her to stop talking so that they could get something from the instruction. She had tried to help me teach a subject of which she was ignorant. She finally became a nurse. Now that she has authority, she listens and does not instruct the teacher.

If Leos have no authority to rule, which is their native trait, they become nuisances, intercepting every remark made and reconstructing it for you, giving it their final O.K. They resent any authority in the hands of another, not listening to a word, setting up rebuttals to confound you. They are the bosses. How dare you take their rightful place!

They are thought to be liars for this reason, for they are the oracles who know it all the time. They pry ideas away from you, making them their own.

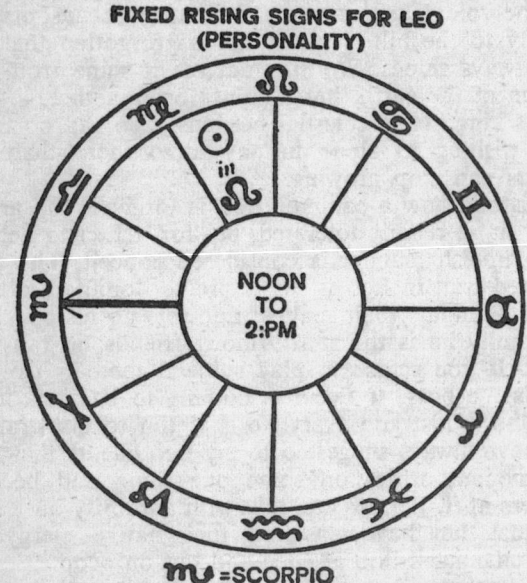

♏ =SCORPIO

NOON–2 PM. The Leo native born at noon will have the strong power-loving sign of Scorpio for a personality. Scorpio loves power; Leo wishes to dominate. That is a self-explanatory picture, isn't it?

Leo is now a strong, wilful personality who will brook no interference whatever. If this combination is not evolved to a high level, this is one of the most difficult persons in the world to get along with. If you need this combination, you must be willing to be dominated, scourged, demoralized, or demeaned. If you refuse to be beaten at every turn, avoid this combination.

Leos born with Scorpio for a personality are very unhappy within. Persons with this double dose of fixed signs never believe they are wrong. They have the self-faith of Leo combined with the jealous power-loving of Scorpio. The reason for the conflict is that Leo must rule. Scorpio will not take a back seat for anyone. The trouble here is which to be—the oracle that knows it all or the one who must be the all-powerful.

If you know something this Leo-Scorpio does not know, he will fight you tooth and nail to get you to admit confidentially that you are a fake and do not know your subject; it is a phony idea or some one thing giving him the power to debunk or expose you. This will lower you to a subject of his realm. It would be impossible to show this combination the error of his ways. Leo does not hear you.

Scorpios cannot afford to admit that you are right, for the power they love would be lost as a consequence of such an admission. The pride of Leo plus the indefatigable desire of Scorpio for power brings the downfall. Mussolini had a Leo-Scorpio personality —Leo, with head held high, though balding, and a chin pointing up to be above you.

MIDNIGHT–2 AM. The Leo born at midnight will have Taurus for a personality, making Leo a sweet and charming person. Domination is reduced for practical purposes; more things are gotten by flattery. Yet fixed signs do not like to yield to each other when confined within one's own walls. The conflict to be reconciled is which to have: money and possessions, or the loved one turned into a possession. The home could be the thing to love here—the home, the castle.

This is a very handsome personality, for the beauty of Taurus now has pride, presence, hauteur, and noble carriage—as well as vanity and pride if the type is unevolved. This would be an overbearing, con-

FIXED RISING SIGNS FOR LEO
(PERSONALITY)

(Chart: MIDNIGHT TO 2:AM, with ☉ in ♌)

♉ = TAURUS

scious beauty. This type will have brown-and-gold hair, auburn coloring, a high, pert nose, a sweet, warm smile, and above all the vain, proud walk.

6 AM–8 AM. The Leo native born with his Sun-sign for a personality is the very strongest Leo, looking like, as well as behaving like, the king of all he surveys. He will be the very rare person whose skin and hair have a golden hue; he will have the best-looking head, high from temple to crown, and a highly bridged nose. The way he carries himself will also be beautiful.

Drama is his best game. The play is on the moment he arrives. He plans to give a good performance. The actor who has this Leo-Leo combination always imposes his personality on the role he plays; he does not

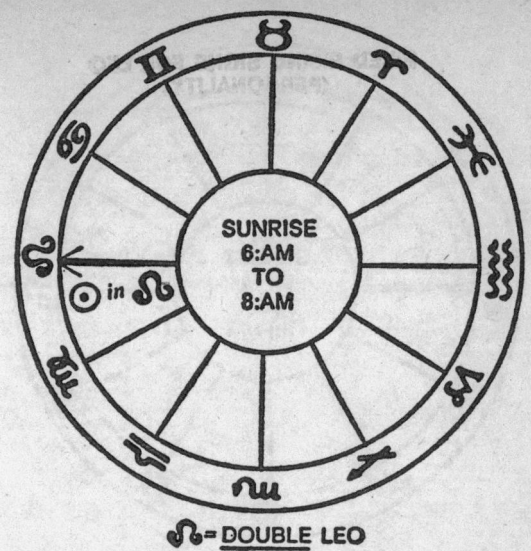

♌ = <u>DOUBLE LEO</u>

assimilate the characterization. His very own personality overwhelms any part. Yet the Leo with Leo as a personality is a generous, warm, loyal person who will give you love for the simple exchange of being moved by you.

6 PM–8 PM. The Leo native born with the opposite sign, Aquarius, for a personality does not look at all like Leo. He is the first tall Leo (Leo is a short sign). The authority that Leo insists is his right will now be disputed. Aquarius is the most argumentative of the fixed signs. Leo argues that he is king. Now he wants his power everywhere.

The superior good-looks of Leo are combined with the unusual, plain construction of the modern Aquarian face. The hollow between cheek and jawline makes Leo's pride less personable. Pride seems to be off in the distant view, and it seems almost of an oracle nature. This is a noble face unaware of the strength and force of its countenance. The warmth of

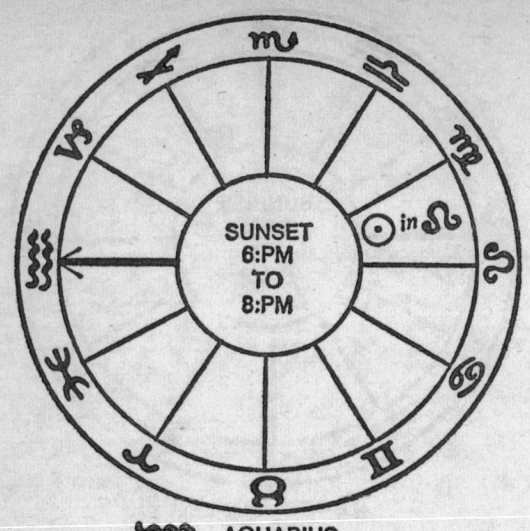

≈ = AQUARIUS

this Leo is cut down to indifference so that it does not matter who gets the love of this odd and strange type. This Leo will carry the fire of the self in the background. Only after prying, or after the friendship is really established, will you get love. You are treated airily until you have fired him into love.

10 PM–MIDNIGHT. If Leo has the first cardinal fire-sign, Aries, for a personality, this will be a splendid type. Aries is fire; so is Leo. Leo does not start out to be self-imposing this time; here Leo starts right —with the head and not with the heart.

Aries is red; Leo is golden. Now you have the titian coloring. The enthusiasm of Aries is combined with the generosity of Leo to bring excitement and life to the scene. This is not a subdued Leo, but one who is expressing excitement eagerly in the good-will cam-

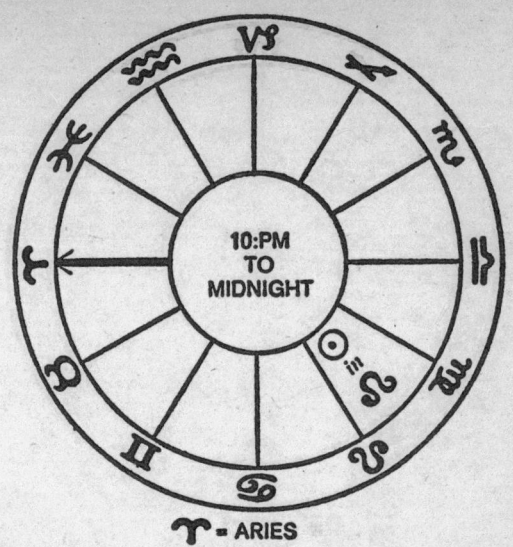

♈ = ARIES

paign for life. Fire signs are starters and consolidators. Leo will be interested in the excitement of your loves and interests, for he now expects you to invest fire for his.

10 AM–NOON. The Leo native born with the beautiful air sign Libra for a personality will now give the beauty an aristocratic bearing. Libra, who has lovely manners, is now combined with the regality of Leo. The result is breathtaking beauty plus graciousness. The ash blonde is pale, golden features will be reflected in even planes, moving up into strength and force behind the beauty. If by any chance there are bad aspects between the two ruling planets, the Sun and Venus being the rulers here, you would still have a person who is described as wonderful.

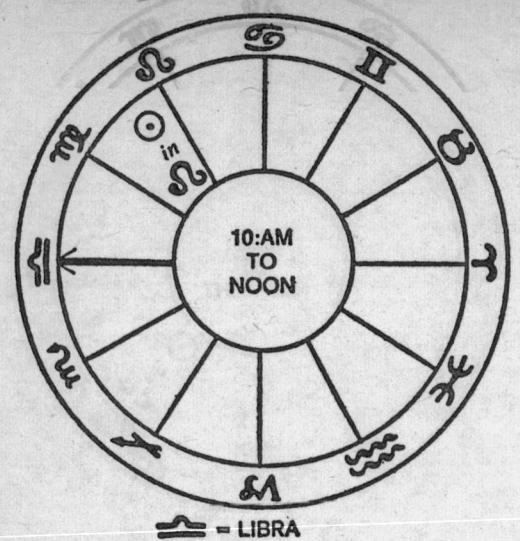

♎ = LIBRA

Marriage would be easy, here, for everyone would want to be wed to this warm, beautiful person. This is the personality who marries one rich person after another, each marriage increasing the native's importance and status.

4 AM–6 AM. The Leo person born with the soft, water sign Cancer for a personality will be a less spirited Leo whose nature has softened, becoming more humble and not imposing its will on you. The coloring is not red or golden, but very fair, having started out as a towhead.

The positive attitude of Leo is subdued with this combination. It is found in the Leo mother who loves the family and children, but not possessively. It is the mother who is treated as a queen; the mother is adored in place of the child.

CARDINAL RISING SIGNS FOR LEO
(PERSONALITY)

4:AM TO 6:AM

♋ = CANCER

Cancer wants to protect; Leo wants to love and guide. This Leo mothers everyone, wishing to improve everyone. Leo needs softening; Cancer needs firming; so this combination makes a sympathetic, loving, harmonious Leo.

4 PM–6 PM. The Leo native born with the very conservative sign of Capricorn for a personality might indeed fool you, for the quietness of Capricorn will completely squelch the Leo enthusiasm. The darkness of Capricorn will hide the sunny coloring of Leo.

Leo is an aristocrat, but Capricorn is a dignitary. This Leo rules with good manners; he has studied ritual and knows the exact time and place to express the well-turned phrase.

Leo might pull rank on you, but Capricorn, who has a high regard for breeding, will not. The quiet, serious Capricorn personality will have a warmth and

CARDINAL RISING SIGNS FOR LEO
(PERSONALITY)

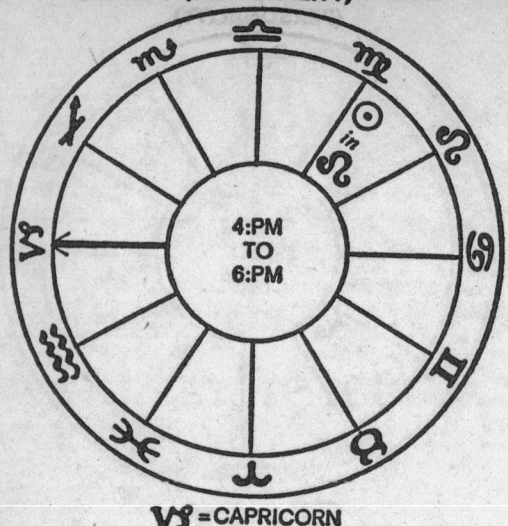

♑ = CAPRICORN

kindness that is in tune with the love that Leo wants you to have and that Capricorn will express in due *time*. You may underestimate this Leo, for the Capricorn caution will not permit love to come forward until the time is ripe.

2 AM–4 AM. The Leo person born with the eternal-youth sign, Gemini, for a personality is very easy to love. The easiness of the personality, plus the warm, loving, speaking voice of Gemini, endears this Leo to all. Leo with Gemini for a personality is very popular in any environment.

This time Leo will talk to anyone and everyone, making friends from the queen to the court jester, tripping gaily through life, making a new friend a minute; for this Leo will not want to dominate anyone.

Leo with Gemini will hear everything you say. His

MUTABLE RISING SIGNS FOR LEO
(PERSONALITY)

2:AM TO 4:AM

♊ = GEMINI

curiosity is keen, for Gemini wants to add to his storehouse of knowledge. Leo wants to be loved and to love. Gemini loves to talk about love. You may hear many beautiful stories about love.

Leo stops wanting to triumph over people; Leo with Gemini wants the love affair he talks about to triumph.

2 PM–4 PM. The Leo born with the third fire sign, the mutable Sagittarius, for a personality has another trine, or harmonious sign, with which to combine. Sagittarius is the third, and last, fire trine-sign. The relationship is such a happy one that this Leo will come off very well. Contact with this Leo-Sagittarius should make one feel instantly the good will of Leo plus the cheerfulness of happy-go-lucky Sagittarius.

This Leo is very tall and dark with reddish-brown hair. The long Sagittarian nose will be shorter; the

MUTABLE RISING SIGNS FOR LEO
(PERSONALITY)

⤺ =SAGITTARIUS

easy-going features have tightened into refinement. The class of Leo is combined with the easy charm of Sagittarius. These are the lawyers winning cases with easy-going authority; the philosophical professor; the lovers of learning. These are examples of this Leo type. The lover would be of another country if Sagittarius had any time left from studying or traveling. Love of metaphysical ideas would suit this native.

8 AM–10 AM. The Leo born now will have Virgo for a personality. Virgo is an earth sign of very practical inclinations that will blight pleasure-loving Leo. Virgo is too businesslike, takes all of the romance out of every transaction, and does not give the dramatic flair of Leo a chance to act out his drama of life.

With Virgo for personality and appearance, this type will stiffen the warm, kind features of Leo. Leo

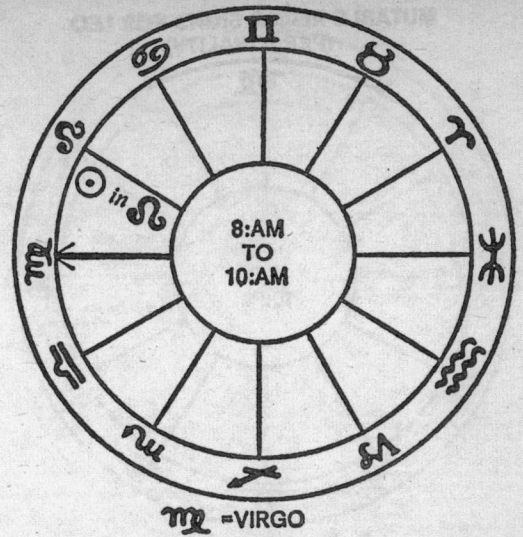

♍ =VIRGO

will slide into the background and refuse to play at all since it can't live it up as he would like.

If Virgo-Leo personality can't be kingpin, he refuses to be relegated to an inferior role; he would then stay at home or go into retreat.

8 PM–10 PM. The Leo born early at night will have the last mutable sign, Pisces, for a personality. This is not a very strong sign to work with Leo. Leo's strength does not get a chance to show up in the personality; it is blighted by indecision. Unless the Leo with Pisces has chosen a type of work that he loves, Leo will lose aim and purpose and become very ineffectual. His will and determination will become confused, and the path ends vaguely.

The strong features of Leo are blurred. Each feature may struggle to be clear, but soft, uneven lines of Pisces prevent it. The glowing complexion of this Leo is light and sallow. The firm chin and high nose are obscured by fleshiness. Warmth and kindness can be

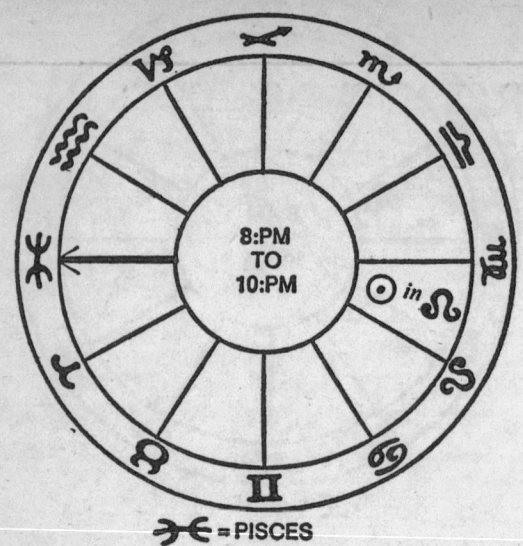

✶ = PISCES

too sticky and maudlin when Pisces combines with Leo. He needs a strong mate to back him up—to give him aim, force, and the desire to succeed.

There is no richer, warmer person than a good Leo. He has heart for any matter, and when happily in love, he wants the whole world to be happy with him.

On the other hand, when Leos are afflicted by unharmonious aspects, they can be very mean, cynical, domineering, and extremely jealous. If their ruler, the Sun, is poorly aspected with the Moon, Leo can change loves like crowns or hats. If the Sun-ruler is afflicted to Venus, the ruler of affections, Leo will love every girl breeze that passes by. If the Sun-ruler is afflicted to Mars, this will make Leo an overbearing braggart. If the Sun-ruler is afflicted to Mercury, this boastful person will make promises that will never be kept.

13

VIRGO: The Sixth Sign
August 23 to September 22

Virgo is the sixth sign of the zodiac, the second mutable, the second earth sign. It is the sign that rules labor and service. It rules health, and it is the sign through which one makes adjustments. In the chart of a country, it rules the army and navy, or the service of that country. Virgo is the dressmaker or tailor (not the designer).

Virgo is the critic, the analyzer, the servant; it is the sign that rules statistics, figures, and details. Virgo is the petty side of life. Virgo is the workhorse of the zodiac. Virgos are happy only when working. The continuous desire to work need not necessarily be constructive, for they can do the same routine duty day after day; it means, many times, only that they must be at it. They will perform the same routine job again and again, compulsively, unaware that they have finished the chore.

One of my Virgo friends insists on emptying ash trays over and over again during her visits. Virgos feel guilty if their fingers are not performing some duty. Another Virgo friend always brings her knitting and works the entire period while visiting in my home.

Just to return to some unfinished task, Virgo will hurry through all forms of pleasure and times of relaxation as though they were a duty rather than an enjoyment. No sign is more unhappy than Virgo when out for the evening. He gives you the feeling that his time is being wasted. Virgos will spend time with you only if you are working for them and their interests or they have to work for you. If the subject veers away from them or their interests, you are promptly dismissed; otherwise they have to leave the scene. They work you, and everything that will benefit them. The moment your usefulness comes to an end, they end their ties with you.

Being an earth sign, everything must have a practical purpose, or it is of no interest to Virgo. Just as you are regarded for your economical values, Virgo too wishes to be useful. He expects the best you can give, and he will give his best, for work and he are one.

Virgo makes a perfectly reliable servant. Virgo can be depended on to do a job because he is a perfectionist, a precisionist. It is against the thoroughness of Virgo's thinking to work against the standard he has set for himself.

Virgos are good critics; they are masters at analyzing. Nothing escapes their critical eye. They understand detail in both deeds and words. They make fine doctors and nurses because of their interest in food and health. Cleanliness is a complex. They are always scrubbing and cleaning; this suits their compulsive busy-ness.

Preoccupation with doing-ness and work makes them one of the most underestimated signs of the zodiac. They are apparently working out details; this deceives you, for they have bigger plans than this world dreams of. As they work, they scheme. The innocent chore they are performing doggedly seems to be filling their mind. While the pleasure-bent boss is off, Virgo is in the office figuring out a way to take over in due time. He makes himself indispensable so that it is hard for anyone to follow him in a job.

Virgo is impossible in love, for his criticism of the loved one cuts him off from receiving the love he would like. How can you love someone who continually criticizes you? Virgo is scathing and very sarcastic. When angered, he points up your weakest point, which his critical eye has noted and summed up upon first meeting you. He lays aside any information for practical purposes. When he needs it to demoralize you, it is brought forward. His opinion of you will be shocking. He may have seen no reason to tell you before, for it was not to his advantage. You can more or less gauge the time when the friendship will be brought to an end by the depths of the mean remarks.

The more you are criticized, the nearer the end of the association. Virgo is very surgical in endings; the break is clean. There are no regrets; you are dead to his mind.

If there is ever a return, it is never the same; it is only a temporary mending—for a new reason to use you. As soon as that is accomplished, you are discarded again. Virgo is notorious for using people. I call it "working you." To counteract this, if Virgo's usefulness is kept in motion, his slack lines will seem straight and redeem his undesirable trait.

Virgo is the worst gossip of the twelve signs. He keeps his own secrets, but not yours. He resembles Scorpio in that you can never do enough for him. As soon as you have accommodated him in any commitment, he has another waiting. Virgos are revengeful too, like Scorpios. A Virgo friend once told me that while working for a skin doctor, she asked for a raise. He refused her the raise she felt she deserved. She systematically suggested to patients that they did not need further treatment—just to deprive the doctor of the amount of money she felt she deserved.

Their cold, classic features have the very long upper lip of the practical talker. The lips are thin, showing little or no sympathy. The straight nose is built neither for defense nor offense; they take the subtle way. They are the tongue-lashers. The narrowness of the face indicates a lack of leniency; the severe lines do not break down under emotional stress, but maintain indifference no matter how aroused or disturbed Virgo may be.

When the mutable signs (Gemini, Virgo, Sagittarius, and Pisces) differ their quarrel is over ideas. Gemini wants the idea resolved into practicality. Virgo wants to work it into a job. Sagittarius wants to analyze it. Pisces cannot make up his mind about how to make the idea satisfy him emotionally. Each wants fulfillment in different forms. Unless these differences can be reconciled and combined, the arguments are interminable.

Mercury rules the sign Virgo, just as it rules Gemini. Mercury is a catalyst. If it combines with Venus you have someone with a beautiful speaking voice, one who writes charmingly. If a Virgo personality has it, he will be a more beautiful and better-dressed Virgo than the general type.

Mercury with Mars makes a vigorous talker; if afflicted, a very quarrelsome type whose sex is tied up in speaking. He enjoys abusing, degrading, or demoralizing others.

Mercury in good aspect to Jupiter—the trine (good luck)—produces pleasant thinking; wonderful ideas are easily expressed. This will be a very complimentary personality filled with hope. Mercury afflicted to Jupiter produces a liar who will never keep a promise—it's just big-shot talk signifying nothing.

MUTABLE RISING SIGNS FOR VIRGO (PERSONALITY)

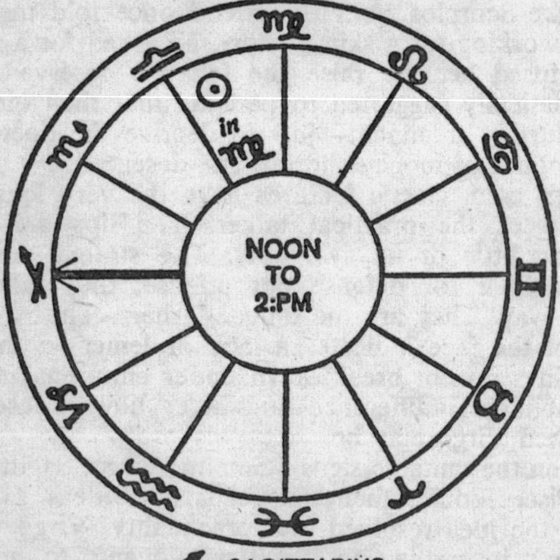

NOON TO 2:PM

♐ =SAGITTARIUS

NOON–2 PM. The Virgo born at about noon will have Sagittarius for a personality. This Virgo will want to make ideas work. The Sagittarius personality makes Virgo tall with features smaller than Sagittarians generally have, but larger than Virgo's.

The large nose of Sagittarius is more finely shaped;

his mouth will be smaller, more controlled. The teeth are much smaller to accommodate the narrowest arch of Virgo. The Virgo born around noon will be the one that enters the communications media. He would make a wonderful ambassador. Mr. Republic, the late Senator Taft, was a Virgoan with this personality spotlighted.

If petty arguments are ever to have importance, this Virgo's will. If these Virgo-born are not evolved, you have the fellow at the bar who knows the answer to everything.

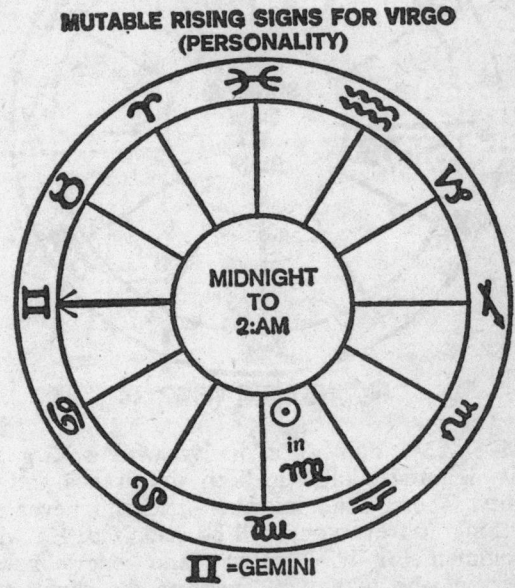

MUTABLE RISING SIGNS FOR VIRGO (PERSONALITY)

MIDNIGHT TO 2:AM

Ⅱ =GEMINI

MIDNIGHT–2 AM. This Virgo-born native with Gemini for a personality changes his mind so often that it would be difficult to keep up with Virgo. *Talk, talk, talk; job, job, job!* It would be best for this Virgo to work in the home, that is, have a profession that could be manipulated in the home, such as counseling or advising.

A client who is a decorator works from her home.

Another client, a beauty counselor, sells skin foods from her apartment. A famous advisor analyzes work from her home. Once the path is found or followed, the charm of Gemini for personality sweetens Virgo so that a likeable personality works with you for your good. In spite of Gemini's youthful appearance, Virgo makes him very efficient.

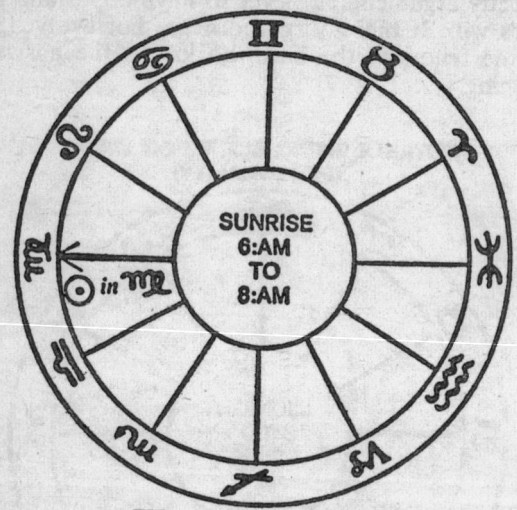

♍ =DOUBLE VIRGO

6 AM–8 AM. The Virgo native with a Virgo personality is unmistakable in both appearance and individuality. There is no mistake—criticism never ends. Everything and everyone will be criticized. He will be the commentator who analyzes and reports news or the person who takes you apart on the slightest pretext. *"You are all right, but. . . ."*

One of my Virgo friends will look over everything you are wearing and will find one thing that she pretends not to like. One evening we were on our way to dinner. She looked me over, obviously with a desire to find fault. Finally she said, "I like everything but your hat." My hat was a simple, plain pillbox; however, she has to comment on something.

Their criticism does not always have merit; they have to find a prop to gain superiority over you, supplant you to gain importance. They have an "importance" complex.

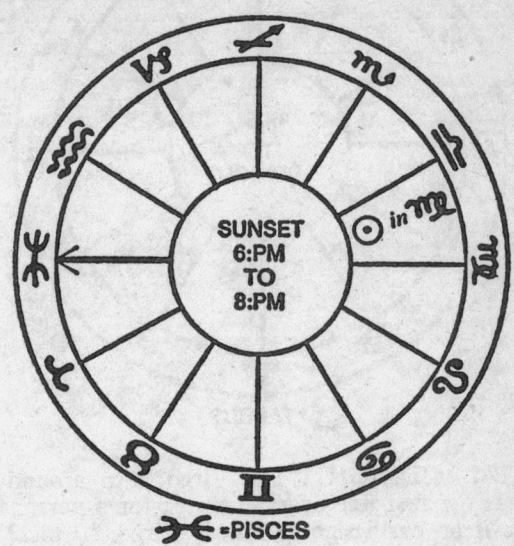

6 PM–8 PM. This Virgo, born with the Sun setting, has the opposite sign, Pisces, for a personality Pisces will cancel everything that has been said about Virgo. First, this is not a trim, neat personality. Virgo with a water sign for personality carries weight, even fat. The hard-working Virgo is now lazy and wants everyone else to work. The features have changed into a soft face with poor outline. The nose, Virgo's best feature, is not good. The face is loose and uncontrolled. The coloring is light and not on the brown side.

The search of this Virgo will be for profession. Still another new idea is always being investigated—not to be put into form, but just to talk about to convince everyone that they are involved in something important.

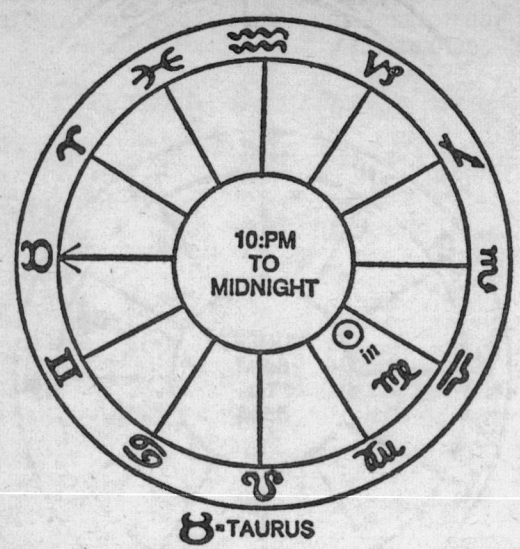

♉=TAURUS

10 PM–MIDNIGHT. The Virgo born around this time has the first fixed sign, Taurus, for a personality. Taurus is an earth sign and so is Virgo; so these two do very well together. Virgo now has greater determination. The working complex of Virgo has settled for the goal of material possessions. The coldness of the Virgoan features is now warmer, sweeter; the gait is less hurried. The personality is more patient, less critical.

The Taurus practicality would want the best pay for a job, but there would not be the wasteful, endless arguments typical of the mutable personalities. Taurus is not a talker. Virgo does not have the ability to associate amicably with people, but charming Taurus would work for you here. You would enjoy socializing and would be more relaxed at work.

The Virgo-Taurus personality might live on a farm and sell everything that was grown. It would be a pleasure to buy from him, for all the items would have been perfect.

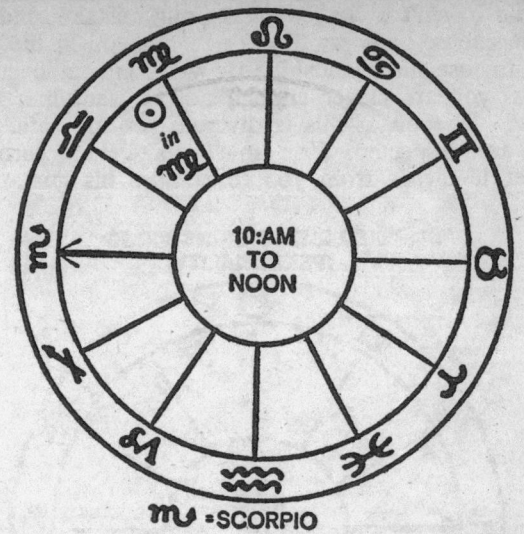

♏ =SCORPIO

10 AM–NOON. The Virgo born with the shrewd water-sign Scorpio for a personality is a tough one. Virgo will work with you, but Scorpio will work you to death. No matter what you do, you could have done it sooner and better, and you have left out the most important thing! There is no way to please this personality. You are criticized from stem to stern, from morning to night, coming and going, *ad infinitum*.

A friend of mine with this combination would survey the dinner table to see if everything was there—salt, pepper, sugar, cream, knives, forks. Then he would shout disgustedly, "My God, you forgot the beer!" Pettiness combined with demoralization. Selfishness combined with using you. This same man would accept hospitality while visiting friends in another town, but never once return it. If the people who entertained him away from home came to town, he would consider it a great imposition if they called him. He would avoid them with the excuse that he was too busy.

Virgo with the personality of Scorpio has a shrewd purpose for every friend. You must be a useful friend, or you haven't a chance. Make one mistake, and that is the excuse he is waiting for to put you in the position to lose his friendship. He will win out over you unless you are clever enough not to want him for a friend. As soon as this is divined, you are safe. Now you are respected. You must make him earn the power he needs from you to achieve his goal.

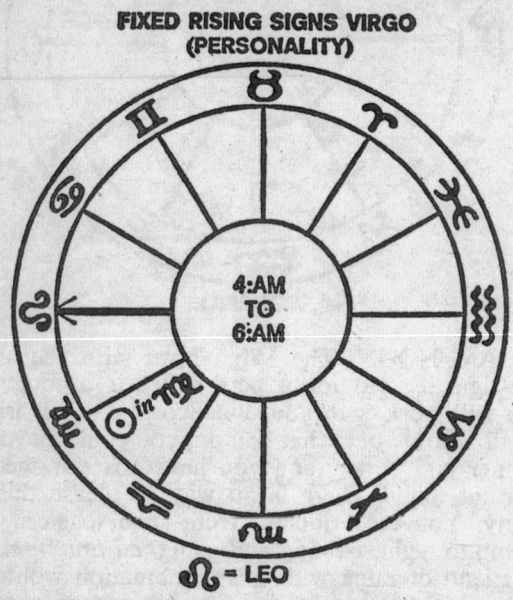

FIXED RISING SIGNS VIRGO (PERSONALITY)

4 AM–6 AM. The native with Leo for personality is as generous as Virgo could possibly be. Virgo is not a generous sign. Leo, the sign of the heart, gives him warmth. He is too big to be petty this time. Leo has to rule. Virgo has to work hard to establish his superiority.

The very straight, severe nose is more highly bridged. The mouth has a curved lip-line instead of the long upper-lip coldness; the eyes are more honest and straightforward in glance; the head is held high. Virgo holds the head as if listening. Cheerfulness replaces the anxious, worrisome nature of Virgo. The busy-ness of Virgo to work every scene for his good is lessened by Leo, who gives a more leisurely attitude to the transaction. The indecisiveness of Virgo has disappeared into "I know where I am going and what I expect when I arrive." The purpose is worked out for money or gain to enjoy life and people, something Virgo by itself knows nothing about.

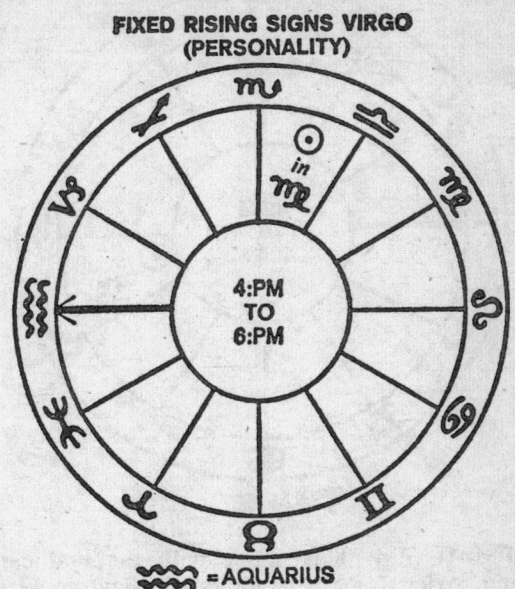

FIXED RISING SIGNS VIRGO (PERSONALITY)

4:PM TO 6:PM

♒ = AQUARIUS

4 PM–6 PM. The Virgo born with the fixed sign Aquarius for a personality would have a difficult time convincing you that he is Virgo. Fixed signs always impose their forcefulness on the mutable signs. Virgo would not have a chance to work all the time. Aquarius would not stand for it. Aquarius wants freedom above all else. A job ties him down. The outcome means changing jobs.

The tall Virgoan with Aquarius for personality has features that are not even or proportioned, but odd. That straight nose has taken an odd slant. Criticism turns to countries, politics, everything on a wide scale.

Work is now for the world, or at least the good of the people all over the world.

The petty criticism of Virgo is directed only toward the mate of the loved ones. This is not too happy a combination, for the petty heart of Virgo is no match for the airiness and indifference of Aquarius.

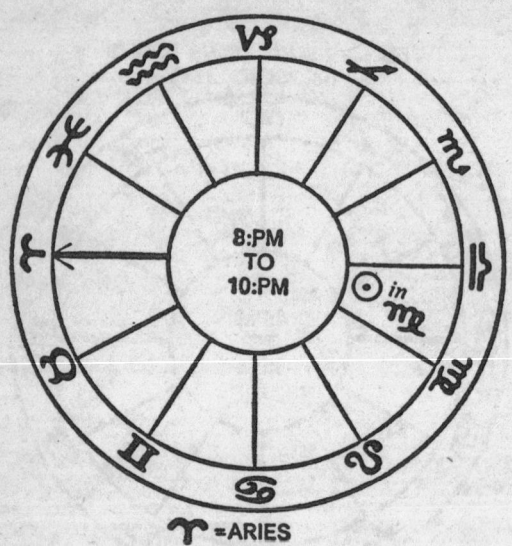

8 PM–10 PM. This native with the first cardinal fire-sign, Aries, for a personality will have more spirit. The activity will center all around people and not continually on the self's interest. The chiseled features will have disappeared for the flat features of Aries.

The criticism will be blunt and brusque in accordance with the broad appearance of Aries. When the body shows special physical traits, do not discount it —it is telling you much about the person. Virgo with Aries for personality will not be obvious. Virgo will show only in that this person is always busy.

Virgo criticism will blurt out a bold remark with intentional lack of tact. Virgo will be combative as well as contentious, for Aries likes quarrels that could end in a fistfight. Virgo will have the conflict of changing jobs because of his brash insults to other employees. The Aries personality is not content as a servant. He may want to lead the strike, for Aries with Virgo is a frontrunner.

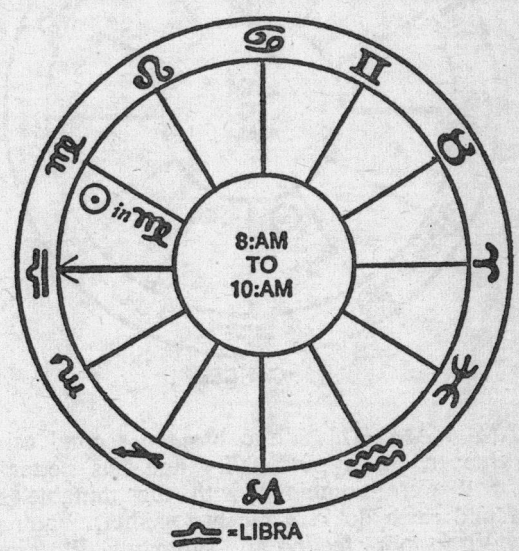

8 AM–10 AM. The Virgo born with the sign of Libra for his personality, the third cardinal sign, will be the very best-looking Virgo. Libra is the beauty of the zodiac. Virgo, when harmonious, has classic good looks. The eyes that seemed too close to the nose are farther apart. The head will look up, for the vision from the expanded view will suggest this.

The social life will pick up—more party-going, a social interest in people, and not a working plan as heretofore. The mate will have to work, for this Virgo will want a good time, good clothes, and fun.

CARDINAL RISING SIGNS FOR VIRGO
(PERSONALITY)

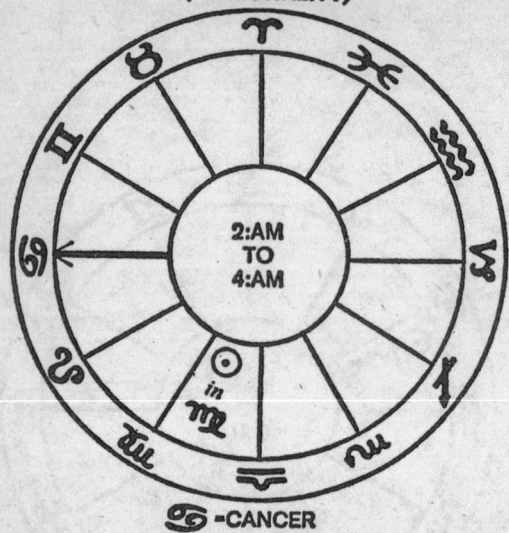

♋ -CANCER

2 AM–4 AM. This Virgo has the second cardinal sign, Cancer, for a personality and has better luck than if it were combined with the mutable signs. Water and earth do very nicely together. Water gives earthy Virgo more feeling and sympathy. Working for the family is the influence of Cancer, who rules domestic life (work is ruled by Virgo). The mind is ever on the family, especially the children. A Virgo client runs her son's house and her son's affairs, even though he is married and has several children. Each time the son moves, the Virgo-Cancer mother goes right to work to settle him in the new neighborhood. Furniture is taken from her house for the home of her son.

The physical features of Virgo are softened by Cancer in this combination. The body seems softer than the prim body construction of Virgo.

CARDINAL RISING SIGNS FOR VIRGO
(PERSONALITY)

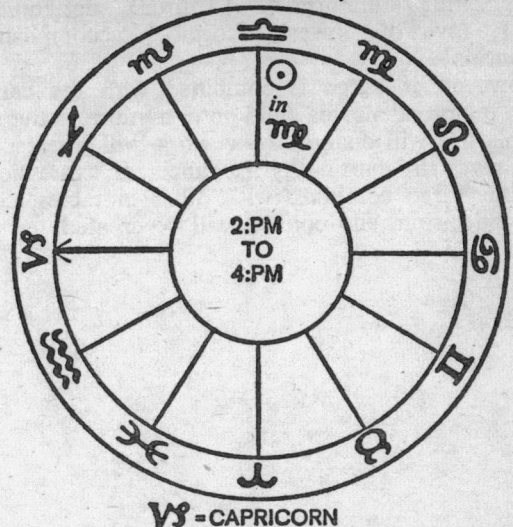

♑ = CAPRICORN

2 PM–4 PM. The influence here is a Capricorn personality, and it is very compatible with Virgo. Virgo will be better educated this time for Capricorn wants to stand high in any community, and Virgo is thorough.

Virgo with Capricorn for personality will produce the very smallest Virgo. The bone structure of Capricorn is tiny, the coloring dark and brunette. The eyes this time will search more; they do not flit about, as Virgo's eyes do. The ability to organize the self as well as plans comes off better.

Hard-working Virgo does not waste time without a goal. Now the program includes a desire to become an executive in an industrial organization, a person of high responsbility. The usefulness of Virgo consolidates with reliability, integrity, and a desire to treat one's fellow with dignity, for Capricorn appraises the worthiness of men.

As always, it is best for a mutable sign to combine with the more determined fixed-sign, for then the goal is always on schedule. Mutables get caught in the rush of abstractions and lose their way—but not if Taurus, Leo, Scorpio, or Aquarius is at the helm incorporating stubbornness (Taurus), determination (Leo), love of power (Scorpio), accomplishment (Aquarius).

However, if Virgo is combined with the cardinal signs, he broadens his field into a more active one, and his life will change. New work will interest him, for it gives the cardinality a chance for expression. If mutable Virgo combines with other mutables, confusion, indecision, and conflict will be created.

LIBRA: The Seventh Sign
September 23 to October 23

Cardinal Libra is the second air sign, the sign of marriage in all forms of partnerships. Libra is most happy in the state of marriage or in a partnership. The cohesive nature of its ruling planet, Venus, draws to it the other people that it needs.

Librans understand associations better than the other twelve signs. It is clear then that Librans are very unhappy in a single state; that is why they marry as soon as possible.

Librans are the beauties of the zodiac. They are the very best dressed. Venus rules color, line, and beauty. It is very difficult to find a Libran who is poorly turned out. Also, if Libra is emphasized in any chart color, line, and appropriate attire will be stressed.

If Libra is having money troubles, though the gown may be old, the remnants of better days will show through—even through shabbiness. The women of this sign can sew and turn a very simple dress into one of distinction through artistic expression guided by the instincts of Venus.

Librans are party-givers. They love to have a place to meet and socialize. It is the marriage mart for them. Giving a party brings in a new flow of friends or potential partners, maybe a mate. When they give a party, flowers, fancies, favors, and extravagances of all sorts run rampant. The dinner party that Libra gives will be lovely and lively; the service will be colorful; the latest food-fad will be served; wines and liqueurs will be expensive. How the bill gets paid, or who pays it, will not deter Librans.

They make the very best decorators, for their sense of color or line is impeccable. As dressmakers or coutouriers they have no peers. They are on the list of the ten best dressed.

One Sunday evening, a Libran invited me for cocktails and dinner. She was a beauty of the calm, quiet madonna type. The restaurant she selected was fashionable and expensive. Sitting at our table, while we were waiting to be served, a very good-looking, tall man passed. He halted and returned to a table nearer us. During the meal, though he was accompanied by a woman, he continued to stare at my Libran friend. Not a word was spoken nor a move made.

The very next Sunday she repeated the invitation. Knowing how Librans operate, I knew something was afoot. Curiosity roused me to study a Libran in action; I accepted. She suggested that we return to the scene of the previous Sunday. The important idea here is that, being a Libran, she wore a spanking-new outfit. She had designed and made the dress, a lovely black sheer dress pleated Greek-style from shoulder to hem. She had gone to a furrier and bought a stunning cape of platina fox that set the black dress off to perfection. The outfit ran into hundreds of dollars. There was no sign of the man, though we dragged the dining out as long as possible without incurring bad taste. No other sign would be this extravagant for a single purpose or as vainly intent upon the idea that she is irresistible. Good manners were expressed in that she made no comment at all about her failure. This is typical of a Libra personality with a Libra birth sign.

Years of work in any profession help the practitioner detect clues that will not fail to show something significant in one way or another. So it is with astrology. Each sign will have an invariable the astrologer can pick up, no matter what the birth hour. For example, many times the birth hour is unknown, yet time is very important in any prediction. If such a client brings me a gift, and he was not born under the sign of Libra, I will know that Libra is the personality. A Libran client, who always had her reading done over the telephone and who did not know her birth hour, came one day with a plant for me—the search was over. She was dressed exquisitely. The gift plus her dress pointed to Libra ascending. All that remained now was to decide the rising degree of her Libra personality.

Librans prefer a calm environment; when a quarrel starts, they are the first to leave the scene even though they may have instigated it. Contention, noise, and vulgar atmospheres completely unnerve them. That is why they have low speaking voices, never shrill ones.

They are early risers; they love the daytime. Venus, their ruler, is an evening star. They are the first to arrive at a party and the first to leave, for their sense of evaluating people has assessed everyone present and made a selection if a worthwhile person is present.

Libra is the beautiful-but-dumb sign—dumb for you, but shrewd for itself. Librans make no attempt at being intellectual. It bores them and takes up too much time. As long as the conversation is light and gay, they pretend to be interested. When and if the subject takes a studious turn, you have lost your Libran. He has moved over to another easy victim.

If Libra stays around, there is something to be gleaned from the conversation: information that he needs or wants for personal advantage. He cannot discipline himself long enough to study. But he can study art or beauty, for the visual sensual enjoyment is fed. Librans are visualizers. For Libra, painting, sketching, and designing are manual forms of expressing their understanding of beauty. They are doers, not thinkers.

Librans have easy, pleasant dispositions as long as they are getting what they want—money, fun, excitement, clothes, and cars. If the tide turns, they seek greener fields. They are so vain that the ugliest Libran can imagine himself beautiful. They are hedonists; they crave pleasure. Their parasitical nature is clearly shown in their gross ingratitude. Their cruelty is the greater for they seemed so very sweet. Not one of the twelve signs has such a completely ungrateful nature as Libra.

CARDINAL RISING SIGNS FOR LIBRA
(PERSONALITY)

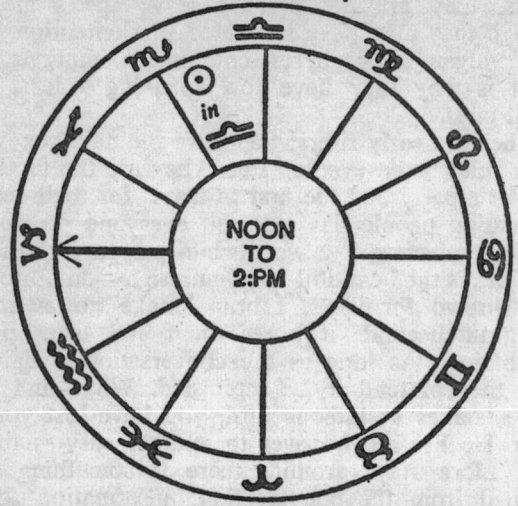

♑ = CAPRICORN

NOON–2 PM. The Libran born at noon will have Capricorn for personality and appearance. Noon births represent prominent people. The most conservative Libran, combined with the cautious dignity of Capricorn, will contradict all that is said about him in the former interpretations.

The big, beautiful eyes of Libra will not stare, but they pierce into people and things. Capricorn goes to the party of "somebodies"; you must be well-to-do for him to accept your invitation. Naturally, this combination will screen the party for importance, not enjoyment.

A Capricorn personality will cut the fairness down to a brown coloring. The bones will be smaller. Like Taurians, Librans usually have large feet. Capricorn will give this Libran smaller feet, more graceful legs and ankles. The clothes will be elegant, not colorful. Librans like muted or light shades. Capricorn prefers black or dark blue. The face here is of fine, clear, classic beauty.

The dinner party given by a Libra-Capricorn personality will be for the "right" people. In the best tradition, the linen will be the finest; the type of food served will be traditional; the china will be special; it will be perfectly timed. After the schedule is run through, you will be dismissed. Everything will be perfect. The most reliable Libran has Capricorn for personality—vanity versus truth.

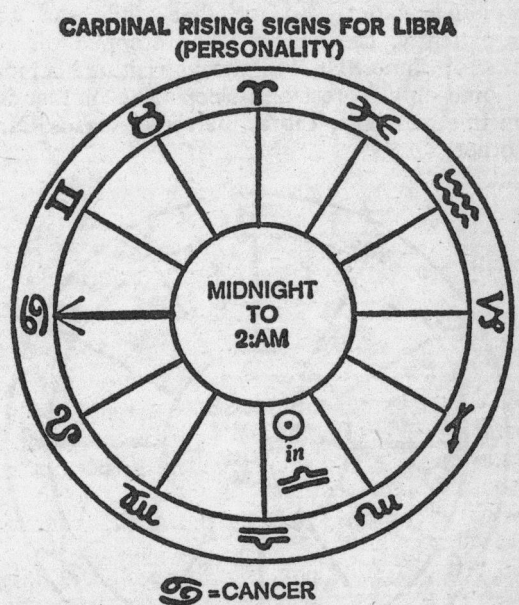

CARDINAL RISING SIGNS FOR LIBRA (PERSONALITY)

♋ = CANCER

MIDNIGHT–2 AM. The Libran with the sign Cancer for his personality will again contradict the fun-seeking Libran. Cancer is too shy to rush to parties. Cancer loves the home; so he may always have something at home to feed you. Cancer loves food. You can drop in, and he immediately puts the kitchen to work. This type is not interested in clothes. In fact, Cancer spills things; so his clothes are not pressed and tidy. His attire is comfortable. Cancer's features cut down on Libra's beauty.

Cancer means to give you enough to eat; so there will be plenty. Don't expect the service to be anything but adequate. This personality is so different from the birth sign that the conflict will be evident. Cancer, wishing to feed the emotions, is the mother compulsively forcing her child to eat. Libra suffers here, being torn between the family and the mate. This Libran marries, but keeps running back home. One of my clients—her husband had this combination—complained bitterly to me that while she waited dinner patiently, her husband had stopped off at his mother's for dinner. He was always visiting his mother, going home only to rest and sleep. The mother is the rival in this marriage, Libra, marriage, versus Cancer, the mother.

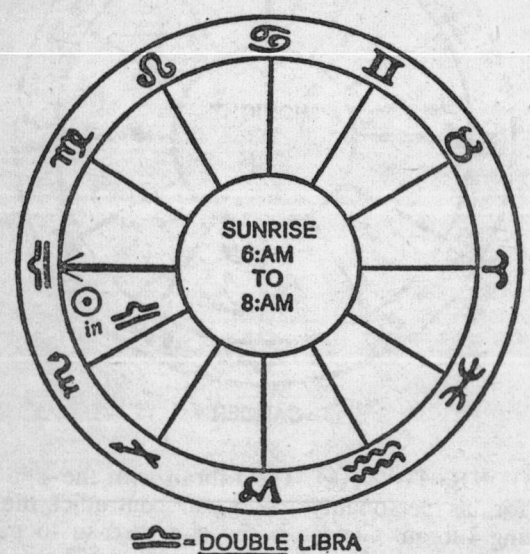

= DOUBLE LIBRA

6 AM–8 AM. A Libran born with the same sign for personality is the strongest-appearing Libra—a double-sign influence—with all of the attributes of the sign. Libra's good looks combined with the character-

istics of the sign personify the party-going type, the active mate-seeker. This Libra dresses for one event after the other; he is clothes-conscious. Money is discussed all of the time. Associates must have money or be willing to spend it.

A Libra personality visited me three times in one day. Each time she wore a different outfit. Another time, in her home, she changed twice. She refused to take me in her car to a party to which we had both been invited, suggesting that another friend take me. She asked me for money; when I objected, she refused to take me. Librans are disloyal and dishonorable when money is involved. They hate to pay debts; they will spend foolishly instead.

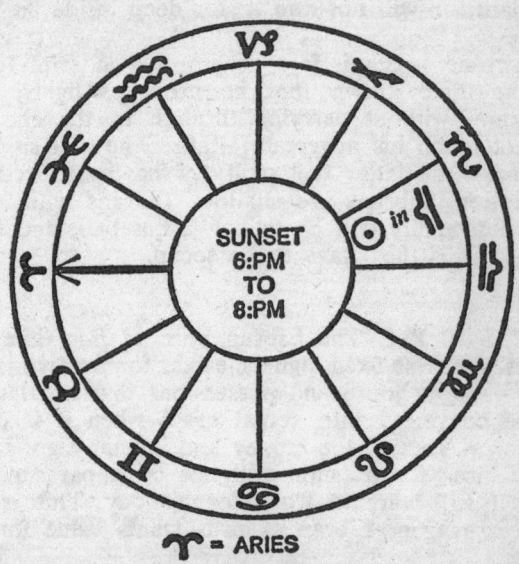

♈ = ARIES

6 PM–8 PM. The Libran born when the sun is setting has Aries for a personality. This is a natural chart (Aries is in the first house, as in the original zodiac), and very little of the appearance of Libra will be seen. The sign of Libra is too far away from the first house of personality or appearance; so Aries combined with Libra will not be refined and polite.

Clothes will mean little. Parties can be noisy and boisterous. He may be a mechanic, caring nothing for art.

But the Aries personality will not lessen the desire for marriage. The beauty now is more masculine, more red; in the face, there are planes that have lost refinement. Still, there will be charm. This is the Libran who may never be at home; he is always on the job or at the back of the house in the workshed. In the home, quarreling stems from the wife complaining that her Libra husband always wants to find her waiting at home, though he is absent. This Libran runs out to the street seeking to stimulate something that doesn't exist. No matter how hard he seeks that stimulant, he will not find it, for deep inside he lacks desire.

Everyone says this is a generous, wonderful Libra, but the mate knows that he provokes fights, then withdraws without carrying through to the end: he will not touch his adversary. Rather, he will sit back and make the latter feel guilty of having started the commotion. Librans are shallow. Librans with Aries for a personality will go to fights, baseball, and football games if they have to be social.

8 PM–10 PM. The Libran born at this time has Taurus, the first fixed sign of earth, for a personality. Libra wants a house and possessions that will last or can be converted into actual cash, when it is combined with Taurus, the money and income sign. Libra with Taurus for a guide will not be a parasite. Instead, it will want to work for his pay. This is the least extravagant Libran. Taurus wants value for his money.

The beauty of both of these Venus-ruled signs keeps the good looks of Libra and adds steadfastness and reliability. Clothes are not pointed up, for money-spending is cut down.

The shallowness of the good looks of Libra has now an added force of richness, warmth, and more sincerity in the features. Beauty can be trusted.

The steadiness of determined Taurus will not desire

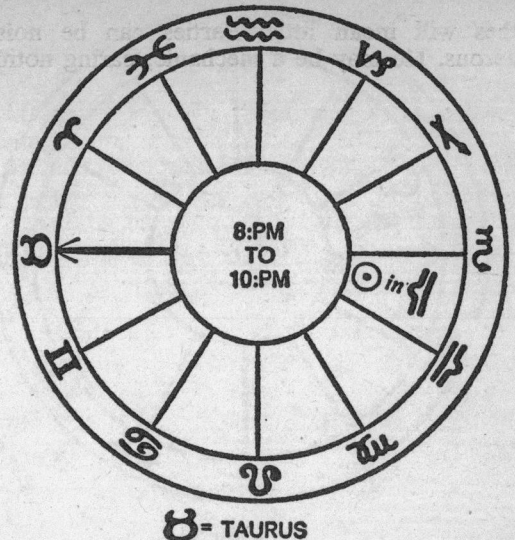

♉ = TAURUS

a change of mates, not wishing to give up anything once it has become his; the Libran trait of the quick divorce will be blocked. This will be the Libran living in the country, buying and selling property. One with Taurus for a personality bought and sold penthouses and a house in the country all within a year.

This influence produces an esthetic Libran. He is a natural lover of green things, perhaps being a gardener working for beauty outside the home as well as within. The vanity of Libra with Taurus's love of money will be expressed through showing off what is owned. The heavier beauty must not allow you to forget that behind it is the parasitical desire to appease the inner vanity.

8 AM–10 AM. The ascendant at this hour has the third fixed sign, Scorpio, on the personality house. Fixed-sign identifications are easy to spot. They are good for cardinal and mutable signs in that they aim for what they want.

Libra is now more determined, less shallow, evi-

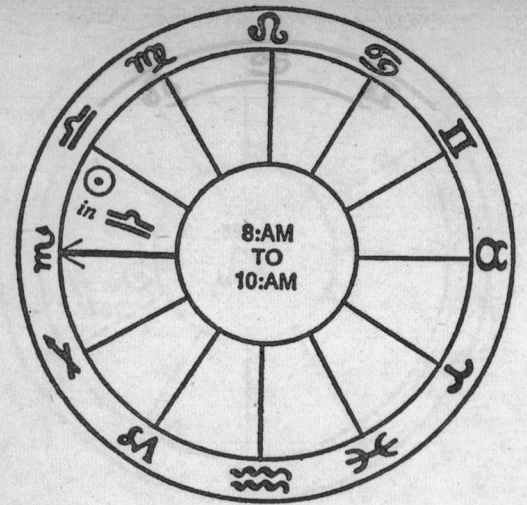

♏︎ = SCORPIO

dencing the relentless pursuit that Scorpio puts into every effort. The beauty of Libra has an aura of mystery and elusiveness. The eyes that were wide are now hooded and penetrating—the unmistakable Scorpio clue. The personality of Scorpio will not waste time in endless, futile, party-going. The party must have a purpose. The charm of Libra will be projected for Scorpio's ruthless or relentless intentions.

This is a very strong Libran. The scheme of Scorpio can be put in the background during the hunt for the money-bearing, powerful mate. Now marriage for the mercenary Libran leads to possessions. The combination of a Libran birth, marrying for money, and the personality of Scorpio magnetism is one of the most difficult to master, either for the person himself or for others who meet him. His charm overwhelms you and obsesses you.

2 AM.–4 AM. The Libran born early in the morning has Leo for a personality. Leo rules love; Libra rules marriage. Leo wants to marry with this combi-

FIXED RISING SIGNS FOR LIBRA
(PERSONALITY)

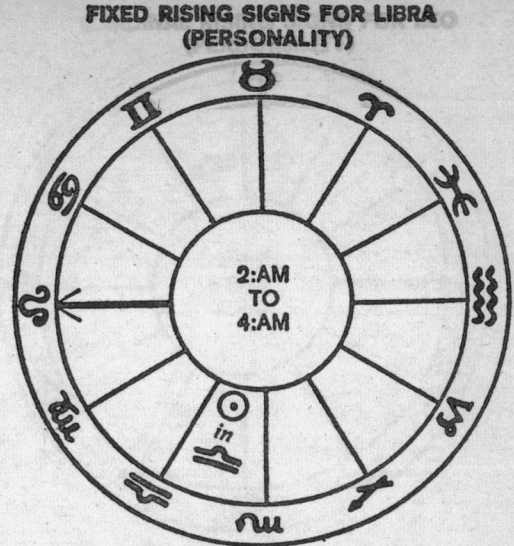

♌ = LEO

nation. The Libran beauty will be warm and noble; its coldness will be gone. The narcissistic Libran will be lost in Leo's kindness and desire to love and be loved. The Libran with Leo for personality wants everyone to love him and will want to love everyone. He will show more consideration than the Libran, who wants everyone to contribute to his comfort and pleasure.

Royal Leo, the aristocrat, gathers power. Libra with Leo will associate with important people instead of being the butterfly type flitting from one social group to another. Libran vanity will now want to associate with the powers-that-be. Leo is completely unhappy unless associating with those on higher levels.

This nature was emphasized to me by a Libran client with Leo for personality. He was working with beauty in flower displays, but was dismissed for telling the head of the company how he thought the greatest advantage could be derived for the show. He could not understand why the boss did not regard him as an equal with the right to advise him.

FIXED RISING SIGNS FOR LIBRA
(PERSONALITY)

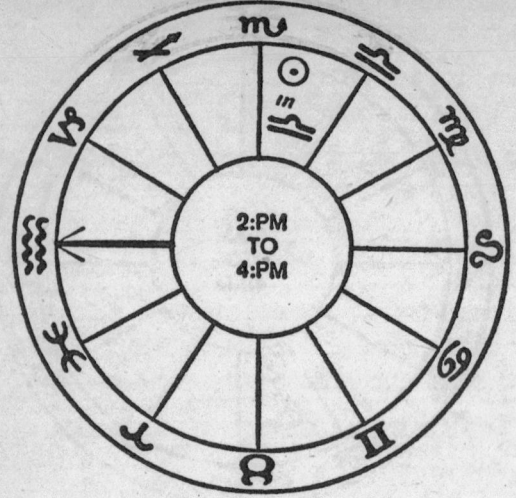

♒ =AQUARIUS

2 PM.–4 PM. Librans born at this time will have Aquarius for a personality. Libra is an air sign, and so is Aquarius. They will harmonize. This is an idealistic Libran who has pursued learning, not vanity. The fixity of Aquarius in investigating universal subjects gives Libra intelligence at last.

Aquarius is tall, and Libra is slender; neither sign carries fat. The beautiful face of Libra, its bone structure standing forward, makes this one of the most beautiful, as well as intelligent, Librans. Clothes are selected with color and line in mind, but worn with casualness and ease. Interests are centered on people, friends, and the love.

It is a lucky Libran who has Aquarius for a personality! This is the model whose photographs circulate all over the world. Both signs being unemotional, Libra is cool here. Thanks to his Aquarian indifference, emotional involvements are cut to nil. This type is loved, but not loving. The trial here would be to arouse this cool Libran. Friends get the best results. This Libran should marry a friend.

♊ =GEMINI

10 PM.–MIDNIGHT. The Libran born at this time will have the Gemini personality. Both being air signs, they will make another idealistic Libran. Beauty combined with the eternal youthfulness of Gemini will produce the teenage, youthful body and a good sense of clothes. It will be useless to try to guess the age of this combination or imagine how many times he will marry. These are the types who drop mates, re-entering marriage without missing a step. How can they help it when someone is always falling in love with them? Their harmonious natures respond to the idea. Libra wants to be loved, and Gemini does not care how many times.

10 AM.–NOON. Here the Sagittarian personality, like all fire signs, brings warmth and kindness to the coldness of Libra, whose beauty is not so chiseled. Here every feature is less controlled and larger. The hair is darker, the nose longer, the smile more personal. He means to make a friend of you. The friend-

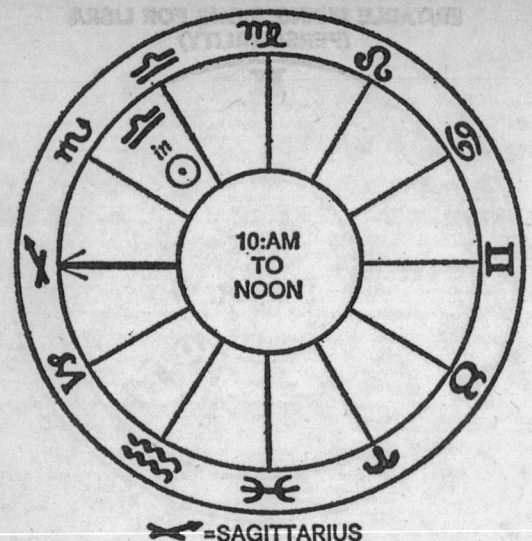

⚞ =SAGITTARIUS

ship of Libra is not lasting, but this combination will make an effort.

As in the case of all mutable personalities, there will be several marriages since Libra likes to marry and Sagittarians repeat everything in the flow through life. Fire and air signs get on very well. This is a very lovely and pleasant combination—so charming in fact that its gets them into trouble when they step to the altar. But they need to be inspired by a new love.

4 AM.–6 AM. The Libran born at this hour brings Virgo to the personality house, and this will somewhat lessen the charm of Libra. Virgo is too practical for Libra, tightening the features into critical lines. The upper lip is too long. The nose dips, and the manner has lost its usual casual charm.

If Librans are money-bent, they work harder. While the love of clothing will change into extreme neatness, it will cost less.

Money troubles will prevail. A friend with a Virgo

MUTABLE RISING SIGNS FOR LIBRA
(PERSONALITY)

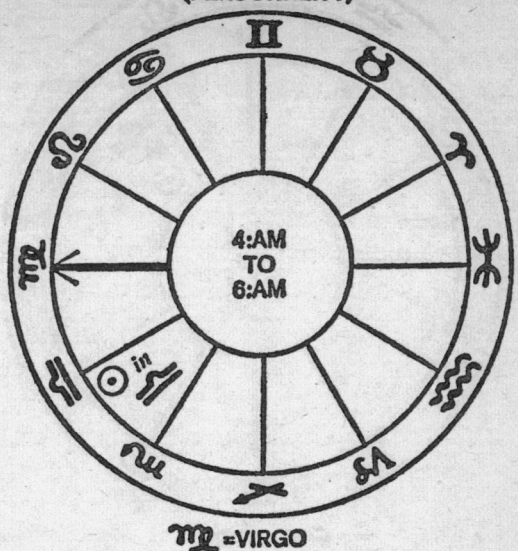

♍ =VIRGO

personality borrowed money from me on one occasion. She refused to pay it back until she knew it was to pay a medical bill. Later I pretended to need money to test her friendship. She dropped me a curt note saying no explanation was necessary even though he had kept hundreds of dollars of mine for seven years. You will lose a Libra friend with Virgo because of money, and then you will be criticized.

4 PM.–6 PM. There are great difficulties for the Libran born late in the afternoon with Pisces for a personality. Pisces is dual, and Libra is cardinal: too much indecision. Active signs need levers to anchor their thoughts. The easy personality of Pisces makes them too light and easy. The beauty of Libra is covered with the indistinct features of fleshy Pisces; the coloring is pale on pale.

Libra is too far from the rising sign here to have enough effectiveness on Pisces's soft features. Librans

MUTABLE RISING SIGNS FOR LIBRA (PERSONALITY)

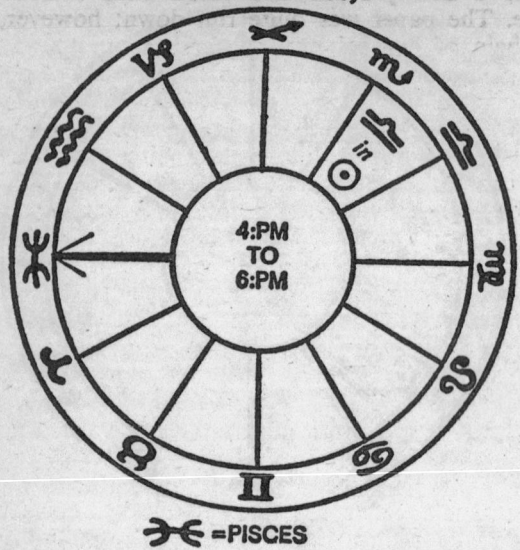

✶ =PISCES

are not talkers; Pisceans do not force an impression. The final result is a vain, emotional person who has no means of commanding the attention he craves. This is the Libran who has no feature to recommend or justify his vanity. Dual marriages will be the result of his chasing those who have a negative influence on him, and he may disappoint his mate by failing to live up to the promise of his good looks.

The other invariable with Librans is their inability to understand why their marriages break up. The failure to prevent broken associations lies in the fact that Librans deny the responsibility required in any relationship. The other fellow must carry the burden so that they may enjoy it.

Change is their nemesis. They think this can be brought about only through someone new. They will work very hard with new persons or new ideas. As soon as all of the potentials are known, they lose interest.

A journalist had me go all the way to Chicago to assess a new job she had taken with a newspaper there. The paper was quite run down; however, with the help of her column, she built it up to an exciting, glamorous paper. But the moment it was about to pay off, she was gone. The owner, when visiting New York, talked with me. He said she was known for this trait; he had hoped to keep her going past this crisis, but had failed. Strangely, she charged the failure up to the owner, even after I told her that she had let her one opportunity slip by. She refused to admit that she had failed herself. The inner vanity of Librans will not permit this.

The desire for change is strong in all cardinal signs. That is what the cardinal influence really implies. Each one uses different reasons for an excuse. With Librans, since people are their forte, those they would part with are at fault. They want you to love them, but that does not mean that they can love you in return. They love the love you offer them, not you. When you begin to see through their narcissism, they must move on, for they know that it will be difficult now to wager for their purposes. They cannot have you break the illusion of their assumed goodness.

A client brought me a friend who was visiting her from California. She asked me to take this friend and organize a plan to prevent a coming divorce. This was the fourth marriage—a Libran, of course!

The man she had left in California would not have her back at any price. She had left him heavily in debt. By working with her chart, we got her married again. Still, I told my friend, the marriage would fail in four years.

As the time drew near, I telephoned her, feeling that perhaps the marriage could be saved. She was preparing to go to Florida and seemed very confident. I withdrew, hoping for the best.

However, her husband wrote her telling her that she was not to return to him; she was to go to Reno for a divorce. She begged me to go to him to effect a reconciliation. I went to the husband, but before I had a chance to plead her cause, he placed a bundle of unpaid bills on the coffee table. He asked me to examine them. I was horrified. Among them were invoices of articles for another man—the favorite trick of Libra: gifts she had already picked out. The gifts were to give the new victim the impression of generosity, the very trait he expects from you.

He said, "I will listen to you, but first let me tell you that I am hopelessly in debt. These bills are nothing in comparison with what I owe. The very money that sent to her to Florida and Reno, I borrowed. If you talk me into taking her back, you will be dooming me. The man she has in mind has nothing. I gave him the money to dine her the night before she departed, for I knew he could not afford the kind of restaurant she would select."

I did not say the things I had planned to say. Upon leaving, we shook hands on a gentleman's agreement. I needed only to say in my wire to her that he was broke. That made her turn from him to a new man.

SCORPIO: The Eighth Sign
October 24 to November 21

Scorpio is the third fixed sign and the second water sign. The water symbolizes emotional expression, but being fixed, it represents fixed emotion. That is why Scorpios are relentless in their emotional demands. You must appease or assuage their desires. They will concede to you only after they see that there is no other way to win. But immediately after winning they return more fiercely to avenge your forcing them to amend. You are never forgiven.

The emotional signs are "feelers," not thinkers. They are ever-searching for the right scene or person in which to "set" their emotions. They will choose you if you can contribute to their power drive; they are the most power-loving of all the fixed signs (Taurus wants money and security; Leo wants a throne to dominate; Aquarius wants to circulate in the international scene and help humanity with his ideas). Scorpio seeks personal power to put the world in its place, as he sees it.

The idea that is unknown to Scorpio is scoffed at. He takes the position that he is a realist, and that such a thing is not real or practical; therefore it is wrong. He likes to use sweeping, final forms of expression that leave no doubt that he does not believe in the idea, mainly because he did not think of it first, or he is irritated if it is your subject and not his. The idea gives you a power that he does not have. He will dispute with you, not so much because the premise of this idea is wrong but because you had it first. Scorpios do not like this; it is an attack on their personal power. Their anger is deep and abiding, bothering them until they find a way to top you.

The underlying reason, in one word, is jealousy.

The jealousy of Scorpio is different from the jealousy of the other water signs, Cancer and Pisces. Cancer does not want you to take his children or his family away from him. These people are his possessions. Cancer is even jealous of his friends. He begrudges sharing a friend. Pisces is jealous that he is not determined enough to attain more or even as much as you. But Scorpio is jealous of everything because it all points to him. What you have, if he does not have it, amasses more power for you. Anything that adds to your personality, position, or knowledge is clearly a thing that might have been useful to him. It angers him that it did not occur to him first.

Scorpio will demean a compliment that you pay to another in his presence. A Scorpio client, the husband of a beautifully groomed wife, will say, "Why not? She lives at the beauty parlor" when you compliment her. Another Scorpio man whose sweetheart is a famous analyst delights in placing her in the position in which she has to defend her theories. He is delighted when she cannot prove a point or win a convert, aiding and abetting the arguments posed against her ideas. She knows something that he does not; he is jealous of this knowledge. No matter how much Scorpio loves you, he cannot overcome this deep-seated jealousy unless he is highly evolved.

Scorpio is ruled by the planet Mars. (In 1930, Pluto, its co-ruler, was discovered, and assigned to Scorpio. But it is best to use both rulers in judging Scorpio.) Mars is a warring planet, war is grist for the Scorpio mill. Mars is always spoiling for a quarrel, for that is the way the planet Mars expresses energy. It is not a planet that thinks; it is a planet that *acts*. Therefore, in order to put action into motion, something must be instigated, provoked, or aroused. Mars rules sex. There are many ways to express sex, for sex is energy. Mars rules energy. Scorpio is given credit for all sex drives, for the eighth house to which Scorpio is assigned in the natural zodiac is the house of sex and regeneration. To regenerate is to form anew, re-do. Scorpios want to re-do your idea as well as you. He does not want to make you over into a nice person, as Leo wants to do. Leo wants you to be a credit to his kingdom. Scorpios want to re-do you for their own usefulness. You must complement them. Scorpio, who must always win over people and the action of the moment, must come out of the fray as a winner.

Scorpio does not care how he wins over you. First, he tries subtle means; that is, he tries to ease you into conquest. If you are a fixed sign like Taurus, Leo, or Aquarius, you resist his subtleties. Then he comes right out and takes for a weapon anything that, during the discussion, he may have sensed is your weak point. He will hammer at that. For example, he may encourage a confidence such as a complaint about an injustice you have suffered. Scorpio will then use this against you, calling you a troublesome complainer. The connotation is out of proportion to your harmless comment. He will distract you while you try to defend yourself, and he will have gone on to triumph in the meantime.

Another reason to provoke you is to find out where you are weak. Leo is his match, for Leo has better manners. Scorpios resent the gentlemanly or ladylike behavior of the latter. If Leo maintains his attitude of being too magnanimous to lower himself to quarrel, Scorpio is unseated.

Scorpio does not have such a hard time with Taurus, for Taurus is the sign opposite Scorpio. It is always possible to get on with the sign opposite yours. Taurus learns his lesson through Scorpio. Scorpio needs the security that Taurians exude. The Taurian steadfastness (and they are not easily ruffled) puts Scorpio's quarrelsomeness to flight. He abandons the fight when he cannot upset slow, quiet Taurus. Taurus does not like the quarrels; he becomes silent, giving Scorpio nothing to work on.

Aquarius loves to argue. Therefore, if an argument starts between Scorpio and Aquarius, it can go on for hours, never being settled. The perversity of Aquarius will not agree. The invincibility of Scorpio will not yield. Aquarius has more reasons for winning. He is more intelligent, being an air sign, and more impersonal. He is not hampered by emotion. For Aquarius, it is simply an idea being knocked around. But if he knows the subject well enough, he has won as far as he is concerned. What Scorpio thinks of him does not matter. This rankles Scorpio, who always thinks that his opinion matters to you. What you think of him means a lot. If you think he is wonderful, he has power over you; if you do not, he cannot manipulate you. The indifference of Aquarius defeats Scorpio's self-importance.

You cannot take Scorpio into your confidence or let him know an uncomplimentary thing about you. In other words, never let him have anything on you, for no matter how long it takes, he will use it against you. The reason for turning on you is that he has exhausted his reason for needing you, or, he has not succeeded in outmaneuvering you. The exposure of a confidence made during the fastness of the friendship is the signal (similar to Virgo) that your usefulness is over for the moment.

When Scorpio abandons you, it is because you have lost power. For the moment, you are *persona non grata*. He does not like losers. It may be that you have found him out; so he discredits you by exposing your secrets. When he starts to make scathing remarks about you, take it as a compliment, for it means he has tried all of his tricks; and you are not beaten. Then out comes the venom of failure, frustration, or hate. Mainly all he has left is to degrade you rather than admit that he has failed to demoralize you into submission.

Demoralizing is native to the Scorpio. He enjoys it. Even the most evolved types are satirists or literary cynics. In fact Voltaire was an exponent of the sarcastic barbs of Scorpio. Great prophecies and forecasts are often made in jest.

Will Rogers' humor carries a bite or sting that is representative of this inclination to demoralize people. This time it is meant to let those who rule know that their phoniness is obvious. Scorpio is not lenient with fakes.

Both Will Rogers and Voltaire were Scorpios. If a crusader for his people, like Ghandi, whose personality was Scorpio (his Sun-sign was Libra), takes up the cudgel of exposure for truth, then this is the higher form of expression of that trait. When really expressed on a higher level, Scorpio is the dove of peace, not the scorpion. The eagle, which is the warring bird and another symbol for Scorpio, flies best in a storm. The only bird to leave the nest in a storm is the eagle. Give the Fight-for-a-cause Scorpio a job to do and he becomes the eagle, flying highest (the flight of intelligence) during a struggle, or dovelike in peace.

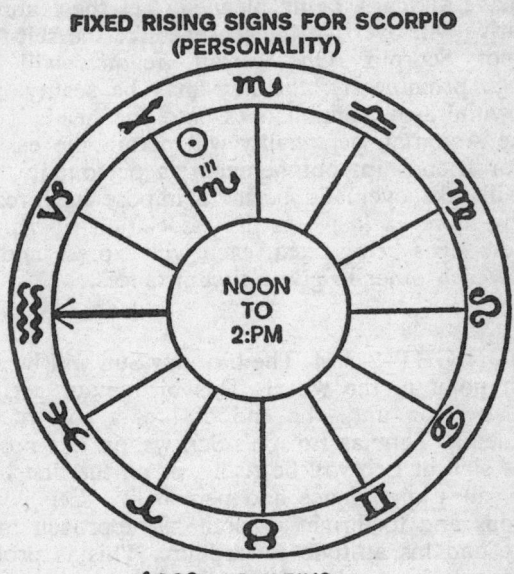

FIXED RISING SIGNS FOR SCORPIO (PERSONALITY)

≈≈ —AQUARIUS

NOON–2 PM. If you are a Scorpio born at noon, then you have the sign of Aquarius rising, or on the first zodiacal house. Your personality will differ from the characteristic traits of Scorpio. You will be entirely different from the textbook descriptions. You will express an Aquarian manner; you will seem less emotional. You will be taller than Scorpio, who is not tall, but heavily constructed. You will be less personal in your approach to people. Your attitude will be casual, not tense. You will have wavy lines in your forehead. Your head will be larger, more dome-shaped around the temples.

The hollows between the cheekbone and jawline will clearly show your face to be more modern in construction, for we are now moving into the Aquarian age; and the face is becoming more intelligent. The Aquarian face is one whose bone structure is clearly outlined and prominent; combined with Scorpio traits, it will seem less casual, keener. As the personality is opposed to the basic traits of Scorpio, both signs will have difficulty being blended. Yet the features of Aquarius will override the tenseness of the self-turned face of Scorpio. One certain feature will come through prominently; the hair may be scanty or the eyes withdrawn, sinking back into the head.

The Aquarian personality will permit the easy first bid for friendship; but behind this personality, Scorpio will take over and begin to impose its force, becoming more exclusive as the association ripens. Both of these signs being fixed, each will express and contradict each other in given circumstances.

MIDNIGHT–2 AM. The birthday Sun will be at the lowest point in the wheel. This birth hour gets very little attention until the end of life, a sort of fame after death. Thomas Edison's Sun was in this position.

The sign of Leo will be rising, or on the first house, which rules appearance and personality. Leo is more generous and forthright in both his approach toward people and his attitude toward life. This is probably so different from what the textbooks say about Scorpio that the Leo personality versus the Scorpio birth erases completely all of the traits ascribed to Scorpio.

The head is high; pride and leadership are clear; the nose has a high bridge and is less beaked; the forehead is wide and not as beetle-browed as Scorpio usually presents. There is less secretiveness. The coloring is florid; the hair tends toward red or golden. The evasiveness and watchfulness of Scorpio has disappeared into an open, sincere desire to be friendly with no axe to grind.

Benito Mussolini was born in the sign of Leo. He would have been a more generous and sincere personality if he had had the Leo sign closer to the rising, or

FIXED RISING SIGNS FOR SCORPIO
(PERSONALITY)

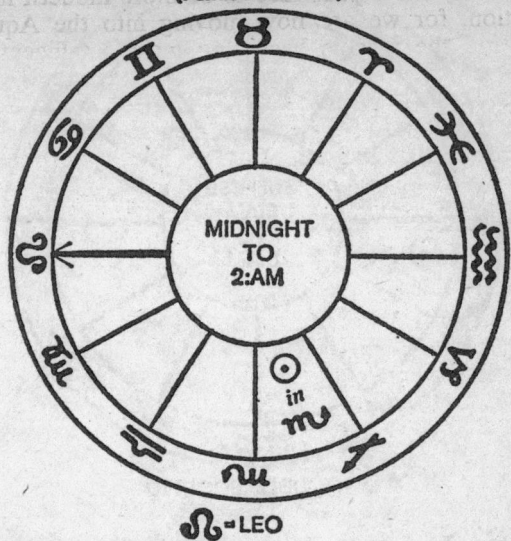

♌ = LEO

personality, house. Instead, Leo's kindness was completely obliterated by his Scorpio personality, the very reverse of the above, cutting magnanimous Leo down to the bone. Scorpio took over and made his entire program one drive for personal power.

6 AM–8AM. This would put the Sun-sign exactly on the rising, or personality house. You now have a Scorpio with an identical individuality and personality. This is the strongest type of Scorpio. All of the force and desire to win are obvious in the personality. This type is always about his own business. There is no letup; you haven't a chance. All of the selfishness is in focus.

No matter what the conversation, this type will direct it back to the self. He will wait for you to come to a comma, put in his words at once, and wring out whatever good he can for his own benefit. Scorpio is always a self-seeking sign. This makes him most

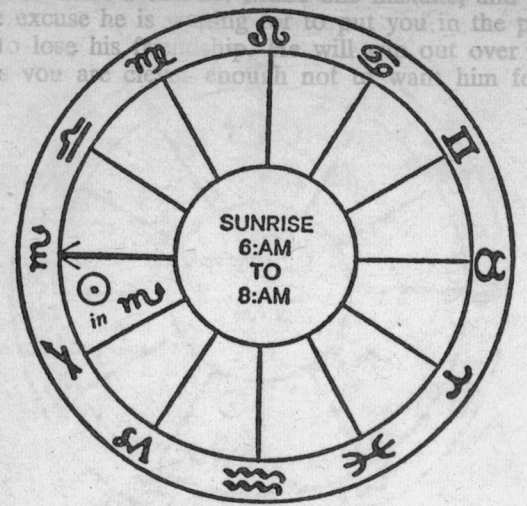

♏ =DOUBLE SCORPIO

offensive. In fact, no matter what sign one is born under, if Scorpio is rising on the first house, this person will monopolize the conversation.

I have a Pisces client who has Scorpio rising. Whenever one of the other signs is being discussed, she continually cuts in with "Am I like that?" even though she knows another sign, entirely different from hers, is being debated.

If Scorpio rises with the Scorpio Sun-sign, you have the heavily built person with a forceful will to attain personal power; then will obstruct the path of everyone and lead it back to himself. All signs have expressions of selfishness, but the Scorpio sunrise births do not hesitate to move toward their goals with you in tow. You must be concerned and work for their attainments; otherwise you will be avoided, dropped, or be treated with contempt. You must be useful to them.

Their acquisitive, beaklike nose, the hooded eyelids (to hide secrets), and their tight compact head, aids in identifying them.

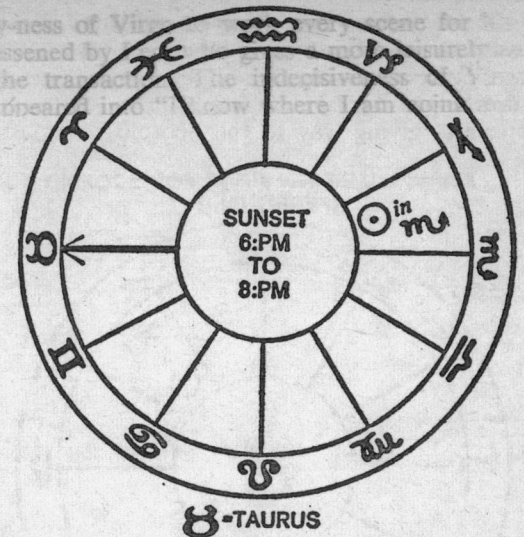

♉-TAURUS

6 PM–8 PM. The opposite sign, Taurus, will be on the first house. Now you have sweet Taurus, whose mien is kindness, sweetness, and more consideration for you, on the first house of personality This is the youthful beauty with the doll-like face. The nose is small, smaller than Scorpio usually effects. The head is very round and small; the neck is very short; thus the head seems to be sinking into the chest or shoulders.

The start of the friendship will be easier; but later, when the bond is well established, the Scorpio traits will seep through—one thing at a time until Scorpio has taken over. At each cue from you to resistance, there will be a waiting period before the next pressure. They never learn through failure, not even with kind Taurus leading them.

A Scorpio friend who has Taurus rising spends all of her time making real-estate deals (Taurus deals in money and land). She telephoned me in in a state of panic, asking me to help her get a penthouse she had lost. In the case of selling the penthouse she was living in, my direction and advice got her even more than she had hoped for. She was delighted. Later on she wanted my help to dispose of another. When I showed resistance, she abused me, telling me that I had not helped her at all. The Taurus sweetness had disappeared, giving way to the Scorpio relentlessness.

CARDINAL RISING SIGNS FOR SCORPIO
(PERSONALITY)

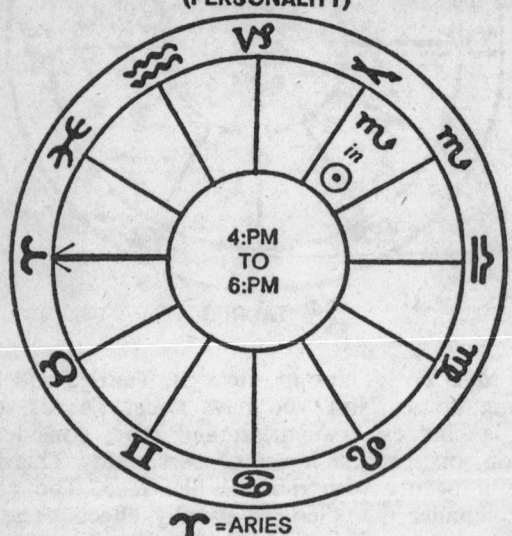

♈ =ARIES

4 PM–6 PM. This Scorpio will have Aries, the sign opposite Libra, rising. Aries, being the first sign of the zodiac, will relegate the Sun of Scorpio far away from the personality house. Thus Scorpio traits will be harder to identify. Aries resembles Scorpio; both have the same ruler, the planet Mars. Aries is very frank. You know where you stand every second. Aries versus Scorpio reinforces the self-seeking Scorpio, but now more openly; with brag and bulldozing, you will be kidded into helping grind his axe; otherwise he will unmercifully make you the butt of all his ribald jokes. Aries is noisy, coarse, and tactless.

The head is large, and features are not rounded. The nose is wide and flat; the space from cheek is wide and flat. The impression is Slavic. Scorpio traits show only in derisive remarks. If the Aries personality is evolved, intelligent Aries's generous personal habits will route the Scorpio's selfishness, making a nicer Scorpio.

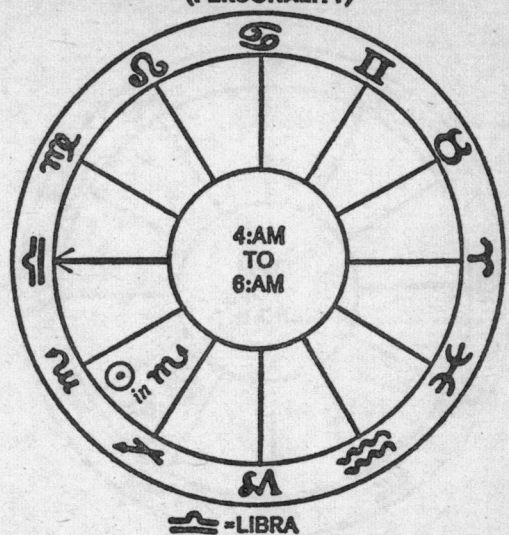

CARDINAL RISING SIGNS FOR SCORPIO (PERSONALITY)

4 AM–6 AM. This Scorpian will have Libra, the cardinal air-sign, rising for a personality—Libran charm, larger eyes, more seemingly open manner. These types make better social material than Scorpio generally presents. Again, after the party-going and social manners are displayed and you are completely taken in, out comes the Scorpio program that was there all the time just waiting for its chance.

This can be most disappointing, for you had seen the attractive, airy, charming good manners of clothes-crazy and party-conscious Libra. You thought that you were going to have a good time with this type of Scorpian; instead, you were lulled into a false security, for now the motive for attracting you is brought into play. The association must benefit this Scorpio. In this case, the Libra with Scorpio personality wants money.

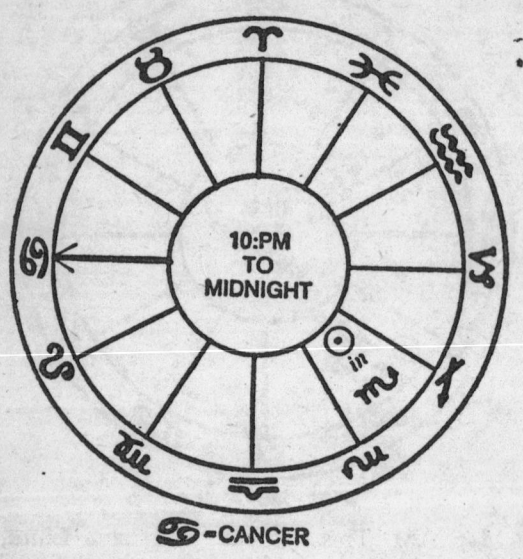

♋︎ — CANCER

10 PM–MIDNIGHT. Scorpio born late at night will have Cancer rising. His personality will express the shy manner of Cancer. This is a very emotional combination, wanting continued satisfactions through emotional channels, childishly wanting attention. A Cancer-Scorpio combination may settle for being mother's pet, sticking to the family, or he may want to be mothered by the mate. The water signs carry so much fat that now you have a very heavy, unevenly distributed Scorpio—pale gray in color and feeding on everyone emotionally. The mouth shows it: it is ugly. These Scorpios seem to be damp, perspiring, never at rest, always wanting something.

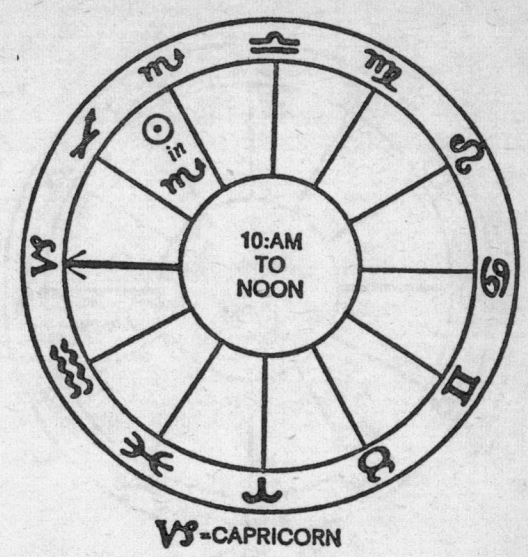

♑ =CAPRICORN

10 AM–NOON. The sign Capricorn will be rising. Conservativeness and breeding will discipline the self-seeking Scorpio while power is still sought. Capricorn thinks too much of his standing to forget this enroute. Capricorn being a small-bodied sign, this Scorpion will not be heavy. The eyes will be less hooded, but more piercing. Capricorn dignity will forego the imposing of the will, waiting patiently until you get around to help him—if he wants your help. Persons with Scorpio Sun-sign and Capricorn personality would rather you thought well of them, and they may never ask your help. If you extend it, they will give you sincere attention, quietly and without display. You can depend on them, for time does not deter them. What they seek now is standing, and they make the effort to earn it. They do not have personal vanity.

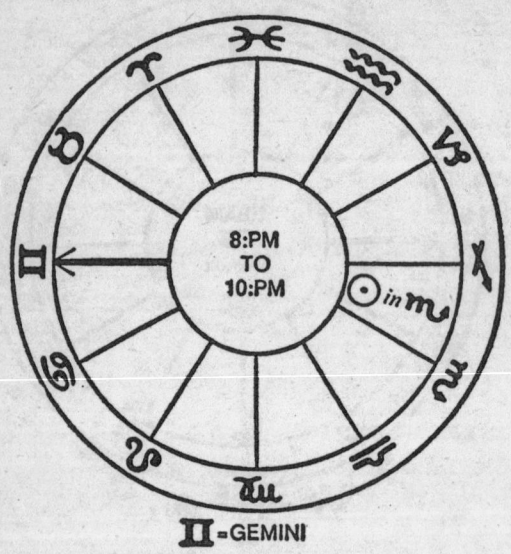

Ⅱ = GEMINI

8 PM–10 PM. Scorpio at this hour has the first mutable sign, Gemini, for a personality. He will be a very effective speaker. This will be the teenage-looking Scorpio, wanting less than the other fixed or cardinal sign combined with Scorpio. Remember, Scorpio wants something every step of the way. Gemini is youthful and easy-going—Gemini belies the heavy brow or body. Scorpio is now more lithe and smaller with really tiny hips. The development characteristics of the fleshy part of the lips have disappeared, and the Scorpio has a very wide smile. Gemini gives one the air when his interest wanes. This will be the only Scorpian who will not wait around to harass you for conquest.

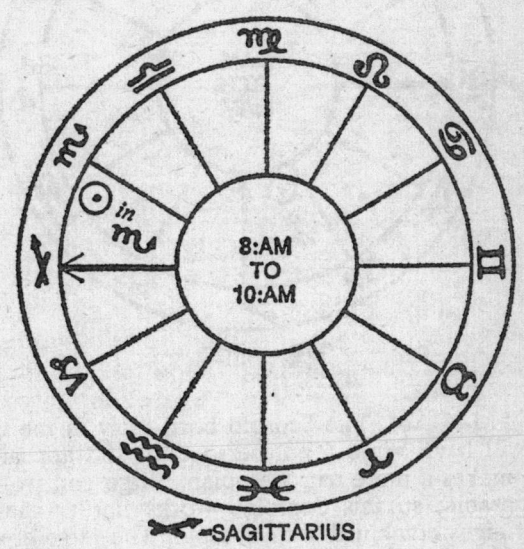

⚹—SAGITTARIUS

8 AM–10 AM. This Scorpio will have Sagittarius, a tall sign, for a personality. Now you have a Scorpian that does not carry weight, whose hair line is thinning at the temples instead of balding. His nose will be longer, less beaked; his face, less controlled. All features are larger to suit the generosity of Sagittarius, who wants less of you than Scorpio generally seeks. Sagittarius with Scorpio would like you to help him sort his ideas. Physical or material gains are not what he wants of you. Microscoping his ideas is his goal.

MUTABLE RISING SIGNS FOR SCORPIO
(PERSONALITY)

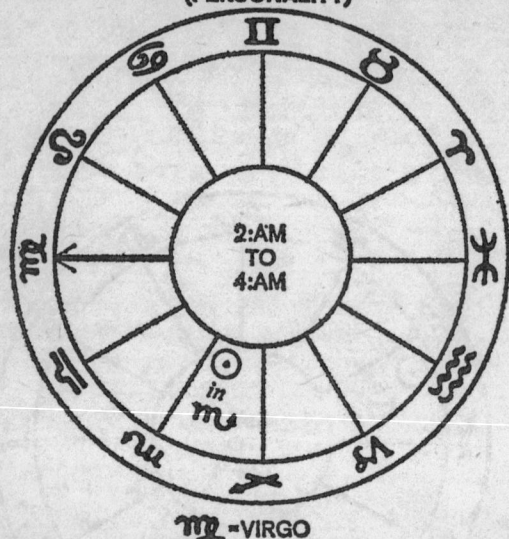

♍ =VIRGO

2 AM–4 AM. The Scorpio born early in the morning will have Virgo for a personality and appearance. This makes a more trim Scorpian. Virgo and work are inseparable; so this Scorpian works harder than the other signs combined with Scorpio. The large area between the base of his nose and his upper lip shows the practical talker. Where this Scorpio talks, it is about his job. He would make a fine labor leader.

His eyes are so close together that they seem to run into each other; the face is too narrow, but there is still force in the beetle-brow. One foot seems to turn into the other, giving the Scorpio-Virgo personality a stumbling gait. When you are insulted by this Scorpian, you never forget it. He will work you to death. You no sooner finish one job for him than another is waiting. Mainly, he wishes you to think like him, so that he can work you for his ends.

MUTABLE RISING SIGNS FOR SCORPIO
(PERSONALITY)

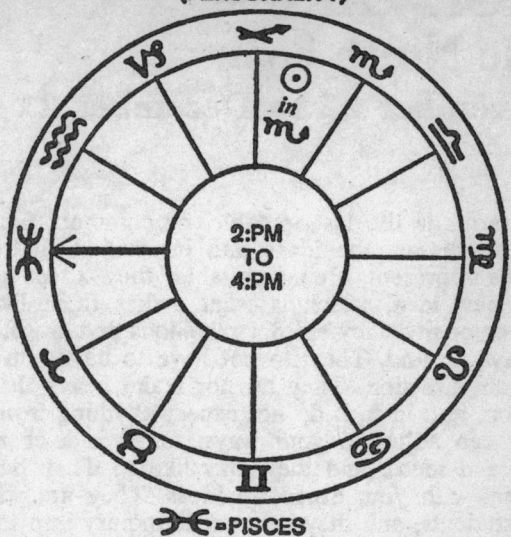

✶✶ = PISCES

2 PM–4 PM. The Scorpio native born at this hour will bring the Pisces personality to the ascendant, or first house. This is the most indecisive of all of the mutable (common) signs. This cuts down Scorpio's determination to win power. This is the last of the common signs. Scorpio is water too; so the emotions are always changing. Like Cancer, he too wants emotional satisfactions, but not from the family.

He swings from negative to positive. The greatest annoyance here is that what he wanted yesterday is canceled out tomorrow. Still, he is always at it. He just wants something. His indecisiveness is shown in the way he carries his body and in his large, spreading, puttylike nose—the fleshiness is uncontrolled and flowing in all directions. Nothing is cleanly cut; emotions are in confusion, and people with Scorpio-Pisces are eternally seeking direction, which they eschew. This is the least successful Scorpian.

16

SAGITTARIUS:
The Ninth Sign
November 22 to December 21

Sagittarius is the last mutable, or common, fire sign. Fire represents the ideas and inspiration that Sagittarians represent. Being mutable, they adapt readily to a new idea, which is what makes them likeable, easy company; they are not rebellious and are pleasant to have around. They do not have to have you move in their direction. They do not make heavy demands on you, and in turn do not expect anything from you. They can adjust to your ways, for it is a change in pace and ideas, and they may like it. They have no quarrel with you, except in ideas. They are scholars and students, and they have made inquiry into the discussion at hand. They can be heated about this discussion; in fact, this is just about their only aspect of determination. They do not give up an idea until it is proved faulty. They do not argue like Aquarius, nor quarrel like Scorpio, nor criticize as Virgo will. They simply refuse to abandon the idea, giving it haven until its workability loses enthusiasm for them.

Sagittarians, like all fire signs, are easy enemies. They soon tire of rigidity, which one needs to remain hostile. Being mentally changeable, their reason for being angry with you is forgiven, though not forgotten. They do not wish to quarrel, for they find it positively unbearable. They avoid anything that could reidentify anxiety between others. Thus they avoid Virgo's ever-critical manner, for they see nothing accomplished in this approach. They make wonderful teachers and professors, for theirs is the friendly approach to convincing you; they do it patiently, with charming words and seductive implications that convert you to their way of thinking, as in the case of Sir Winston Churchill. No idea is too much trouble for Sagittarians to present in the most romantic fashion. They can woo and win you with words that carry powerful ideas and prophecy. They are forecasters.

Sagittarians have more vision than similar signs. Gemini, for example, is concerned with immediate results. Virgo is tied to practicality; Pisces is not sure of his interest.

Sagittarians think in terms of the future. They make good lawyers; they understand the law and that it will secure your future forever. They write with an eye to posterity; for they want what they say to be useful to future generations. They love the law—the law of God mainly, for it is spiritual philosophy. They make good priests and ministers. Their idea of religion is less rigid and formidable than that of administrators. Sagittarians understand that you bend ideas in your own direction; they are sensitive to your way of accepting ideas; it arouses their humanity, with which they are amply blessed.

Sagittarians are not very good at keeping appointments. Spain and its people come under this sign. They are notorious for tardiness. In fact, an idiom of the Spanish language is *mas tarde*—later. Time that restricts them seems a tyrant; they express leisure even in their walk. The expression "conversation piece" must have been coined by a Sagittarian. He enjoys more than anything else to sit before the log fire, easily explaining away an idea.

Sagittarians excel in all forms of athletic expression, for this is an idea put into motion. It has to be calculated with their sense of gamble. The chance element is the prophecy put to test. Faith as an idea is put on trial. The promise of life is appraised. Hope is the chase to the fulfilled. The poet Milton, a Sagittarian, questioned the laws of God—putting the laws on trial—in his writings. It was always a discussion between him and his God; he never tired of it. The true love of Sagittarians is ideas. When all else fails, he will return to an idea. A Sagittarian will travel to the ends of the earth if at the end of the journey he is rewarded with a wonderful idea.

MUTABLE RISING SIGNS FOR SAGITTARIUS
(PERSONALITY)

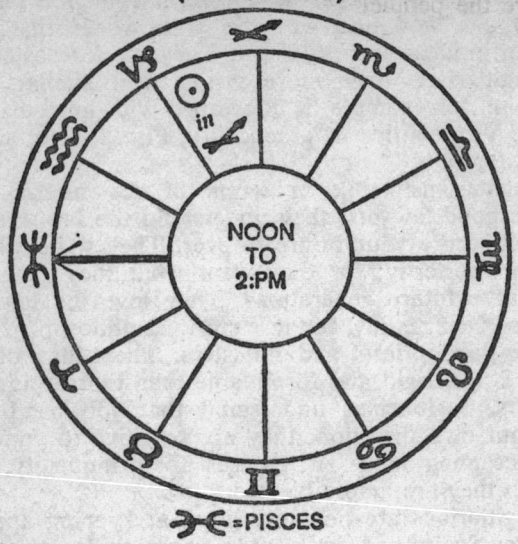

⌇⌇ = PISCES

NOON–2 PM. If a Sagittarian is born at noon, then Pisces, the last mutable sign, will be the rising on the first-house cusp. He will have the individuality of Sagittarius and the personality or appearance of Pisces. This will present a lighter person than the dark Sagittarian. The scholarly air has given way to a more vague approach to life. Ideas are not quite as clear, nor are the facial features.

The color of the skin is pastel. The lower jaw is shorter than the usual Sagittarian's. His face is long with a bony jawline. The teeth of a Sagittarian, like the horse's, are very large, especially the central or front teeth. Pisces changes this; the teeth are not seen when speaking.

This native is not definite in making a statement. Sagittarius makes statements. Sagittarius is lean, but Pisces carries fat or is fleshy. Here you see a good example of the personality detracting entirely from the textbook description of a sign. This Sagittarian will be prominent before the people. But the Pisces affliction may cut down his success—even a doorman stands out before the people!

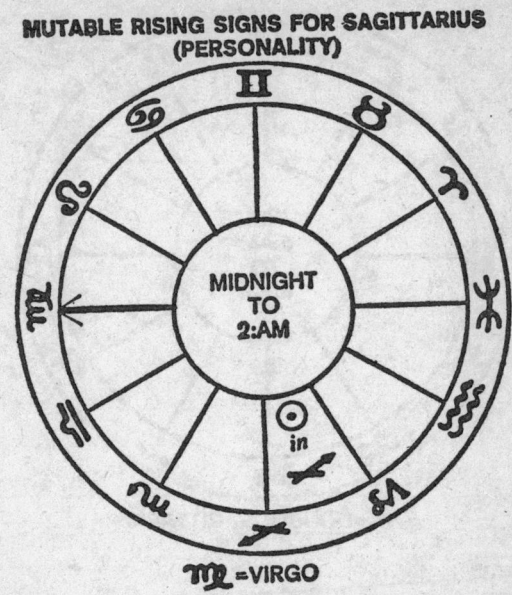

MUTABLE RISING SIGNS FOR SAGITTARIUS (PERSONALITY)

MIDNIGHT TO 2:AM

♍ =VIRGO

MIDNIGHT–2 AM. The Sagittarian will have Virgo, the critic, on his first house of personality. The very instincts of the Sagittarius are against Virgo because of the latter's insistence on being a workhorse. Sagittarians detest this and can be very unhappy. The conflict is great because the Virgo personality reduces him to menial work. But he will find a way out. He will talk his way into being aide-de-camp to the boss in order to avoid the tasks of the servant.

Sagittarius loves to travel. That is why he makes an ideal newspaperman. Sagittarians chase or travel for ideas. If the idea they are in love with is demeaned by someone they wish to impress, their hurt is very great.

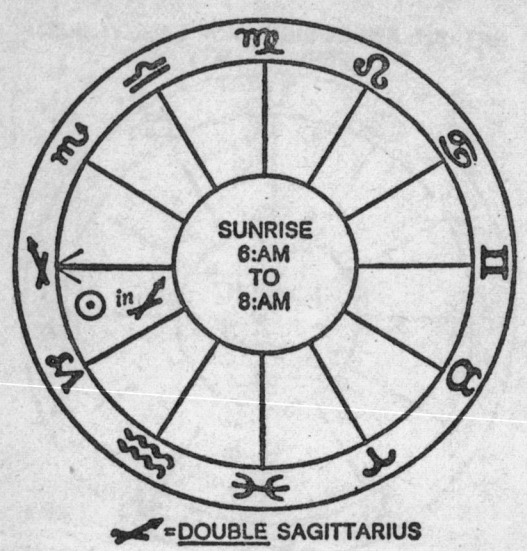

➳ =DOUBLE SAGITTARIUS

6 AM–8 AM. The Sagittarian born at sunrise has the individual and personal traits re-identified. This is the strongest Sagittarian, both influences being one. He will be a tall person with a strong jawline, large, cleanly cut teeth, and the every-ready wide-smile. The mouth is generous, and the lips curved, every-ready to speak and enunciate. The head is narrow. Early in life the hair is long and abundant, becoming scanty at the temples later in life.

Their personality being studious, these Sagittarians are perennial students. When they lose a mate, it is because their studies come first. Unmindful of neglecting the mate, they have their long noses stuck in a book. The lost mate finds out too late that that is the price paid for so easy and charming a person.

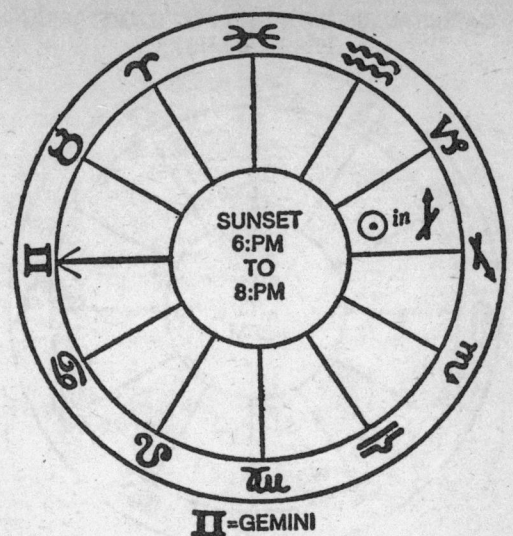

♊︎ = GEMINI

6 PM–8 PM. The Sagittarian born at six in the evening has the opposite sign, Gemini, in his first house of personality and appearance. The teenage sign makes this Sagittarian shorter. His face is not long; the teeth are like those of a child who has not yet lost the baby teeth. The gum line shows in the smile. The hair curls rebelliously at the temples. The youthful look is never lost. These are the Sagittarians whose age you cannot guess. Their youthful charm endears them, for they are inclined to be very friendly.

Both signs "never met a stranger." Easy to know, hard to hold, they want little and do not stay long enough to ask for much. They treat each venture with the inquisitive attitude of an enraptured child seeing a thing for the first time. But, the Sagittarian who does not seem to notice something has really photographed it for later uses. Though the chatter of the Geminian personality might throw you off, the Sagittarian heart has claimed the venture for his encyclopedic future.

CARDINAL RISING SIGNS FOR SAGITTARIUS
(PERSONALITY)

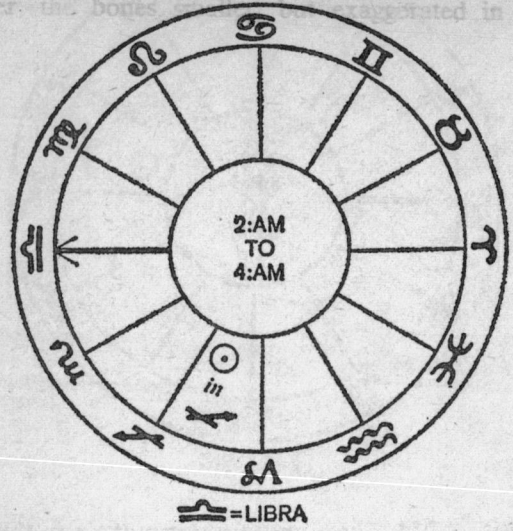

♎ = LIBRA

2 AM–4 AM. Sagittarius born this early in the morning has the charming, lovely personality of Libra. Forever marrying, these people marry four or five times. The charm of Libra leads them into marriage. They have really married before making a decision; their charm has betrayed them.

They are beautifully groomed, most gracious, and give you a wonderful time. They dine and wine you every second. They are handsome and tall with the lovely eyes that Librans are known for, plus the easy, happy disposition that is the Sagittarian's best trait. But later the indecisiveness of Sagittarians sets in. They are never home; they are always on their way to something, pursuing some idea, or putting over a big deal. They have to dine the boss, or take his sister, wife, or mother to the opera. As a symbol of the idea they married, you must continually re-arouse them; sell them all over, otherwise, they will marry again. You must keep alive the idea you represented.

CARDINAL RISING SIGNS FOR SAGITTARIUS
(PERSONALITY)

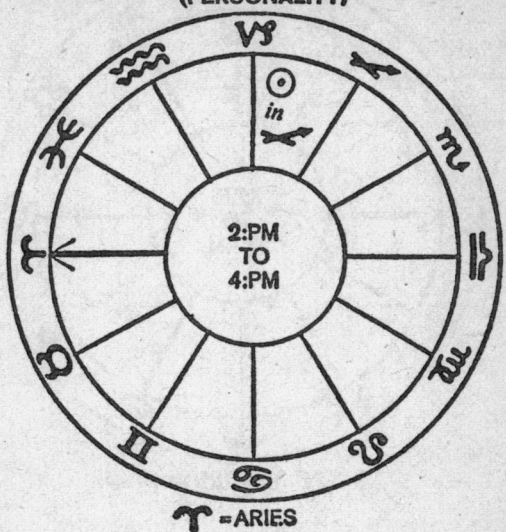

2 PM–4 PM. The Sagittarian born in midafternoon has Aries on the first house of personality. This is the go-getter. He is a traveling salesman selling ideas. The personality is active, blustering to suit the early enthusiasms of Aries. This Sagittarian is more muscular and less scholarly-looking. He moves fast—a real pitchman.

His coloring is ruddy; he might even be sandy-haired. The Aries personality wants a fast answer. He expresses his generosity in a kidding manner, making a joke of giving. Sentiment bothers Aries. But, like all fire signs, generosity is being expressed one way or another.

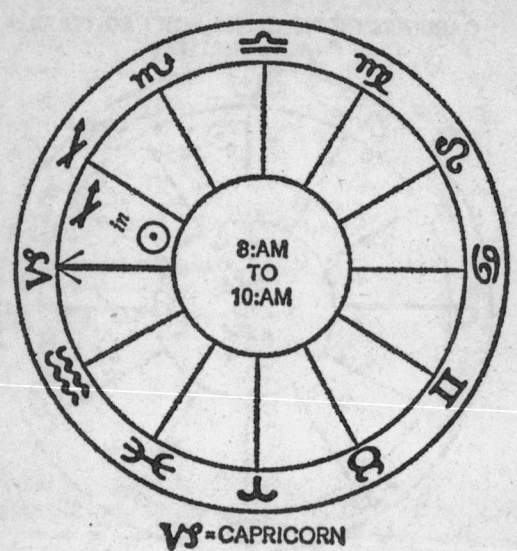

♑ = CAPRICORN

8 AM–10 AM. The Sagittarian born in the morning has Capricorn on the first house of personality. This gives the most conservative, quiet Sagittarians of all. Their ideas are all cataloged, one for every occasion. They are the smallest Sagittarians and are small-boned, hating the noise that the Sagittarian can make. They are exquisite, for they do not want to know the rank and file, but rather prefer the well-to-do. They have keen eyes and see the worth in people. They dress well but conservatively, which recommends them to the discriminating. They insist on quality in making a selection. Sagittarius with a Capricorn personality gives tone and class to a sign that is known for its gregariousness.

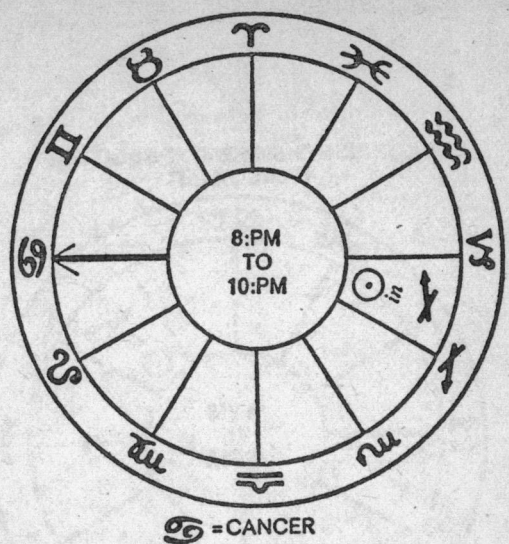

♋ = CANCER

8 PM–10 PM. The night birth of a Sagittarian brings Cancer to the first house of personality. The water sign makes Sagittarius heavy in build. Since Cancer is a pale sign, Sagittarius is lighter, less talkative.

Sagittarius does not come off very well in the shy, sensitive Cancer sign. He is too easily hurt. He refuses to travel; he stays at home with his parents or children. The only way to get rid of his ideas is to gossip about the family or neighbors, for Sagittarius must talk about something.

This Sagittarian makes a very good mother. Home (Cancer) is fulfilled through children. This makes this type carry weight; he is fat, for Cancer loves to eat. Since Sagittarians do everything expansively, he eats too much. These Sagittarians take many short trips to someone's home. They can serve the public in jobs that employ the rank and file. This is the least productive Sagittarian, who is victimized by the emotional swamp of the neighborhood and family.

FIXED RISING SIGNS FOR SAGITTARIUS
(PERSONALITY)

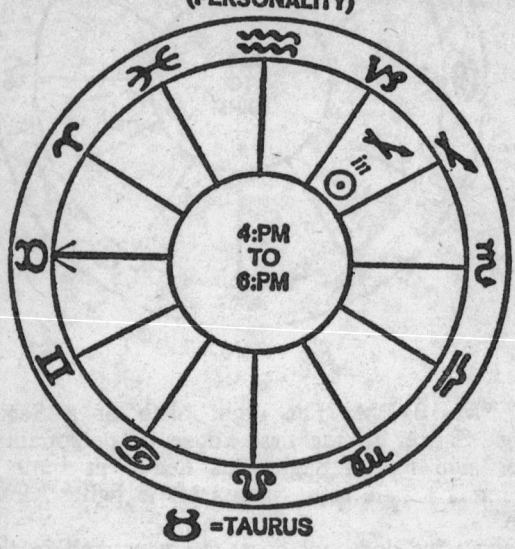

♉ =TAURUS

4 PM–6 PM. This Sagittarius birth will put Taurus on the first house of personality. Now you have a quiet, settled, reliable Sagittarian, wanting things at last: money and land. His ideas will be practical. Taurus will cut the height down. Determination is shown in the round, firm chin of the Taurian. The jawline of Sagittarius, with its prominent bone structure, helps to identify scholars. This Sagittarian will not talk much; his gamble is always to make money. He will not travel for ideas, but for values. Sagittarius with Taurus for a personality sorts out many ideas or ways to make money for practical purposes.

FIXED RISING SIGNS FOR SAGITTARIUS
(PERSONALITY)

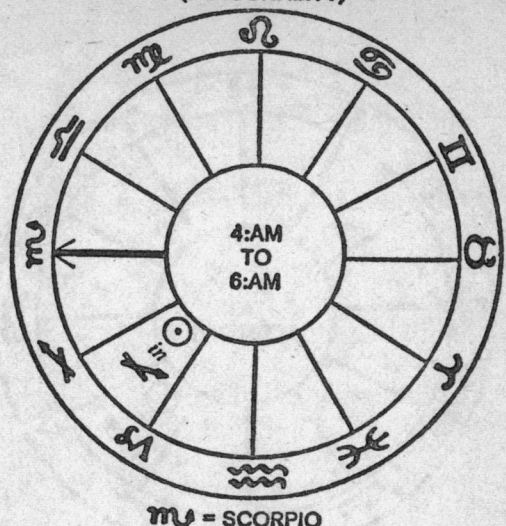

♏ = SCORPIO

4 AM–6 AM. The Sagittarian born early in the morning will have Scorpio for personality. This is a horse of a different color: Scorpio will impose his force over the easy nature of the Sagittarian. This meeting of two signs produces a different relationship. Scorpio is not accessible, and Sagittarius is hampered now by the weighty calculations of Scorpio. He wants to be friends, but his personality puts up storm warnings, for he makes demands you may not be willing to meet. Sagittarius is now shorter; the smile is slower. The hair is not abundant, but is finer. Ideas are examined and rejected, and since it is your idea, it is rejected. Later it may be paraded, for it has now become the Scorpio's idea: that makes it logical.

Sir Winston Churchill was a great statesman whose chart had Scorpio giving power to his every utterance, even though his Sagittarian birth gave him words and ideas.

Ω =LEO

10 PM–MIDNIGHT. Sagittarius born at this time of night has Leo, the second fixed sign, on the first house of personality. This is a more determined Sagittarian. Leo is good for Sagittarius because it steadies the indecisiveness of Sagittarius; Leo gives more reliability.

Sagittarius is now quite short. Not as dark, his hair is chestnut or auburn. The nose has a higer bridge. The smile is very warm, yet directed to smile *on* you rather than *at* you.

Leo does not like you to get too personal, so there will be an aloofness in this Sagittarian. Stay your distance. Ideas will be expressed only after your capacity for understanding has been gauged. Sagittarius with Leo for personality will consolidate his love for you, making it the real thing, knowing that he wants it. These are the aristocrats among the Sagittarians.

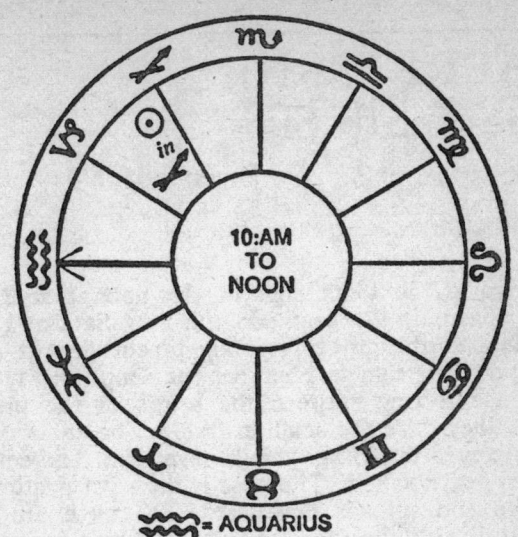

≈≈≈ = AQUARIUS

10 AM–NOON. The Sagittarian born at this hour of the morning has Aquarius rising. The personality of Aquarius combined with the fire of Sagittarius will circulate the many and varied ideas of the Sagittarian. This is a fortunate combination. Fire needs air to make it burn. Sagittarius loves a reason for expression; if he can get into circulation the idea represented by the Aquarian, he is in business.

The breezy Aquarius personality suits the light traveling Sagittarius. He catches ideas on the wing and leaves them behind in the same way. Very tall men have this combination. I have always thought Howard Hughes had this twosome. Lanky is more the word to describe it.

Sagittarius now has the most individual of faces. Our greatest president had it: Abraham Lincoln had a Sagittarius-Aquarius combination. His features were rugged, his strong bones well-defined. The interest in ideas must comfort and appease the people.

CAPRICORN:
The Tenth Sign
December 22 to January 19

Capricorn, the tenth sign of the natural zodiac, is symbolized by the goat and ruled by Saturn. It is a cardinal earth-sign representing practicality. It is the most difficult sign to identify. The simplest way is to note the furrow between the brows or the piercing eyes. They have the smallest frame. The ankle is very dainty; even in old age this is never lost. The coloring is dark, even sallow. The nose is the most unattractive feature and spreads downward. The teeth are good and strong. When they smile, their whole face seems to light up.

Their cautious attitude stems from the fact that they hate to make mistakes or a *faux pas*. Etiquette and decorum is important, for Capricorn is a very formal sign. They understand form. Law is innate in their nature; so they do well in the church. The clergy is full of Capricornians. Organization and well-thought-out plans suit them. Hitler had his Moon (the mentality) in the sign of Capricorn. He used the word *order* incessantly. It was absence of order that regimented his mentality.

Capricorn is completely lost without a plan. Even one day is very difficult to handle if there is no plan to follow. To be entertained by a Capricorn is a great pleasure. A very well-to-do Capricornian invited me to spend Christmas with friends in her Connecticut home (the house was built in 1778). She made arrangements to have each guest picked up by car. Cocktails were served the minute our things were put away. Dinner was served exactly on time, so that we could watch motion pictures of special shrines in

Buddhist countries like the sites of the Angkor-Wat or the Angkor-Thom shrines at Pnom-Penh—the sort of thing that is precious and a great treat for those interested in metaphysical subjects. That Capricorn understood that this would have special meaning at Christmas. The pictures lasted for the better part of the visit. All was planned and *timed* for the special happiness of the guests. The car that took us delivered each and every one back to his doorstep. It was a perfect evening—and it was perfectly timed with no effort for the invited guest, except to enjoy himself.

Capricorn is thoughtful in any occasion, for esteem is balm to his troubled soul. He respects you. To show disrespect to him means losing him forever. The quickest way to lose ground with Capricorn is to underestimate him. At the first move toward a slight, he has dismissed you from his consciousness. He has the ability to blank you out completely if there is a breach in manners or respect.

Friendship with these persons has a spiritual quality. They feel responsible for you: you are part of their duty; they expect to look after you. If anything goes wrong with their friendships, depression sets in until the love they feel dies of its own will. You are not thought of again. A sadness takes place, giving them the melancholy expression for which they are known.

Since Capricorn gives anything of sentiment a religious aura, the loss of a love, a friendship, or an idea is looked upon as being deathlike; it cannot be replaced; it is a thing that is lost forever.

NOON–2 PM. The noon birth hour for Capricorn is a very fortunate one, for then the personality house has Aries rising. This is the natural sign to rule the first house. You do everything right. Aries is the start-of-everything sign.

Your appearance and personality being Aries, you will contradict what the textbooks say about the appearance of Capricorn. You will be taller, even though Capricorn is a short sign. Instead of being dark, you should be on the red or golden side, with

CARDINAL RISING SIGNS FOR CAPRICORN
(PERSONALITY)

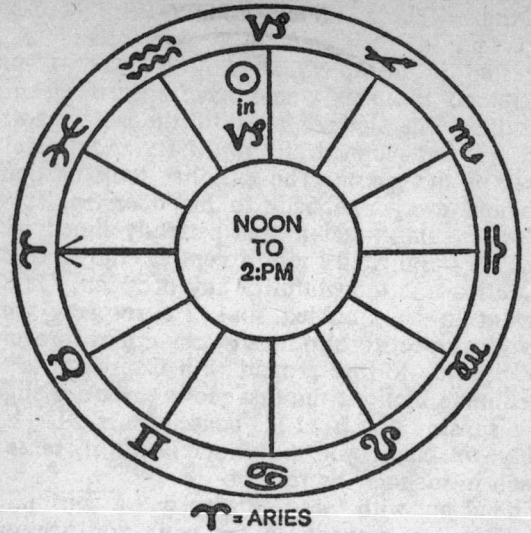

♈ = ARIES

ruddier skin than the Capricorn brunette. Your attitude is more lively. Your head is larger, as opposed to the small head of the Sun-sign. You will be very active, and uncontrolled in habits like Capricorn. This indeed is a perfect example of the time of birth changing both appearance and personality. The struggle to express the conservative Capricorn individuality versus the Aries personality will pose many problems. One side of you wishes an organized way of life, while the other side is rushing here and there in pursuit of any new venture.

A salesman representing a broadcasting station has this aspect. At the drop of a hat, he drives long distances for two and three days at a time, trying to promote a business deal. Nothing happens. He should never have left the desk of the big company he works for. He is just missing out all around, for he has some misconceived idea that as long as he is rushing (an Aries trait) he is accomplishing his aims. He has never reconciled this combination, yet he is clever, for he delights in telling of these adventures.

CARDINAL RISING SIGNS FOR CAPRICORN
(PERSONALITY)

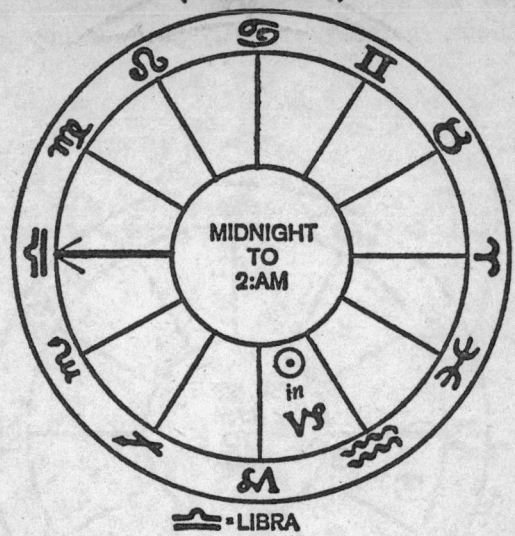

MIDNIGHT–2 AM. Having been born under the Sun-sign Capricorn at midnight, you will have Libra rising on your house of personality and appearance. It will give you more of the beauty for which Capricorn is known. Capricorn's good looks are wistful, quiet, and even sad. Librans are raving beauties with great big eyes, fine bone structure, and square frames that show off the planes of the face.

This Capricorn is more vain and gives more attention to clothes. He is a party-goer and will marry often —or even make marriage a career. Making a reputation or pursuing a business career will be lost to this type, even though Capricornians are fine businesspeople. One Capricorn client, a doctor, has done just that—married one society woman after another, one richer than the last. He pays very little attention to his patients.

The Capricornian born with the Sun at the lowest point in the wheel, as it is placed here, does not come into his own until late in life. He then becomes very career-conscious, making a name in the last quarter of his life. Finally, this Capricorn versus Libra person will be well groomed, have fine manners, be socially ambitious, charming, and very good-looking.

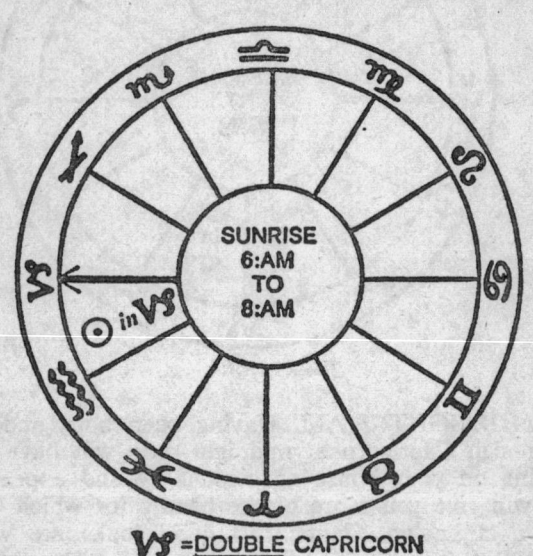

♑ =<u>DOUBLE</u> CAPRICORN

6 AM–8 AM. Having Capricorn for both a birth sign and a rising sign produces the truest Capricorn type: small, quiet, good-looking, dark, serious, very symmetrical. The odd thing about the true Capricorn is that, though small-boned, he is very well proportioned and neatly put together, which makes him trim and delicately composed. A good example of this type is Ava Gardner.

Personal ambition and reputation will be his drive. It will be most important to fulfill the self for the self's sake, not for what the world may think. Self-esteem will dominate every motivation. If anything goes wrong with this, he looks forward to death.

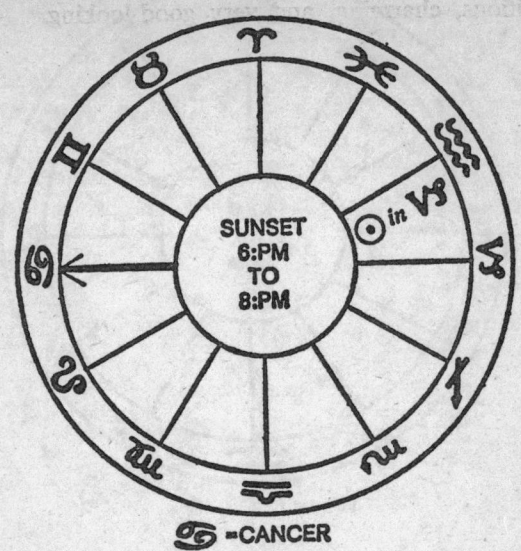

♋ =CANCER

6 PM–8 PM. The Capricornian born at the end of the day now has the opposite sign, Cancer, for personality and appearance. This again will test the textbooks. His appearance will not be dark, but pale. Cancer has the tissue-paper-white skin, and his features are babylike. He will have an infantile forehead, as if that part of the face did not mature with the rest. His mouth is always pouting. It is, for Cancer is a complainer; Capricorn is not.

The nose is his best feature: small and delicate to suit the sensitive personality. He is always being hurt or imagines so. Capricorn is not seen at all, except in the drive to fulfill his ambitions. Capricorn is always chasing a goal—quietly.

A Cancer personality versus a Capricorn birth cancels the drive for ambitious pursuits. Cancer is too busy with his personal problems; his sensitive nature accumulates them. Marriage is the chief trial.

FIXED RISING SIGNS FOR CAPRICORN
(PERSONALITY)

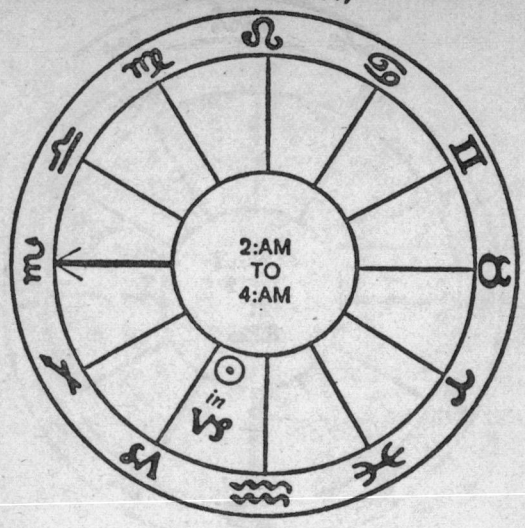

♏ = SCORPIO

2 AM–4 AM. This early-morning birth will bring Scorpio to the house of personality and appearance. Fixed signs will strengthen cardinal signs, cutting down their changeability, making them more determined. Scorpio is power-loving; Capricorn is ambitious. This is indeed a very important Capricornian!

2 PM–4 PM. Capricorn born at this time has the first fixed sign, Taurus, for personality and appearance. This makes a much heavier Capricorn; weighted with practicality, he combines ambition with money. Now we have a Capricorn who wants to make money as well as a name. Taurus sweetens Capricorn so that he approaches all business matters with charm, wheedling others with his knowledge.

FIXED RISING SIGNS FOR CAPRICORN
(PERSONALITY)

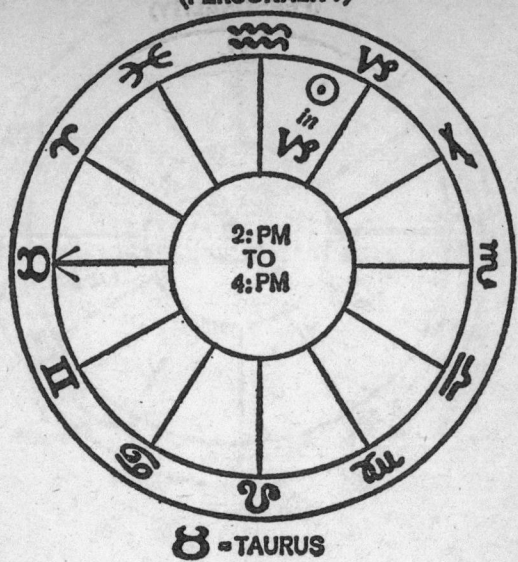

♉ = TAURUS

This is a very good combination. Both are earth signs; Taurus complements Capricorn, giving good looks, dignity, and quality while bringing money into the ambitious strivings of Capricorn. A textbook example might be the handsome banker with a beautiful voice that suggests, with great dignity and formality, the right stocks and bonds for you to buy.

8 PM–10 PM. This Capricorn native will have the second fire sign, Leo, for personality and appearance. Leo is the sign of royalty. Leo will make Capricorn, who hates display, dramatize things. Leo will give Capricorn more pride and hauteur. The coloring will be lighter; he will have a larger head; his build will be more commanding. The nose is better, higher, not so spreading. The smile is very warm. Dignity and formal-

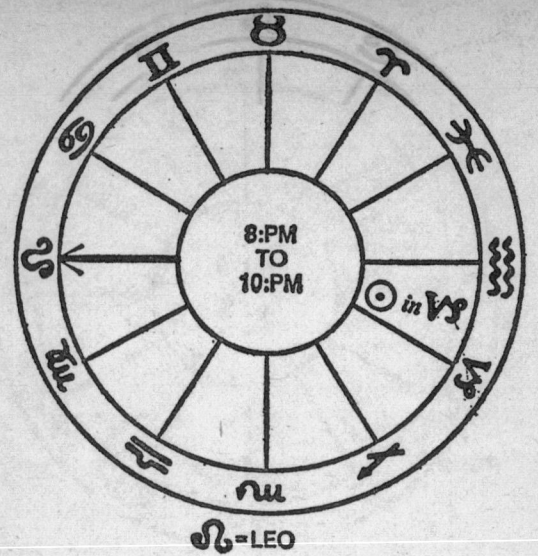

ity ease into the aristocratic nature; he feels compassion and understanding. This Capricorn wants to love you.

8 AM–10 AM. Capricorn born at this time has the sign of Aquarius on the first house of personality and appearance. He is very tall for a Capricornian. The bone structure is larger, though the joints, the knees, and the ankles will remain tapered and small. The features are stronger, the head larger, the brow higher and with wavy forehead lines in the frown; there is no furrow between the brows. The face is more square than oval. The eyes are not piercing, but raised at the corners. The coloring is lighter, the attitude less self-involved.

His interests are directed toward people, and he is concerned with the human race in general. He has

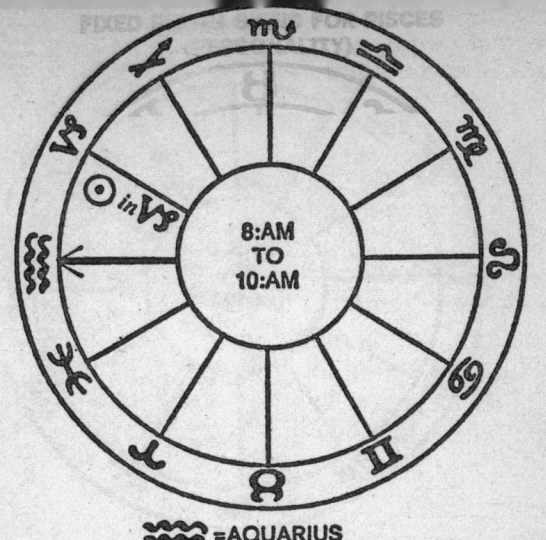

≋ =AQUARIUS

ceased motivating for the self. Humanitarian causes, especially hospital work, are typical.

The Capricorn with an Aquarian personality makes friendships his personal business. His heart beats for his mate. To marry the one he loves means he has arrived.

4 PM–6 PM. The first mutable sign, Gemini, will control the personality and appearance of this Capricorn. Gemini is the youthful sign, and this combination will always look young. This is the very smallest Capricorn.

Gemini is a practical thinker, and what he thinks will control his personality and appearance. Gemini combines its trim, neat, well-dressed look with the dignity of Capricorn. Flighty Gemini will be controlled. The smile will be ready, but with more concern over the reason for smiling. Formality, a

(PERSONALITY)

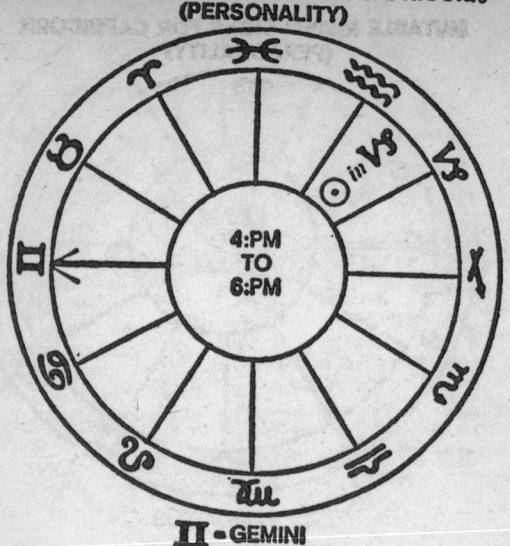

II - GEMINI

Capricorn trait, will show as a spontaneous personality eager to win. Gemini makes Capricorn talk more, discussing every subject imaginable, for Gemini is a talker, and Capricorn is well informed.

4 AM–6 AM. Capricorn born at this hour has Sagittarius rising which gives the personality and appearance height. This one is charming—the tall, dark, and handsome type. Sagittarians are the easiest-going people in the world. Capricorn gives them depth and sincerity, qualities they ordinarily do not have.

This combination helps Capricorn to lighten up and become more pleasant; it is also more substantial because ambition is the drive of idea-conscious Sagittarius. This native is a talker with well-organized ideas; he evaluates you by what you stand for.

Sagittarius makes Capricorn very attractive. The

MUTABLE RISING SIGNS FOR CAPRICORN
(PERSONALITY)

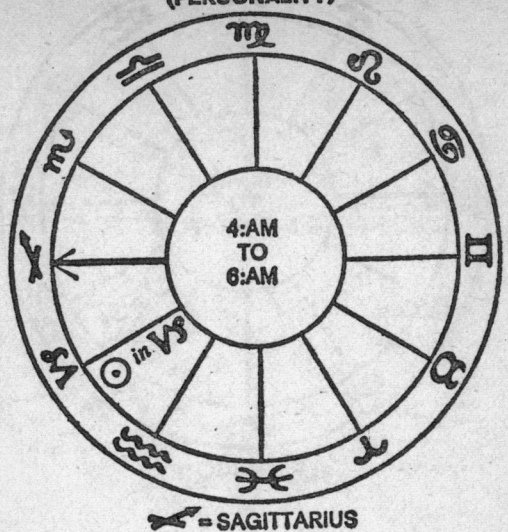

⟵ = SAGITTARIUS

coloring is a lighter brown, and the mouth less controlled. There is no frown; the eyes are merrier, seeming to laugh even when the mouth is immobile. Still, the teeth are large and prominent. He will marry more than once, and money will come late in life.

10 PM–MIDNIGHT. Capricorn born late at night will have Virgo in the first house of personality and appearance. These earth signs suit each other, making a very satisfied Capricorn, but not necessarily an attractive one. At first brush, you think you will like this mutable Capricorn until you find out that he talks about nothing but his work. His practicality is cloying. If you visit or dine with him, he is busy with the ash trays or in the kitchen most of the time. You are the guest, but he is the servant. I once visited one such person on her Maryland farm. I never saw her during the visit except at mealtime, for her other duties came first.

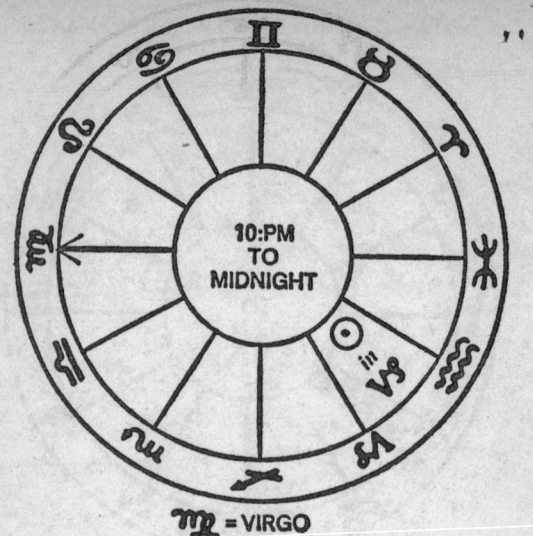

♍ = VIRGO

Virgo works you; Capricorn wants to interest you in his ambitions, which makes him very poor social material. He is bored in atmospheres where he cannot practice his ideals. This will be a very neat Capricorn, for Virgo is a very clean sign.

Capricorn controls the features and Virgo scrubs them, leaving no softness or leniency in the eyes or mouth. This type henpecks the mate and runs the children. In all community affairs, he supervises the program. "The hair combed back tightly" best describes these persons.

10 AM–NOON. The last mutable, or dual, sign, Pisces, rises on the first house of personality and appearance at this time. While Pisces, a water sign, gets on enough with the Capricorn Sun, it is not a strong enough sign to help Capricorn attain his ambitions.

With his personality, he slows down into a state of indecision. He is unsure of what he wants and what

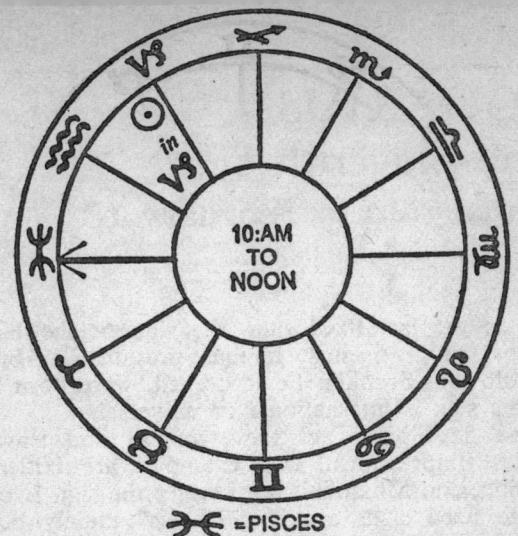

✹ = PISCES

he started out to achieve—unless other aspects reassure him with more strength to all his efforts.

The coloring is indistinctive; the hair becomes mousy, the eyes less piercing; for now they are not focused on any goal. The mouth, which is uneven in line, has lost control. The bone outline is not seen at all, for the face has jowls. The nose of Capricorn tends to spread out. Combine these two signs, and Capricorn has lost his ambitions in a labyrinth of indecisiveness.

AQUARIUS:
The Eleventh Sign
January 20 to February 18

This is the last fixed sign, the sign of the Hall of Fame. Our two most famous presidents, Abraham Lincoln and Franklin D. Roosevelt, were born under it. The sign is international or universal.

The fixed signs are the strongest and leave the greatest impressions. Two examples are Hitler, the Taurian, and Mussolini, born under the sign Leo.

The fixed signs are "big wheels" mainly because they want what they want more determinedly, wilfully, and resolutely. Taurus is stubbornly plodding toward his goal; Leo is wilfully controlling dominions. Scorpio is dead-set on what he wants. The determination of Aquarius may seem to waver at times. Being an air sign, he is less emotional about winning; he is also more intelligent. The nature of Aquarius is to change everything. In so doing, he might strike out in a new direction should others cease to arouse him intellectually.

Aquarius is the most difficult of the fixed signs to keep, for air is hard to control. Divorce or alienation is native to Aquarians. In fact, no matter how close the attachment, they give people, or ideas, the air every now and then. Crisis is a thing they create to arouse a new start. Just when you think all is well with you and the Aquarian, suddenly—without you having done anything—he will alienate you. Do not blame yourself: you do not have to do anything to provoke his alienation. Aquarius is a spiteful sign.

Aquarians simply do not like things to go along smoothly. They have to start something; so it may as well be you as anything or anyone else. It is their native perversity. The truth is, Aquarians are contrary. When they become contrary, give them the air first; you will earn their respect. They are contemptuous of those who tolerate their perversity. The fact that you beat them to the gun shortcircuits their intention to put you in the position their perverse natures enjoy.

The planet that rules Aquarius is a Judas planet. It will fail you if you depend on it. If you expect it to fail you, it will not; instead it will turn the tide in your favor. Uranus, the ruler of Aquarius, is unpredictable. If this planet Uranus is joined to your birthday Sun, it will make you the most contrary person on earth.

An Aquarian girl with the planet Uranus joined to her birthday Sun turned on her mother and eloped. She then told all of her friends that her mother did not want her to marry, which was not true. She did this to make a complete break with the parent. She wanted to express her rejection of a previous way of life and to enter safely into a new path; so she told scurrilous lies, projecting her guilt on the parent.

If Aquarius is afflicted by Taurus rising or by Scorpio rising (especially by Scorpio), you will have the most argumentative Aquarian possible. Aquarius loves to argue. Cooperation is the good Aquarian; the negatives are uncooperative and love to go against the given situation purely for the excitement of being different. It gives them an importance their egocentric natures crave. Aquarians are odd and peculiar.

They are against time, behind it, or ahead of it, but never *in* time. That is why they invent, originate, or innovate. The sign rules circulation, which means Aquarians like to circulate—if not the self, then their interests. They make wonderful newspaper-people for this reason.

They dress differently, but their clothes are never in style. Either they are ahead of the style, which makes them designers, or behind it, wearing odd things of bygone years.

Both the dome-shaped head swelling at the temples and the hollow Lincolnesque cheekline give them a gaunt expression. This is the facial feature that best identifies them. They are the best friends in the zodiac. Friendship is their best relationship, for that is not limiting. They will not be compelled to relate. Aquarians must be free to express themselves at their top level.

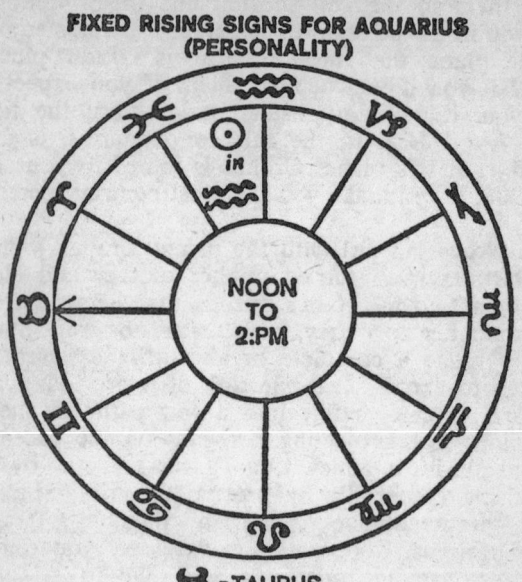

FIXED RISING SIGNS FOR AQUARIUS (PERSONALITY)

NOON TO 2:PM

♉ =TAURUS

NOON–2 PM. The Aquarian born at noon will have a Taurian personality. Taurus, being sweeter, will reduce the eccentricity of the Aquarian. The body will be more compact, more solidly put together. Aquarius is a bony, rangy type. Aquarius, a very tall sign, will be shorter with the Taurus personality, kinder, more thoughtful, and less alien. Taurus will give the facial features a softer line than the Aquarians usually have. The bone structure will be strong, but with more flesh to add roundness. The eyes will be more beautiful, wide and round.

The stubbornness of Taurus will blend with the contrariness of Aquarius. So, very sweetly, this combination will listen quietly to your argument and then do exactly what he started out to do. The arguments will be less heated, for Venus, the planet that rules

Taurians, loves peace. Therefore, argument being against the grain of the Taurus personality, these Aquarians will have their say determinedly, smile sweetly, and say no more.

The moon birth is the most prominent, or public; so the sweetness of the Taurus personality will get this Aquarian where he wants to go through charm. Flattery gets him everything.

FIXED RISING SIGNS FOR AQUARIUS (PERSONALITY)

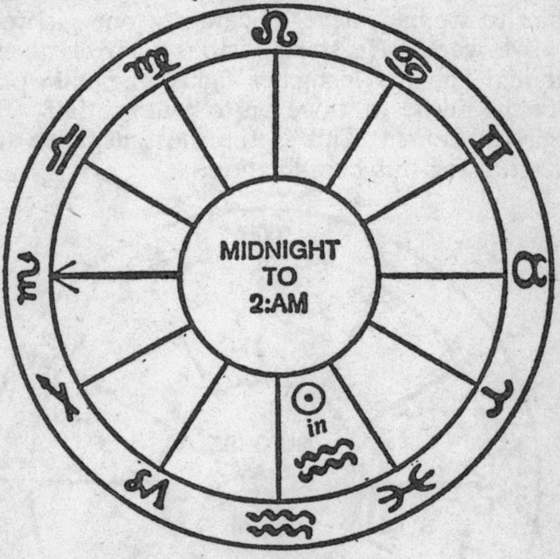

MIDNIGHT TO 2:AM

♏ =SCORPIO

MIDNIGHT–2 AM. The Aquarian born at midnight puts Scorpio on the rising house of personality and appearance. This make a much stronger Aquarian, who combines power with creativeness like Thomas Edison.

He will invent or create, for the Scorpio makes him want to investigate. Argument will now be expressed as a powerful desire to prove an intellectual idea. The Aquarian with Scorpio for a personality will not have the dome-shaped head—it will be smaller, more compact, and it will be bald. The body will not be tall and rangy, but more tightly put together. Scorpio is a secret sign; so this Aquarian will not talk as much and especially not just for argument's sake. He will contend for a personal reason, and he will have a real purpose that must end in a material thing. If there is not a physical or material goal ahead, then this combination will argue fiercely, scathingly, channeling this tremendous force into mean, vicious quarreling. Scorpio, ruling sex, will incline the person to pursue all kinds of odd Hollywood-style sex-experiences that lack real quality.

A client who has this combination runs from woman to woman, never sticking to one girl for more than five weeks. He starts vicious quarrels to end the affair and actually instigates fights in public places to justify the desire to move on to a new affair—blaming the girl of course. This is the most negative form of expression for this combination.

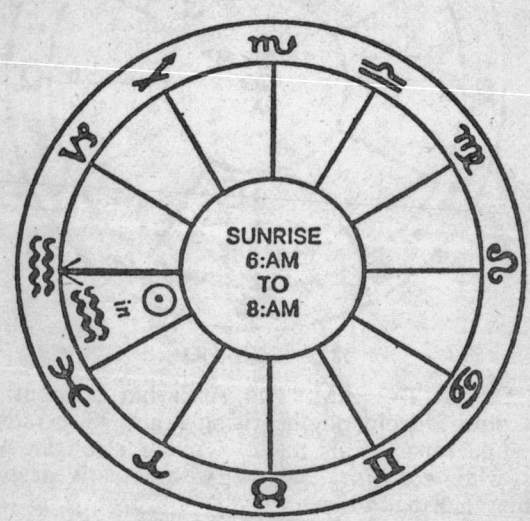

≈ = DOUBLE AQUARIUS

6 AM–8 AM. All signs that have their own sign rising, as here, on the personality or appearance house are true types (double signs). The individuality and personality are identical. Life is in their hands, and they are not the victims of fate. They are exactly

what they seem to be. They are Aquarian in personality and Aquarian in character. They are tall, lean, and moving continually. They possess all the facial characteristics for which the sign is known: unusual features, a rugged sort of handsomeness, exaggerated bone structure, large head, and inquisitive eyes.

The attractiveness lies in the very casual, almost indifferent manner. You feel free with this type, as if anything you do or say will be readily understood. You cannot shock him. His emotional lack is reassuring.

Argument is now always personal: it concerns him or is tied up in his action. The really odd ones become personally egocentric towards the end of life. They retire to the country or suburbs with a hobby that is like them—odd.

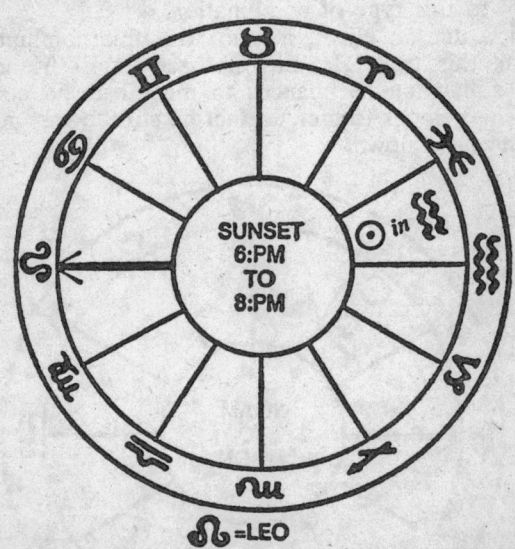

6 PM–8 PM. The sign of Aquarius is on the opposite side of the wheel, bringing Leo into the personality or appearance house. This is a short sign, so Aquarius has lost height. The warmth of Leo routs the indifference of Aquarius. The head is not dome-shaped, but higher. Sometimes the width and height are com-

bined and you have a gnomed, big head, too large for the body, and seeming to dominate the body. This type shows more drama in the personality, and gives more attention to love than Aquarius generally expresses. The desire to circulate is for love and in search of dramatic experiences. Aquarius with Leo for personality is very domineering, wanting to rule everyone. Friends are now ruled with an iron hand.

An Aquarian girl with Leo ruling the personality house would argue furiously with friends who did not do exactly as she directed. They had to go out with people she chose, or they had to account to her for having done something without consulting her. All male friends were treated like mates. Even if she introduced one to a girl friend, she still expected the man to treat her as someone special. Everyone "belongs" to this type of combination.

An Aquarian client, a man with this combination, repeats this trait. He may not see a girl friend for ages; still when he chances to meet her, he behaves as if she belongs to him. In fact he still "owns" all the girls he has known.

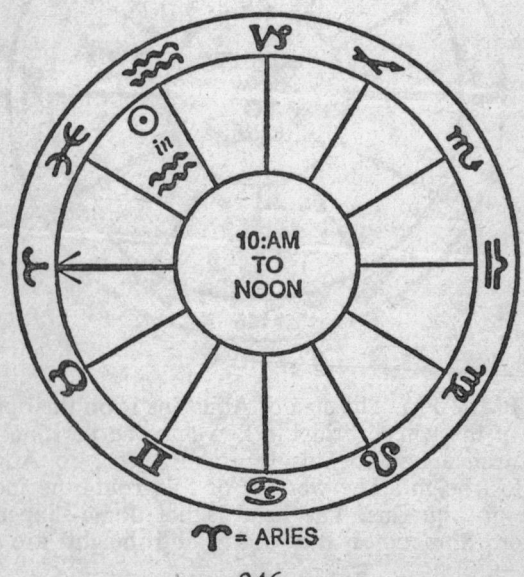

♈ = ARIES

10AM–NOON. The Aquarian born at this hour has a natural chart; that is, Aries, the first sign of the natural zodiac is on the personality first-house. Aries is a very athletic sign. Aquarius with this sign for a personality will not only be tall and rangy, but muscular with heavy shoulders. The facial features will be less prominent, the coloring more red. The brusque Aries will be warmer, giving Aquarius a desire to show more personal interest in everyone he meets; his attitude will not be casual. Every new hope or wish is now entered into with great enthusiasm. A great deal of activity is shown at the start, but soon dissipated when the idea becomes routine.

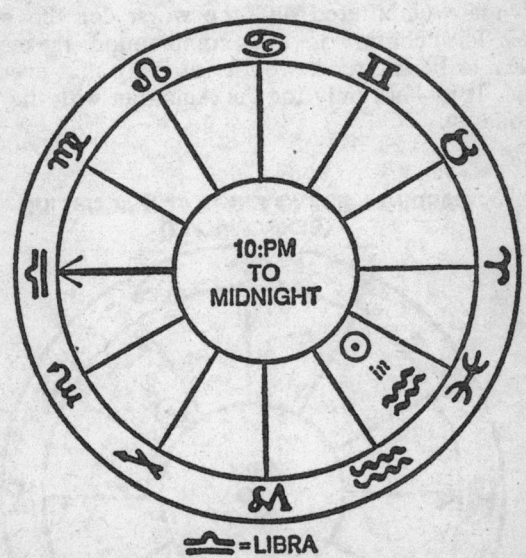

≏ =LIBRA

10 PM–MIDNIGHT. Aquarians born at this house have the beautiful sign Libra, a trine air-sign, for a personality. Both are air signs. This is a very fortunate Aquarian, for he can make marriage his career. Aquarians' good looks get them everything. Signs of the same element trine each other, that is, bring luck to each other. The unusual features make for extreme beauty—the prominent bone-structure, the square jawline, and the wide, beautiful eyes. The skin coloring will be very clear with the nose and mouth chiseled and cleanly cut.

A client who married five times moved from one husband to another with the resiliency of someone stepping from one room to another—but not until after each victim was stone-broke. This is the one Aquarian who combines the spendthrift habits of Libra with the cold indifference of Aquarians; he also has the ability to divorce you the moment his interest wanes. The parasitical vanity of Libra will be unsatisfied if you cannot assuage their craving for extravagance.

The Aquarian with Libra for a personality leaves each mate embittered and the worse for the experience. The charm of this combination makes him appear to be the most wonderful thing that ever happened. It is—but only for the Aquarian with the Libra personality.

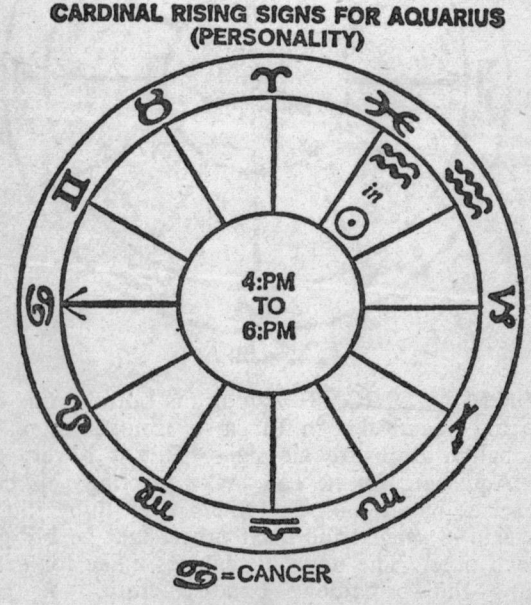

CARDINAL RISING SIGNS FOR AQUARIUS (PERSONALITY)

4:PM TO 6:PM

♋ = CANCER

4 PM–6 PM. The Aquarian born in the late afternoon has Cancer on the personality house. This makes a very odd appearance, for Cancer is a water sign. Since the Aquarian sign is air, this type does not come off very well in appearance.

The soft, childish face of Cancer is now exaggerated, for it is like a child whose face looks too old. Every feature that was small seems grotesque. Cancer, a short, fleshy sign, will give Aquarius a rolling gait and more fat to cover the bones. The eyes may "frog out" and the mouth slant sideward. Much more emotion is expressed in the features than Aquarius likes to show. The conflict is that Cancer versus Aquarius is too emotional about friends. Cancer wants to mother everyone, and friends may not want to be mothered!

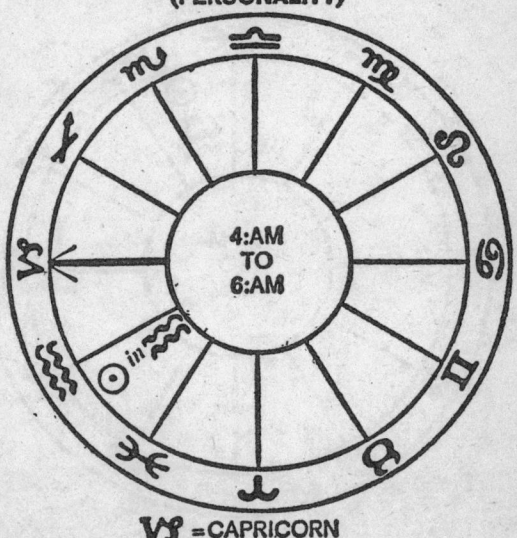

CARDINAL RISING SIGNS FOR AQUARIUS (PERSONALITY)

4:AM TO 6:AM

♑ =CAPRICORN

4 AM–6 AM. Early-morning birth will bring Capricorn to the first house of personality and appearance. He will be the smallest and shortest Aquarian. Capricorn will discipline the useless running around of

Aquarius, who seems to think that unless he is on the go, fame will pass him by. The wavy lines in the forehead will also be furrowed. The coloring will be darker, the bones smaller, but exaggerated in some way, such as the calf of the leg seeming too developed for the ankle.

This is the first Aquarian who is disciplined, orderly, and organized to make money. Every motion will be made for gain. He is the only Aquarian who will stay put, and he will be bored by running around. Being the president of a radio or television station would work out very well here. Or this Aquarian may expect his friends to figure prominently in his financial affairs. Friends will be screened for what they have rather than what they are; this is the Capricorn interest.

MUTABLE RISING SIGNS FOR AQUARIUS
(PERSONALITY)

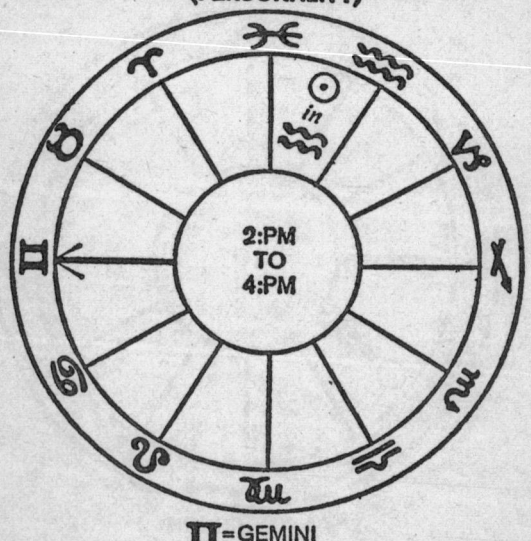

♊ = GEMINI

2 PM–4 PM. A midafternoon birth will give this Aquarian the youthful sign Gemini for a personality. Both being air signs, they will complement each other. This Aquarian will be just as beautiful as the

Aquarian-Libra combination born around ten or twelve o'clock at night.

Gemini is the teenage sign with Aquarius. This would give a model who is as slim as a reed; she would have beautiful features that remain girlish, a very small waistline, and no hips to worry about. Easy-going and so very casual, she is in demand for every party.

The head is smaller; the features always seem to smile with deep expression-lines around the mouth. The eyes will be even more curious than is usual for Aquarians. There is inquisitiveness there too, giving an almost oriental lift, that looks pixyish. Gemini is always taking short trips, and Aquarius circulates continually. You would never find this Aquarian at home, but traveling on another honeymoon, marrying as much as the Libra personality.

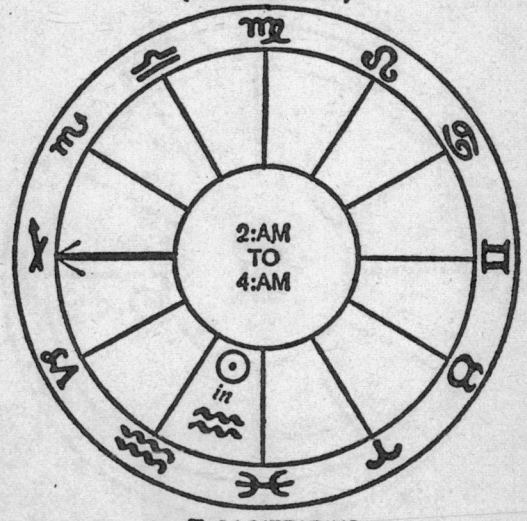

2 AM–4 AM. The early birth of Aquarius with Sagittarius for a personality brings the warmth and easygoing nature of the hail-fellow-well-met Sagit-

tarian. Airy yet warm, very tall, and moving through life with the greatest of ease, this one is a charmer. He is good-looking and has attractive manners, going some place every step of the way with a new idea that should be circulated. In fact that is the reason for his continual traveling—to come home, write about it, and have it published for all the world to read. He is a very international character. There will not even be time to dress properly. This Aquarian comes to the formal party in a business suit, but one doesn't usually care as long as this unusually good-looking, tall, smiling Aquarian, who says something nice to everyone, arrives.

The Aquarian with the Sagittarian personality will coin phrases. His language will be different, odd, new. The mate will be lucky to see him at all, but letters will come to explain his absence. He might even be divorced while on a trip, for this Aquarian marries many times. Being bachelor-born, he is not bothered by it at all.

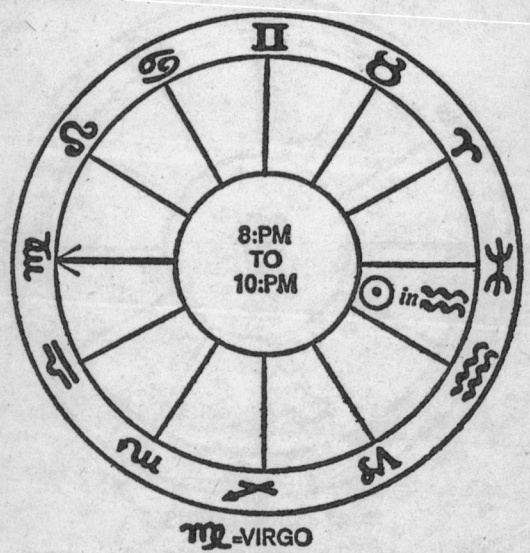

8 PM–10 PM. An Aquarian born this late at night will have Virgo, the sign of labor or service, for a per-

sonality. This is the first hard-working Aquarian. The severe features of Virgo will reduce the large head; the body will be smaller and neat. Attention will be given to cleanliness. Aquarians care nothing for clothes or overgrooming. They are a take-as-is type that prefers casual or sport clothes.

Virgo will tend this Aquarian towards doing a job. Whatever the work, it will be done very differently. If writing is called for, it will be about an odd subject. It might even be a hobby that has now turned into the real profession. He works at odd hours, such as the night shift in a hospital; he is the specialist who practices in an odd branch of medicine; the baby doctor who is called out in the middle of the night.

This is the one Aquarian who is interested in health instead of running all over the world. He could be the food faddist who circulates magazines about vitamins or the newest thing in foods, or he could write a cook book with new recipes. Whatever the fad, there will be no other subject that will interest the Virgo Aquarian other than his present form of specialized labor.

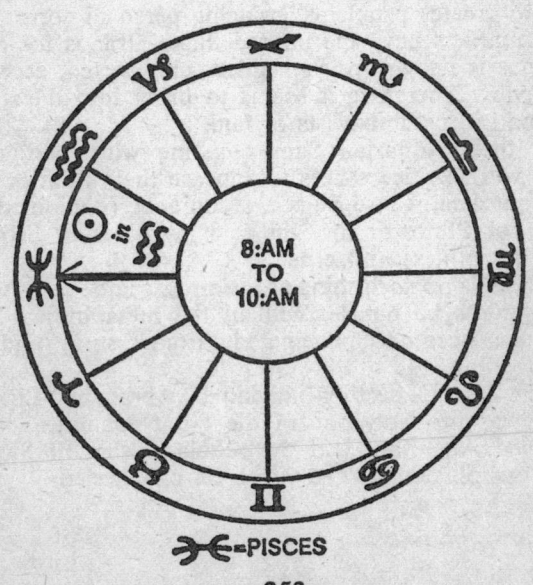

⊱⊰=PISCES

8 AM–10 AM. The last sign on the zodiac, Pisces, is the personality for the Aquarian born at this time. This is the least argumentative Aquarian, for Pisceans are too vague to maintain a positive stand for a long time.

The Aquarian with a dual sign for a personality will have the softest features of any Aquarian, for he will be weaker than the stronger Aquarian. The color is vague, just as the personal attitude is. The hair might be light brown, and it may gray early. The strong bones are obscured under the fleshy, soft features with indistinct lines, but one feature will be overly prominent—for example, a heavy jawline that is out of proportion to the head.

This Aquarian will marry someone who works for him and thus place his own social position in jeopardy. This is the least important Aquarian. Even if he holds a responsible position, he is not given full credit for his efforts. He is a behind-the-scene worker being sacrificed personally by a boss who takes all the bows. The mate seems to be working him in every way possible. Or he might be married to someone whose health creates problems, bringing personal sorrow.

Aquarians have the unpredictable Uranus for ruler. Uranus is known for its sudden, unexpected, eccentric behavior. Therefore it seems to bring into their lives the odd turns and twists of fate.

If their Aquarian Suns combine with vain signs, they will sacrifice others to appease their vanities.

Aquarians whose Suns are conjunct (conjoined) to Mars or Pluto, or in signs such as Aries or Scorpio, can be ruthless and cruel.

There is no such thing as a simple, plain, easy Aquarian unless he has learned all the metaphysical laws and has become emancipated through study and understanding.

The great destiny-individual Abraham Lincoln, who was probably one of the finest examples of the evolved Aquarian, had the scholarly sign of Sagittarius complementing the vision he prophesied.

PISCES: The Twelfth Sign
February 19 to March 20

Pisces is the last zodiacal sign. It is a mutable water-sign. The water makes it emotional, but being a mutable (common) sign, it will express itself dually.

The outstanding feature identifying them is the inclination to carry the arms up against the body in fin-like fashion, a sort of hugging-the-body affection. They seem not to know what to do with their arms. They can be very dainty and have either delicate features that are all Dresden doll or be gauche and heavy with huge noses dominating—like the famous Jimmy Durante. The eyes in youth are starlike, the lashes double or very long.

Their disposition is inclined toward the flexible, soft temperament; they are willing to please and unresisting towards an idea, welcoming any stimulating thought. This is a double-edged sword; once you have convinced them of an idea, someone else can come along and change their minds; they are very unreliable; the new idea just seems better, and they do not mean to fail you.

Their greatest difficulty is bringing their dreams down to a practical level. The highly evolved types are visionaries. They feel and see things long before the events happen. They have very long spiritual-feelers sensing the times or trends. They believe they have hunches, but really they pick up vibrations from the cosmic-consciousness which they do not trouble to sort out or analyze. That is why many of them believe themselves psychic and become mediums, for they are able to feel the rate of flow of good or evil in the personalities of those with whom they come in contact. They seem so close to sorrow at all times that an apprehension is created; it is identifiable as discontent. The poorly directed are spiritually unfulfilled divine-discontents.

Their states of indecision make them prey to stronger signs that see they cannot stand firm. The female Piscean is easy prey for unscrupulous males, who manipulate them. The male types are Casper Milquetoasts for overbearing wives. They seem to gravitate toward these viragos. It may be that they want around them the reassuring strength that they lack.

This gives the impression that they are masochistic, but it may actually mean that they are so emotionally geared that the storms of life disorganize them completely. In order to stay out of emotional swamps, they drift into the ocean to avoid the pressures, to escape, thus getting themselves misunderstood or maligned. This can be misleading to those who do not know that this is their weapon of defense and that they are not necessarily escapists.

It is really difficult to land blows on them, however, for what you strike at is really not there; they create a mirage for you. Their most characteristic behavior is to masquerade against the world by taking a chameleonlike personality; this frees them from taking issue with you or defending themselves.

Pisceans are past masters at creating illusion. They are makeup experts. Like the stars, they come out at night. A Piscean can look beautiful when in love or newly inspired. The planet Neptune, which rules Pisces, rules photography, perfumes, mist, and fog. Pisces can also create a mysterious atmosphere about the self, mystifying you or putting you in a fog with no other effort than just willing so. As the Chinese say: They are like a feather wall; the harder you hit them, the higher they fly.

MUTABLE RISING SIGNS FOR PISCES
(PERSONALITY)

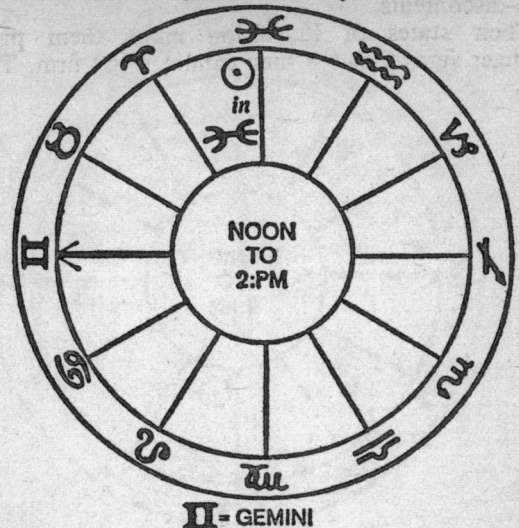

♊ = GEMINI

NOON–2 PM. The Piscean born at noon has the mutable sign Gemini on the first house of personality; he thus has two dual signs. Gemini wants to do both things, and Pisces wants to go both ways. This creates quite a conflict in being and in constructive action.

I always advise my clients with dual signs to do two or more things to take up the slack of indecision. For example, Pisceans like to do something that gives them inner satisfaction. Gemini prefers a hobby that requires study or investigation. If a Piscean wants to sing, he usually can since people with water signs have lovely voices. Caruso was a Piscean. The mutual personality would express another versatility by playing an instrument, especially in the case of Gemini, for Gemini rules the fingers and arms.

Gemini, being the youthful or teenage sign, will keep this Piscean young. As Pisces tends toward the light aura, this will be the golden, dainty type, with starry eyes soft as cotton and sweet as honey. There would be more than one marriage. This combination is at its best as a motion-picture actor or actress.

MUTABLE RISING SIGNS FOR PISCES
(PERSONALITY)

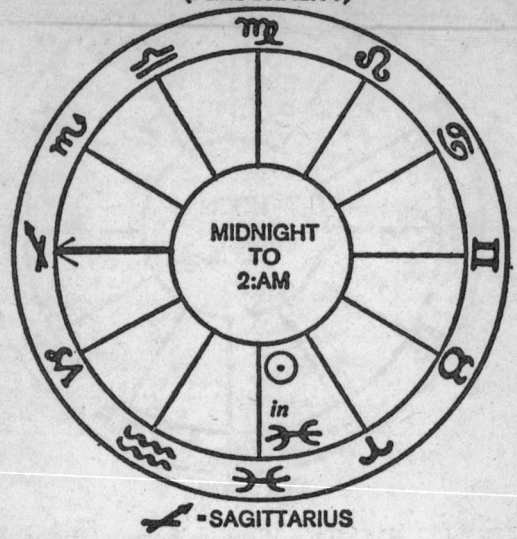

♐ - SAGITTARIUS

MIDNIGHT–2 AM. If a Piscean is born at midnight, the sign Sagittarius will give the personality and appearance traits. This will be a very, very tall Piscean, he is more agile than the slow-moving Piscean; he is dark and has a prominent nose.

The dual personality of this individual might cause him difficulty in choosing a profession. The sign Sagittarius rules law; Pisces rules hospitals and prisons. The lawyer (Sagittarian) could help those caught in the web of Piscean troubles. This lawyer could spin quite a yarn about his unfortunate client, for a person born under Sagittarius would make a very capable storyteller. Sagittarius creates ideas while Pisces can create illusive pictures.

6 AM–8 AM. Pisces would be rising here; so the individuality and personality would make this the pure Piscean type; the appearance and inner state being the same gives as strong a Piscean as can be found.

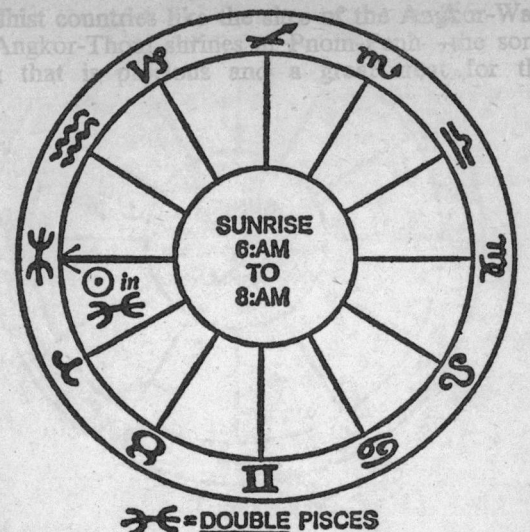

⨯⨯ = DOUBLE PISCES

Confusion is also one of the states for Pisceans. There may be a strong tendency towards embroiling those they contact, snaring or beguiling them like the sirens of old. An ability to fascinate exists.

Pisces rules the feet. One of my most beautiful clients, a famous ballerina, has Pisces for a personality. She has skin so fair that it seems translucent. On the stage she creates the illusion of being ethereal. Although she is very tall and quite husky, she can give a doll-like impression at will. In real life she does more than one thing: she teaches choreography in addition to starring in musical shows.

6 PM–8 PM. Pisces individuality is far removed from the first house of personality and appearance because the opposite sign, Virgo, colors the attitude. Virgo is too practical for Pisces and does not give Pisces a chance to express itself. This sign opposite Pisces acts as a lever forcing the true individuality back and causing Pisces to be completely misunderstood.

A case in point is that of a couple who came to me

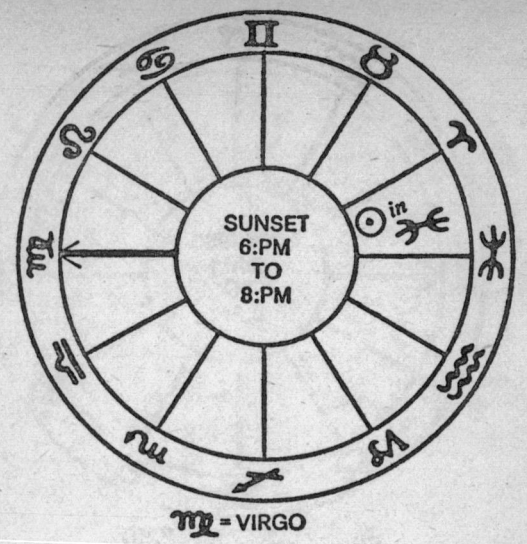

♍ = VIRGO

constantly with their marital problems; the wife had this aspect. The husband complained that he could not seem to get her to respond to him. She insisted that she cared for him, but could not seem to express her emotion. She did not realize that the chaste Virgo personality turned her critical attitude in on the self so that she was awkward and self-conscious to the point of being unable to do the one thing she was well equipped to do—love her mate in a very spiritual way.

8 AM–10 AM. The Piscean born in the morning will have an Aries personality. Aries is a very muscular and active person. The color for the Aries person is red. Pisceans are pastel in coloring. Combine these, the coloring will be golden red. Water signs have soft features. Aries is a very masculine sign. Thus, a Piscean born with an Aries personality will be a muscular, strong, active type.

Pisceans born at this time will have flat features. They may be tall, but they will have powerful mus-

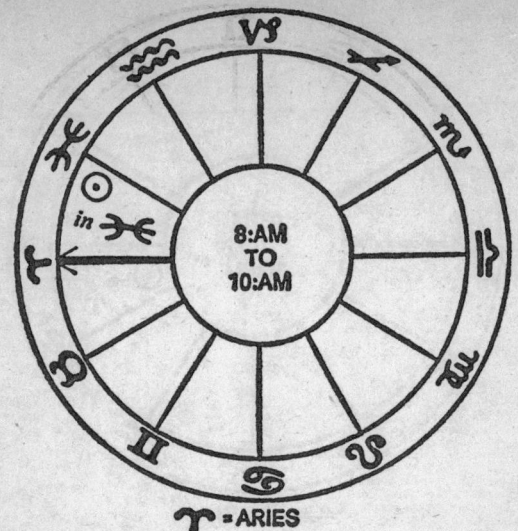

♈ = ARIES

cles and a bigger frame. They will have large noses with very little bridge-development and large mouths with an indistinct lipline. The forehead is flat and wide from temple to temple.

Pisces starts everything right now, for Aries rules the head, and that is where all ideas are conceived. There is no indecision about these Pisceans. They know what they want and go right to it. Aries is a cardinal sign, and the active signs help the mutable signs to make motion. Good or bad—they act!

8 PM–10 PM. Pisceans born at this time have Libra, the sign of beauty, on the first house of personality and appearance. They will be truly lovely. The softness of the water sign plus the casualness of the air sign give them their quality. Pisceans with Libra for personality will not worry much about ideas. They will treat life casually. Yet marriage or the idea of mating will consume much of their time. They will want to work for the good of the mate, giving atten-

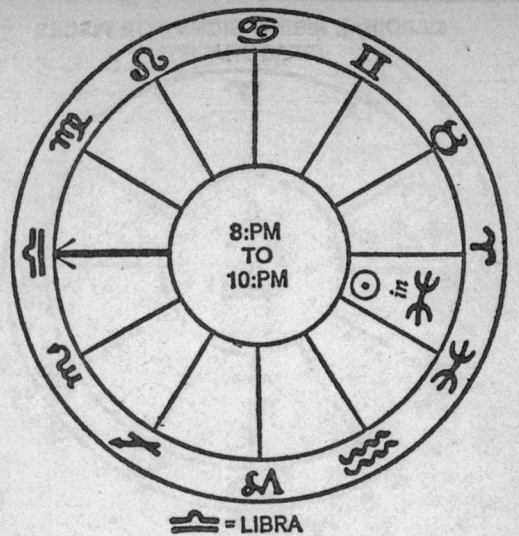

⎯ = LIBRA

tion to the health and well-being of the marriage partner.

The beautiful face of Pisces with Libran features is more firm, the facial construction more clearly formed. Pure Librans have large eyes, and pure Pisceans have dreamy eyes; if these are combined, the eyes will be the best feature. The calmness of Libra will reduce the emotionalism of Pisces. Since Librans entertain very well, Pisces will find this a channel.

2 PM–4 PM. Pisces is very much at home with the water sign Cancer on the first house of personality. Both being water signs, they complement each other. The same element expresses harmony. Cancerians have delicate features; they have the whitest skin with silky hair. The threat of heaviness is present, for Cancer loves food, and Pisceans console themselves with it when emotionally hungry. Water signs are always seeking emotional satisfactions.

These Pisceans will want a higher education; they enjoy intellectual adventures. Writers have this com-

CARDINAL RISING SIGNS FOR PISCES
(PERSONALITY)

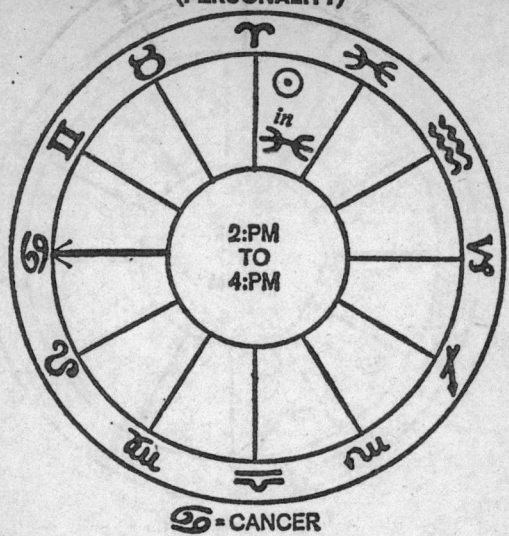

♋ = CANCER

bination, for the imagination travels to other countries to feel what the common man needs, thinks, or wants from life. Cancer rules the home life; Pisceans will theorize about it.

A client, an advertising man, had this combination. Apart from writing ads, he wrote TV scripts concerning marital life and child behavior (Cancer rules the baby) toward the parent. Cancer is the best sign for an understanding parent. One day he brought his beautiful child for a visit; the relationship between him and his son was a thing of beauty. Pisces birth with Cancer for personality is a splendid combination.

2 AM–4 AM. The most practical Piscean, who always has a definite plan, has Capricorn on the first house of personality. The darkest Piscean, he has no hint of fat; any indecisiveness is completely erased. Capricorn, a very restrained sign, will minimize the emotional struggles of the Piscean; it will be all ex-

CARDINAL RISING SIGNS FOR PISCES
(PERSONALITY)

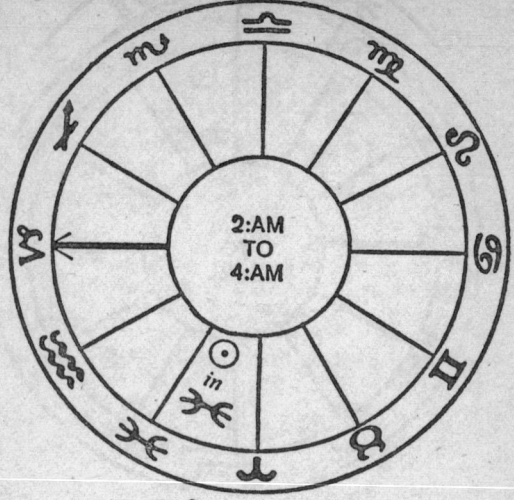

♑ = CAPRICORN

pressed in writing or speaking. Rudyard Kipling had this combination. His works are mystical with many metaphysical examples of man pitted against the elements.

The piercing eyes of Capricorn will be softened, but they will seem always to be surprised and alert. The dignity of Capricorn takes a conciliatory turn that seems to use easy conversation to direct one through emotional harrassments into clear waters. He is usually a spiritual director or organizer.

10 AM–NOON. Pisceans born in the late morning have Taurus on the first house of personality; they should be very attractive, for earth signs come off well when combined with the softening effect of a water sign like Pisces. The practicality of earth minimizes the emotional waste. The trend towards accomplishment is clearer. Taurus wants things, so Pisces is put to work to acquire them.

Taurus, a Venus-ruled sign, is very good looking.

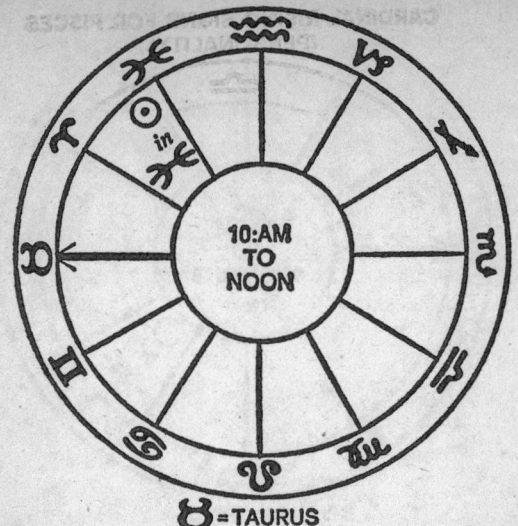

ȣ = TAURUS

The vague expression of Pisces must give way to the determination in Taurus's clear-cut features—firm chin and round, compact head with large, fringed, starlike eyes.

The birth hour being so near midday presages a public figure such as someone in the theater or motion pictures.

10 PM–MIDNIGHT. The Pisces Sun-Sign combined with the power-loving Scorpio on the first house of personality gives the strongest Piscean possible. Indecision is swept aside, for Scorpio wants love in this combination. If that fails, the theater or motion pictures (Elizabeth Taylor is born under Pisces; her Moon is in Scorpio) would be the best way to channel this emotionally harmonious combination. This combination makes a strong beauty. The magnetic attraction of Scorpio combined with the persuasive beauty of Pisces has strength and invincibility behind it. When they go after you, you must succumb. The resourcefulness of this lover is limitless.

Scorpio is the vampire, the siren, of the zodiac. The

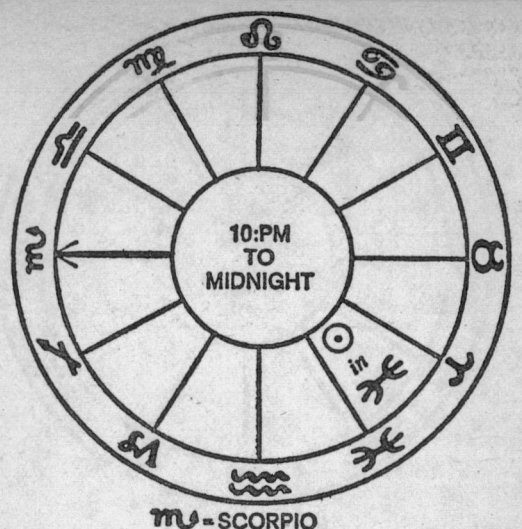

♏ = SCORPIO

apparent flexibility of Pisces may give the impression of softness. However, the unyielding Scorpio really knows what he wants. The harmony of this trinity reduces the demoralizing characteristics of Scorpio; it gives Pisceans a force and an effectiveness.

4 PM–6 PM. Pisceans born when fixed signs rise on the personality house are the stronger Pisceans. Fixed signs strengthen this mutable, who really wants to express himself in many ways: fixed signs force them into making a choice. (Cardinal signs: Aries, Cancer, Libra, and Capricorn are not as helpful; common signs Gemini, Virgo, Sagittarius, and Pisces find it very difficult to make decisions.)

This house places Leo on the first house of personality and appearance. Leo is a very strong sign that gives the Piscean definite ideas. Such a Piscean, while short in build, will have a meaningful carriage. Leo walks like a king or queen, the head held high in accordance with the high-bridged nose. The features are more arrogant than the self-effacing Pisceans. Leo will resist the indecisiveness of Pisces and take a firm

FIXED RISING SIGNS FOR PISCES
(PERSONALITY)

♌ = LEO

stand. The dramatic personality of Leo will make Pisceans put on an impressive show. Crisis and climax (Leo rules the fifth house of love and drama) are the instruments that are manipulated by this combination of Pisces and Leo.

A client, a lovely Pisces girl who changes loves from month to month has this combination. She is really in love with love, a Leo trait. The mental changeability of the Piscean becomes emotionally discontent with those who do not fit their dreamy ideas.

A Piscean boy and his mother, both my clients, took me to the beach one day. The boy has Leo for his personality sign. His mother ran back and forth at the beach bringing us cold drinks. The Leo personality behaved like a king. The mother, a Cancer type, enjoyed treating her grown son as a baby. Throughout the day the Piscean boy accepted this treatment vaguely, never quite sure that this was what he wanted.

Leo is a sign of authority. Leo is a king or queen

or ruler. A Piscean pupil (the uncertain sign) with a Leo personality invariably finds some error (imagined, of course) in my calculation during a lesson. The Leo is the authority, not I. Yet the Piscean individuality cannot be sure; thus we have the repeated performance.

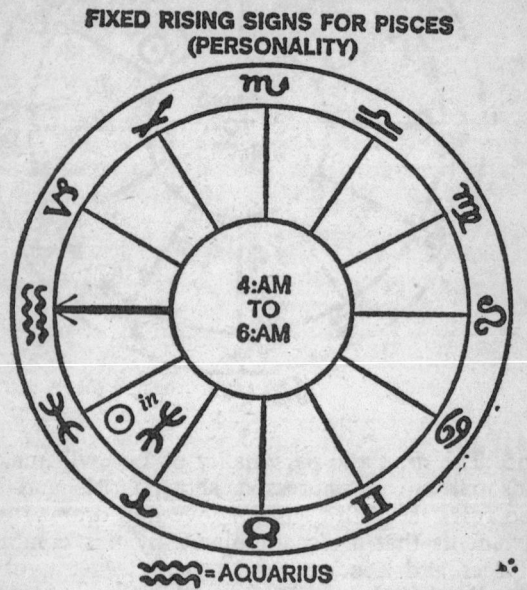

FIXED RISING SIGNS FOR PISCES (PERSONALITY)

4:AM TO 6:AM

≈≈≈ = AQUARIUS

4 AM–6 AM. The Piscean who has Aquarius, the friendship sign, on the first house of personality feels that friends are his true possessions. He is so personally involved with his friends that he sacrifices his own accomplishments on their behalf.

Aquarius's personality and appearance gives a lean, tall Piscean whose peculiarities might result in eccentricities; or he might be the hermit type, who disappears and goes into exile if the love he is determined to give to friends is not warmly received. One of my clients with this combination studies rare plant-life as a hobby (it takes her into isolated woods or forests); she has given up the dream of fulfillment through friends.

20

Discovering Your Sun and Personality Sign

Each sign has a virtue; each sign has a fault. Every sign can tell you something and teach you a lesson. If it tells you something you wish to hear, you may herald the sign. If it causes you a sore lesson, you may dislike the sign, but it has served its purpose, for it has evolved you to a higher level through the trial. You will recognize this test in a future brush with life.

If a sign expresses itself negative, it is on the unevolved side and cannot give you what it does not have. Do not expect more from a sign than either it can give you. Light, airy signs cannot express deep feelings any more than a sign of depth can treat lightly the relationships or experiences that are met in life.

The fire signs, being the most generous, forget what it was you said that they did not like.

The earth signs are too practical to give words space to live emotionally in their consciousness.

The air signs just give words and you a very airy treatment.

The water signs give offense water to grow in, dropping it down into their subconscious for further use. Being collectors, water signs cannot bring themselves to throw hurt away. Cancer may have use for it later when he needs you; Scorpio keeps it as the dividend for something he knows about you. Pisces keeps it for years; later it may serve to put a vision into practical motion for realization.

For example, a client told me about a trip she was about to go on. She explained that a friend had asked her to visit her in California. I suggested good periods that might inspire a marriage which she sought. I complimented her on this interesting plan, endorsing it as the idea was apt and suitable to the present state of her chart. As we parted she asked, "What are you doing for vacation?" I replied, "I plan to spend my vacation in Europe." She exclaimed with much sarcasm, "What in the world are you going abroad for?" These negative traits were habitual patterns in her character; they prevented her understanding that success might come to another and were ready to defeat her in any of her endeavors. Needless to say, her visit brought nothing new into her life.

A client once sought astrology to aid her in the one thing she wanted more than anything in the world—a happy marriage. She explained she could not afford the lengthy consultations that were required to bring about the result. I hit upon a plan. She was a secretary. I asked if she would like to tidy up lectures and notes that needed classification (about ten days of typing). She answered that she was an expert and could very easily do it to pay for my services.

In approaching her problem, her own attitude, the aftermath of an unsatisfactory marriage, had to be readjusted. We set about our program. She began by finding fault with the typewriter. Next, she said that it would take months (it was spring) and that she could not possibly finish until fall. Each session was one of continual complaining about the handicaps the chore involved.

It was clear that this girl did not want to do anything. The inability to give is of course the reason she could not get a husband. She had nothing to give. Or rather, she wanted as much as she could get from others without giving anything of herself. The men she met sensed this (men see much more in women than they are given credit for) and gave her a wide berth.

She had a majority of lightweight signs, but just enough of the heavy, or fixed, signs to be too unyielding to change, even to her own advantage.

Another airy-sign client shows sympathy and interest in friends until he finds out what the current quest of their plans may lead to. He feigns deep interest until each detail if the idea is exposed, then he turns on you and enumerates each and every reason why it cannot be accomplished by you.

This compulsion is the extreme negative side of the light signs. So completely is this personality imbued with failure that he strains in the direction of failure for everyone he meets. He has failed—so, why don't you? If you have not failed, he has the perfect formula for how it can be accomplished. Failure is just as much a goal for the negatives as success is for the positives.

But on the positive side, a lovely girl, whose chart showed a definite marriage, came to me. In fact, she had a progressed New Moon showing that a new man was on the scene and leading to marriage. I asked if she had met a new person. "No," she answered. In fact she had been going steady with a boy for five years. What did I think about the boy's chart? One look convinced me he was not to be her mate. I turned from that to the new man on the horizon. But she showed no interest; however, I repeated my prediction. I said, "There is a very wonderful new person coming your way; why not open your mind to a new friend?" She accepted this, but I was troubled. Here was a very active chart leading to progress, but she was determined to remain behind and wait for a man that would never be hers.

I put my consciousness on this very deserving girl. She promised to accept more social engagements and to take a weekend vacation on the very good periods that I had pointed out. Two weeks later she telephoned. To my great delight, she reported meeting a new friend whom she found to be more desirable and who had asked her to marry him. I asked anxiously, "But, will you?" "Oh! yes, I like him much better," she answered to my real satisfaction.

A very bright girl, a buyer, became involved with a man who had had two marriages, but who was then separated and back playing the field. One look at his chart indicated that even if she married him, it too would fail, for the man was not marriage material. She was very much in love. I asked her, as I do all my clients, "Is he what *you* want?" She assured me that he held the key to her happiness. I said, "Very well, we will campaign for your happiness." I did not mean that man, however.

This girl lived in another city, and I saw her about three or four times a year. The man lived in another city so that he came to her town just about as frequently. That gave me a chance to see her after he had visited her. I worked the friendship out astrologically to last about two years, considering the distance between visits. He was the type that lasted about ten or twelve dates with any girl. I felt that, during that time, I would be able to lead her gently into the fact that *she* would make the decision against wanting to marry him, rather than tell her the reason he would not divorce the present wife. He did not live with this wife, but she was insurance against another marriage.

Meanwhile, when her chart was appropriate, I suggested that it would be nice to have an escort in her own community to take her about. She thought this a pleasant idea; in fact she was now eager to meet new friends, her confidence assured by the fact that she had (she thought) a steady beau. After many visits, I gave her one question to ask the married man. The answer, I knew, would tell her all she needed to know to bring her to end this futile affair. Simply, "What was marriage?"

He told her that thirty days was all there was to any marriage—that, after that, it was simply routine! She was a Leo girl, and love meant everything to her. This statement broke the illusion. Her escort was a fire sign; he really loved her. She turned to him, for by this time the married man had left empty spaces, and the escort could be depended upon.

One day I received a letter from the Leo girl that made my heart sing. She had made the decision; she had wrapped the letters and pictures of the married man into a neat bundle and put them in the storage cellar. Then she had written him a letter, lettting him down very tactfully. She was wonderfully relieved and would marry the escort in October.

For every negative sign, there is a positive sign—and there are both traits in each sign. Unless you need the lesson, run from the negatives. The first lesson negatives teach you is all you need to know; they will then continue to repeat. Cultivate the positives. There are many ways to test them. Of each and every sign that comes along, accept the good of the sign and forget that side of the sign that may not suit you. Remember, there may be a negative side of you that may be tiresome.

You cannot change fixed signs; take them or leave them. Another way to take them is at great intervals; steady diets of them may be difficult. If you are not prepared or conditioned to be burdened by their assertiveness, treat their friendships casually. If you find that a fixed sign or the shallowness of a light sign is imperative to your happiness, remember that what attracted you is the very thing that you may not be. This is what really fascinates you.

In any situation, whatever you don't like may be the very experience that you need to widen your view or to bring new interests or horizons to the crux of your existence.

If you are a timesaver wishing to fill your life with that which is worthwhile and progressive, have at least one good reading from a qualified, competent astrologer. Find out what you are like. If, in the predictions, you are not told that you are destined for great things, at least get acquainted with yourself. This may cut down on the mistakes you make. This is a time-saver. If you attract the wrong people (many charts attract those who would crucify them) or are engaged in the wrong field, it is never too late to try a new path. Develop and live up to the best side of your *Sun and Personality*.

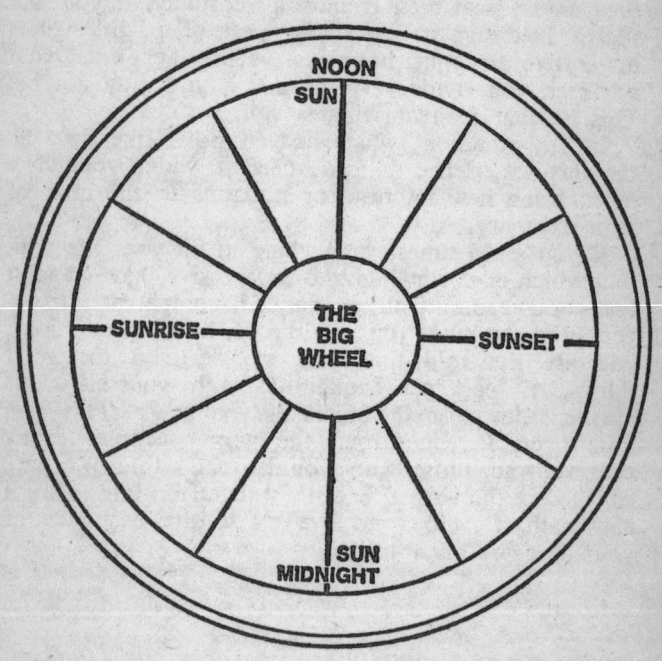